THE STORY OF THE BIBLE

The Story of The Bible

Written and Drawn by
Hendrik Willem Van Loon

Garden City Publishing Company, Inc.

Garden City, New York

CL

1941

GARDEN CITY PUBLISHING CO., INC.

THE STORY OF THE BIBLE

To

GEORGE LINCOLN BURR

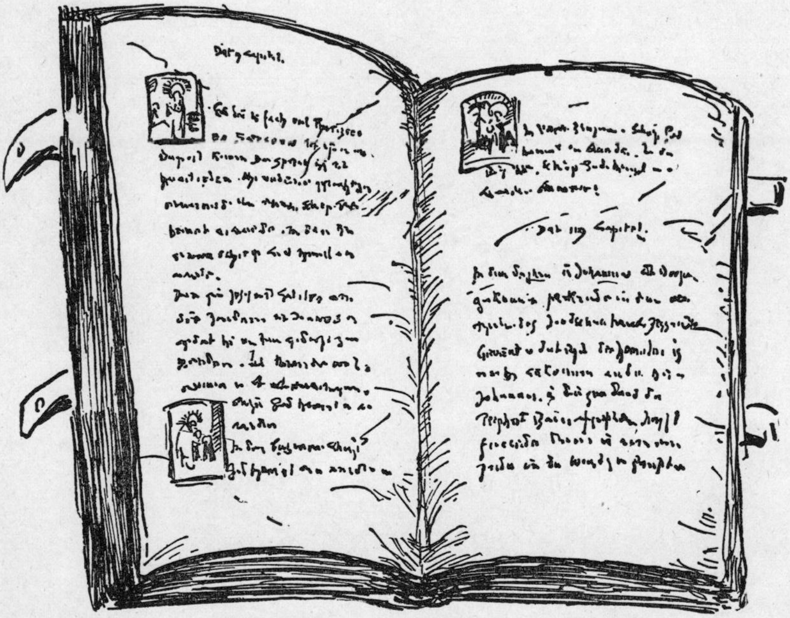

FOREWORD FOR HANSJE AND WILLEM

Dear Boys:

THIS is the story of the Bible. I have written it because I think that you ought to know more about the Bible than you do, and I really could not tell you where to go for just the sort of information I want you to have. Of course, I might ask you to read the original, but I am not certain that you would. For many years, little boys of your age have been frightened away from it by the solemn faces and forbidding attitude of those who believe that the Holy Volume has been entrusted to their particular care. And yet you never can be thoroughly educated without knowing these stories. Besides, at one time or another in your lives, you may badly need the wisdom that lies hidden in these ancient chronicles.

This book has been a most faithful companion of man for several hundred generations. A few of the chapters were written as long as twenty-eight hundred years ago. Others are of much more recent date. For many centuries, it was almost the only book your ancestors possessed or cared to read. They knew it by heart. They made the Law of Moses the highest law of the land. Then, when the age of modern science came, there arose a conflict which gave rise to a bitter warfare between those who held the book to be of Divine origin, and those who regarded it merely as an account of certain historical events. And for a time, the Bible was hated as cordially by many men and many women as it had been loved and revered before by their fathers and grandfathers.

Of all this, I shall tell you nothing.

I am not preaching to you. I am not defending or attacking a cause. I shall merely tell you what you ought to know (in my own opinion—and Heaven forbid that I should ask others to agree!) that your lives may be more full of understanding, of tolerance and of love for that which is good and beautiful, and therefore holy.

It will be comparatively easy to write about the Old Testament. It is the story of a certain tribe of desert people who after many years of wandering, finally conquered a little corner of Western Asia where they settled down, and founded a nation of their own. Then we come to the New Testament. That is going to be very difficult. The New Testament centres around one single figure. It tells the story of a simple carpenter of the village of Nazareth, who asked nothing of life and gave all. There may be other stories more interesting than that of Jesus, but I have never read any. And so I shall give you a very simple account of his life as I see it, not a word more and not a word less. For that, I am sure, is the way he would like to have me tell it.

HENDRIK WILLEM VAN LOON.

CONTENTS

CONTENTS

LIST OF PICTURES

LIST OF PICTURES

THE STORY OF THE BIBLE

A few facts are at our disposal, and of these I shall try

A LITERARY INHERITANCE

CHAPTER I

HOW THE OLD AND THE NEW TESTAMENT CAME TO BE WRITTEN AND WHAT HAPPENED TO THE HOLY BOOK IN THE COURSE OF MANY CENTURIES

HE pyramids were a thousand years old.

Babylon and Nineveh had become the centres of vast empires.

The valley of the Nile and that of the broad Euphrates and Tigris were filled with swarming masses of busy people, when a small tribe of desert wanderers, for reasons of their own, decided to leave their home along the sandy wastes of the Arabian desert, and began to travel northward in search of more fertile fields.

In time to come, these wanderers were to be known as the Jews.

Centuries later, they were to give us the most important of all our books, the Bible.

Still later, one of their women was to give birth to the kindest and greatest of all teachers.

And yet, curious to say, we know nothing of the origin

8

of those strange folk, who came from nowhere, who played the greatest rôle ever allotted to the race of man, and then departed from the historical stage to become exiles among the nations of the world.

What I shall therefore tell you in this chapter is somewhat vague in its general character and none too reliable as to detail.

But the archæologists are busily digging in the soil of Palestine. They are learning more and more as time goes by.

A few facts are at our disposal, and of these I shall try to give you a trustworthy account.

Through the western part of Asia run two broad rivers.

They take their origin among the high mountains of the north. They lose themselves in the waters of the Persian Gulf.

Along the banks of those two muddy streams, life was very agreeable and quite lazy. Therefore the people who inhabited either the cold mountains of the north or the scorching desert of the south all tried to get a foothold in the valleys of the Tigris and the Euphrates. Whenever they had a chance, they left their old homes and wandered into the fertile plain.

They fought each other and conquered each other, and founded one civilisation right on top of the ruins of another that had gone before. They built large cities like Babylon and Nineveh, and more than forty centuries ago they turned this part of the world into a veritable paradise, the inhabitants of which were envied by all other men.

But when you look at the map you will see many millions of busy little peasants tilling the fields of another powerful country. They live on the banks of the Nile and their country is called Egypt. They are separated from Babylonia and Assyria by a narrow strip of land. There are many things which they need and which they can obtain only in the distant countries of the fertile plain. There are many things which the Babylonians and the Assyrians need, and which are manufactured only in Egypt. The two nations therefore trade with one another, and the highroad of commerce runs through the narrow strip of land which we have just mentioned.

Nowadays we call that part of the world Syria. In olden days it was known by many names. It is composed of low mountains and broad valleys. It has few trees, and the soil is baked by the sun. But a number of small lakes and many little brooks add a touch of loveliness to the sombre monotony of the rocky hills.

From the earliest times on, this region of the ancient highroads has been inhabited by different tribes, who have moved hither from the Arabian desert. They all belong to the Semitic race. They all speak an identical language. They worship the same gods. Often they fight each other. Then they make treaties of peace with each other, and fight each other again. They steal each other's cities and each other's wives and each other's flocks, and generally behave as such wandering tribes will behave when there is no higher authority in the land than the violence of their own will and the strength of their own good sword.

In a vague way they recognise the authority of the Kings of Egypt or the Kings of Babylonia or Assyria. When the tax-collectors of those mighty potentates come down the road with their armed retinue of men, the quarrelling herdsmen become very humble. With many profound bows, they acknowledge themselves the obedient servants of the Pharaoh of Memphis or the King of Akkad. But when His Excellency, the Governor, together with his soldiers, has gone, then the old life of tribal warfare continues as merrily as before.

Please do not take these struggles too seriously. They were the only outdoor sport these ancient people could enjoy, and the damage done was usually very slight. Besides, it kept the young men in good trim.

The Jews, who were to play such a great rôle in the history of the human race, began their career as one of the quarrelling, fighting, wandering, stealing little tribes who were trying to maintain themselves in the land of the High Roads. Unfortunately, we really know next to nothing of the beginning of their history. Many learned men have made many learned guesses. But a plausible guess does not fill an historic gap. And when we read that the Jews originally came from the land of Ur on the Persian Gulf, this may be true, but also it may be false. Rather than tell you many things which were not so, I tell you nothing at all, and only mention a very few facts, upon which all historians agree.

The earliest ancestors of the Jews probably lived in the desert of Arabia. We do not know in what century they left their old homesteads, that they might enter the fertile plain of western Asia. We know that they wandered for many centuries, trying to get hold of a bit of land which they could call their own, but the road which they followed has been lost. We also know that at one time or another, the Jews crossed the desert of Mount Sinai and that they lived for a while in Egypt.

From that moment on, however, Egyptian and Assyrian texts begin to throw some light upon the events which are enumerated in the Old Testament.

The rest of the story became a familiar tale—how the Jews left Egypt and after an endless trek in the desert, were united into a strong tribe—how that tribe conquered a small part of the land of the High Roads, called Palestine, and there established a nation, and how that nation fought for its independence and survived several centuries until it was absorbed by the empire of the Macedonian King, Alexander, and was then turned into part of one of the minor provinces of the great Roman state.

But when I mention these historical occurrences, bear one thing in mind. This time, I am not writing a book of history. I am not going to tell you what (according to the best historical information) actually happened. I am going to try to show you how a certain people, called the Jews, thought that certain things had happened.

As you all know, there is a great deal of difference between the things that "are facts" and the things which we "believe to be facts." Every text-book of history of every land tells the story of the past as the people of that particular country believe it to be true, but when you cross the frontier and read the text-book of the nearest neighbour, you will therein find a very different account. Yet the little children who read those chapters will believe them to be true until the end of their days.

Here and there, of course, an historian or a philosopher or another queer person will read all the books of all the countries, and perhaps he will come to an appreciation of something that approaches the absolute truth. But if he wishes to lead a peaceful and happy life, he will keep this information to himself.

What is true of the rest of the world is also true of the Jews. The Jews of thirty centuries ago and those of twenty centuries ago and those of to-day are ordinary human beings, just as you and I. They are no better (as they sometimes claim) and no worse (as their enemies often state) than any one else. They possess certain virtues which are very uncommon, and they also have certain faults which are exceedingly common. But so much has been written about them, good, bad and indifferent, that it is very difficult to come to a correct estimate of their just place in history.

We experience the same difficulty when we try to learn the historical value of the chronicles which the Jews themselves kept and which tell us their adventures among the men of Egypt and among the men of the land of Canaan and among the men of the land of Babylonia.

Newcomers are rarely popular. In most of the countries which the Jews visited during their endless years of peregrination, they were newcomers. The old and settled inhabitants of the valleys of the Nile and of the dales of Palestine and those who lived along the banks of the Euphrates did not receive them with open arms. On the contrary, they said, "We have hardly room for our own sons and daughters. Let those foreigners go elsewhere." Then there was trouble.

When the Jewish historians looked back upon those ancient days, they tried to place their own ancestors in the best possible light. Nowadays we do the same thing. We praise the virtues of the Puritan settlers of Massachusetts and we describe the horrors of those first years when the poor white man was forever exposed to the cruel arrow of the savage. But we rarely mention the fate of the red man, who was exposed to the equally cruel bullet of the white man's blunderbuss.

An honest history, written from the point of view of the Indians, would make mighty interesting reading. But the Indian is dead and gone, and we shall never know how the coming of the foreigners in the year 1620 impressed him. Which is a pity.

For many centuries, the Old Testament was the only history of old Asia which our grandfathers could decipher and understand. But a century ago, we began to learn how to read the hieroglyphics of Egypt, and fifty years ago we discovered the key to the mysterious nail-writing of Babylon. We now know that there was a very different side to the stories which were related by the old Jewish chronicle writers.

We see them commit the mistakes of all patriotic historians and we understand how they perverted the truth to increase the glory and the splendour of their own race.

All this, however (I repeat it), does not properly belong in my book. I am not writing a history of the Jewish people. I am not defending them, or attacking their motives. I am merely repeating their own version of ancient Asiatic and African history. I shall not study the critical texts of learned historians. A little Bible, bought for a dime, will provide me with all the material I can possibly need.

If you had used the word "Bible" to a Jew of the first century of our era, he would not have known what you were talking about. The word is comparatively new. It was invented in the fourth century by John Chrysostom, the patriarch of Constantinople, who referred to the general collection of Holy Books of the Jews as the "Biblia" or the "Books."

This collection had been growing steadily for almost a thousand years. With a few exceptions, the chapters had all been written in Hebrew. But Hebrew was no longer a spoken language when Jesus was born. Aramaic (much simpler and widely known among the common people) had taken its place and several of the prophetic utterances of the Old Testament were written in that language. But please don't ask me "when the Bible was written," because I could not answer you.

Every little Jewish village and every little Jewish temple possessed certain accounts of its own which had been copied on the skins of animals or on bits of Egyptian papyrus by pious old men, who took an interest in such things. Sometimes small collections were made of different laws and of prophecies for handy use among those who visited the temple.

During the eighth century B. C., when the Jews had settled down to their life in Palestine, those compilations grew larger and larger. At some time or other between the third and the first century before our era, they were translated into the Greek language, and were brought to Europe. Since then they have been translated into every language of the world.

As for the New Testament, its history is quite simple. During the first two or three centuries after the death of Christ, the followers of the humble carpenter of Nazareth were forever in danger of trouble with the Roman authorities. The doctrines of love and charity were thought to be very dangerous to the safety of the Roman state, which had been founded upon the brute strength of the sword. The early Christians, therefore, could not go to a book store and say: "Please give me a 'Life of Christ' and an account of the acts of his Apostles." They got their information from secret little pamphlets which were passed from hand to hand. Thousands of such pamphlets were copied and re-copied, until people lost all track of the truth of their contents.

Meanwhile, the Church had been triumphant. The persecuted Christians became the rulers of the old Roman state. First of all they brought some order into the literary chaos caused by three centuries of persecution. The (head of the) Church called together a number of learned men. They read all the accounts which were popular, and discarded most of them. They decided to keep a few of the gospels and a few of the letters which had been written by the Apostles to the members of distant congregations. All the other stories were discarded.

Then followed several centuries of discussion and dispute. Many famous Synods were held in Rome and in Carthage (a new city built upon the ruins of the famous old seaport) and in Trullo, and seven hundred years after the death of Christ the New Testament (as we know it) was definitely adopted by the Churches of the East and by those of the West. Since then there have been countless translations made from the original Greek, but no very important changes have occurred in the text.

CREATION

CHAPTER II

HOW THE JEWS BELIEVED THAT THE WORLD HAD BEEN CREATED

HE oldest of all questions is this: "Where do we come from?"

Some people ask it until the very day of their death. They do not really expect to get an answer, but they are happy in the courage that makes them face the realities of life, and like brave soldiers, facing a hopeless task, they refuse to surrender and they pass into eternity with the proud word "why" upon their lips.

This world, however, is full of all sorts of men and women. Most of them insist upon a plausible explanation of the things which they do not understand. When no explanation is forthcoming, they invent one of their own.

Five thousand years ago a story which told of the creation of this world in seven days was common among all the people of western Asia. And this was the Jewish version of it.

They vaguely attributed the making of the land and of the

sea and of the trees and the flowers and the birds and of man and woman to their different gods.

But it happened that the Jews were the first among all people to recognise the existence of One Single God. Afterwards when we come to talk of the days of Moses, we shall tell you how this came about.

In the beginning, however, the particular Semitic tribe which later was to develop into the Jewish nation, worshipped several divinities, just as all their neighbours had done before them for countless ages.

The stories of the creation, however, which we find in the Old Testament, were written more than a thousand years after the death of Moses, when the idea of One God had been accepted by the Jews as an absolutely established fact, and when doubt of His Existence meant exile or death.

You will now understand how the poet who gave unto the Hebrew people their final version of the beginning of all things, came to describe the gigantic labour of creation as the sudden expression of one single and all-mighty will, and as the work of their own tribal God, whom they called Jehovah, or the Ruler of the High Heavens.

And this is how the story was told to the worshippers in the temple.

In the beginning, this earth floated through space in sombre silence and darkness. There was no land, but the endless waters of the deep ocean covered our vast empires. Then the Spirit of Jehovah came brooding over the sea, contemplating mighty things. And Jehovah said, "Let there be light," and the first rays of dawn appeared amidst the darkness. "This," Jehovah said, "I shall call the Day."

But soon the flickering light came to an end and all was

as it had been before. "And this," Jehovah said, "shall be called the Night." Then he rested from his labours, and so ended the first of all days.

Then Jehovah said: "Let there be a Heaven, which shall spread its vast dome across the waters below, that there may be a place for the clouds and for the winds which blow across

LET THERE BE LAND

the sea." This was done. Once more there was an evening and a morning, and there was an end to the second day.

Then Jehovah said, "Let there be land amidst the water." At once the rugged mountains showed their dripping heads above the surface of the ocean, and soon they arose mightily towards the high Heavens and at their feet the plains and the valleys spread far and wide. Then Jehovah said, "Let the land be fertile with plants which bear seed, and with trees that bear flowers and fruit." And the earth was green with a soft carpet of grass and the trees and the shrubs enjoyed the soft caress of the early dawn. And once more the morning was followed by eventide, and so the labour of the third day came to an end.

Then Jehovah said: "Let the Heavens be filled with stars that the seasons and the days and the years may be marked. And let the day be ruled by the sun, but the night shall be a time of rest, when only the silent moon shall show the belated wanderer across the desert the true road to shelter." This too was done, and so ended the fourth day.

Then Jehovah said: "Let the waters be full of fishes and the sky be full of birds." And he made the mighty whale and the tiny minnows and the ostrich and the sparrow, and he gave them the earth and the

THE SUN, THE MOON AND THE STARS

ocean as their dwelling place and told them to increase, that they and little minnows and little whales and ostriches and sparrows might enjoy the blessings of life. And that night, when the birds tucked their tired heads underneath their wings and when the fishes steered into the darkness of the deep, there was an end to the fifth day.

Then Jehovah said: "It is not enough. Let the world also be full of creatures that creep and such as walk on legs." And he made the cows and the tigers and all the beasts we know unto this very day and many others that since have disappeared from this earth. And when this was done, Jehovah took some of the dust of the soil, and he moulded it into an image, resembling Himself, and he gave it life, and he called it man, and he placed it at the head of all creation. So ended the labour of the sixth day, and Jehovah was contented with what he had wrought and on the seventh day he rested from his work.

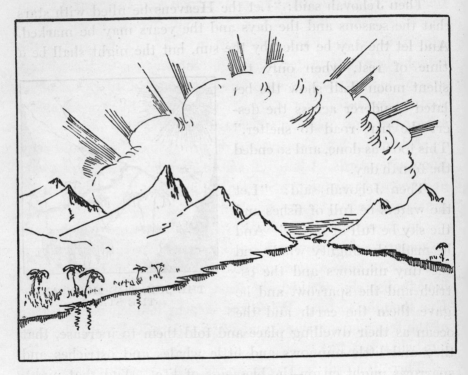

THE FIRST SABBATH

Then came the eighth day, and Man found himself amidst his new kingdom. His name was Adam, and he lived in a garden filled with lovely flowers, and with peaceful animals who came and brought their kittens and their puppies, that he might play with them and forget his loneliness. But even so, Man was not happy. For all other creatures had been given the companionship of their own kind, but Man was alone. Therefore, Jehovah took a rib from Adam's body and out of it, created Eve. Then Adam and Eve wandered forth to explore their home, which was called Paradise.

At last they came to a mighty tree and there Jehovah spoke to them and said: "Listen, for this is very important. Of the fruit of all the trees in this garden you may eat to your hearts' content. But this is the tree that gives forth the knowledge of Good and Evil. When Man eats from the fruit of this tree, he begins to understand the righteousness or the wickedness of his own acts. That means an end to all peace of his soul. Therefore, you must leave the fruit of this tree alone, or accept the consequences, which are very terrible."

Adam and Eve listened and promised that they would obey. Soon afterwards, Adam fell asleep, but Eve remained awake and began to wander. Suddenly there was a rustling in the grass, and behold! there was a crafty old serpent.

In those days the animals spoke a language which could be understood by man, and so the serpent had no difficulty in telling Eve how he had overheard the words of Jehovah, and how foolish she would be if she were to take them seriously. Eve thought so too. When the serpent handed her the fruit of the tree, she ate some, and when Adam woke up, she gave him what was left.

Then Jehovah was very angry. At once he drove both Adam and Eve from Paradise, and they went forth into the world to make a living as best they could.

In due course of time they had two children. They were both boys. The name of the elder was Cain, but the younger was called Abel.

They made themselves useful around the house. Cain worked in the fields and Abel tended his father's sheep. Of course they quarrelled as brothers are apt to quarrel.

One day, they both brought offerings to Jehovah. Abel

had killed a lamb, and Cain had placed some grain upon the rude stone altar which they had built as a place for worship.

Children are apt to be jealous of each other, and they like to brag about their own virtues.

The wood on Abel's altar was burning merrily, but Cain had trouble with his flint.

Cain thought that Abel was laughing at him. Abel said no, he was just standing by and looking on.

Cain asked him to go away. Abel said no, why should he? Then Cain hit Abel.

But he hit him much too hard, and Abel fell down dead.

Cain was terribly frightened and ran away.

But Jehovah, who knew what had happened, found him hiding in some bushes. He asked him where his brother was. Cain, in a

THE DEATH OF ABEL

surly mood, would not answer. How should he know? He was not a nurse-maid, supposed to be looking after his little brother, was he?

But of course, this lie did not do him any good. Just as Jehovah had driven Adam and Eve from Paradise because they had disobeyed his will, so he now forced Cain to run away from home, and although he lived for many years, his father and mother never saw him again.

As for Adam and Eve, their lives were very unhappy.

Their younger son was dead and their older boy had run away.

They had many more children and they died when they were very old and bent down with endless years of toil and misfortune.

*　　*　　*　　*　　*

Gradually the children and the grandchildren of Adam and Eve began to populate the earth. They went east and they went west and they went northwards into the mountains and they lost themselves amidst the sandy wastes of the southern desert.

But the crime of Cain had set its mark upon the early race. Forever the hand of man was lifted against his neighbour. People murdered each other and they stole each other's sheep. It was not safe for a girl to leave her home, lest she be kidnapped by the boys of the neighbouring villages.

The world was in a sad state. A false start had been made. It was necessary to begin all over again. Perhaps a new generation would prove to be more obedient to the will of Jehovah.

In those days there lived a man called Noah. He was the grandson of Methuselah (who lived nine hundred and sixty-nine years) and he was a descendant of Seth, a younger brother of Cain and Abel, who was born after the family tragedy had taken place.

Noah was a good man who tried to be at peace with his conscience and with his fellow men. If the human race had to begin once more, Noah would make a very good ancestor.

Jehovah therefore decided to kill all other people, but to spare Noah. He came to Noah and told him to build a ship. The vessel was to be four hundred and fifty feet long and seventy-five feet wide and it was to have a depth of forty-three feet. This made it almost as large as a modern ocean liner and it is difficult to see how Noah constructed such an enormous craft entirely out of wood.

THE BUILDING OF THE ARK

But he and his sons set to work with a will. The neighbours stood by and laughed. What a funny idea to be building a ship, when there was not a river or a sea for (a thousand) miles around!

But Noah and his faithful workmen stuck to their job

They cut down the mighty cypress trees and laid the keel and built the sides and covered them with pitch, that the hold might be dry. When the third deck had been finished, a roof was built. It was made of heavy timber, to withstand the violence of the rain that was to pour down upon this wicked earth.

Then Noah and his household, his three sons and their wives, made ready for the voyage. They went into the fields and into the mountains and gathered all the animals they could find that they might have beasts for food and for sacrifices when they should return to dry land.

A whole week they hunted. And then the Ark (for so the ship was called) was full of the noise of strange creatures who did not like their cramped quarters and who bit at the bars of their cages. The fish, of course, were not taken. They could look after themselves.

On the evening of the seventh day, Noah and his family went on board. They pulled in the gang plank and closed the door.

Late that night, it began to rain. It rained for forty nights and for forty days. At the end of this time, the whole earth was covered with water, and Noah and his fellow travellers in the Ark were the only living ones to survive this terrible deluge.

*   *   *   *   *

Then, however, Jehovah had mercy. A violent wind swept the clouds away. Once more the rays of the sun rested upon the turbulent waves as they had done when the world was first created.

Carefully Noah opened a window and peered out. But his ship floated peacefully in the midst of an endless ocean and no land was in sight.

Noah sent out a raven, but the bird came back. Next he sent out a pigeon. Pigeons can fly longer than almost any other bird, but the poor thing could not find a single branch upon which to rest its feet, and it came back to the Ark and Noah took it and put it back into its cage.

He waited a week, and once more he set the pigeon free. It was gone all day, but in the evening, it returned with a

IT BEGAN TO RAIN

freshly plucked olive leaf in its beak. Apparently, the waters were receding.

Another week went by before Noah released the pigeon for the third time. It did not return, and this was a good sign. Soon afterwards, a sudden bump told Noah that his vessel had struck ground. The Ark had landed on top of Mount Ararat, in the country which is now called Armenia.

* * * * *

The next day Noah went ashore. At once he took some

THE ALTAR

stones and built an altar and killed a number of beasts and birds and made a sacrifice. And behold, the sky was bright with the colours of a mighty rainbow. It was a sign of Jehovah to his faithful servant. It was a promise of future happiness.

Then Noah and his sons, Shem, Ham and Japheth, and their wives, went forth and once more they became farmers and shepherds and lived peacefully among their children and their flocks.

But it is very doubtful whether the danger through which they had just passed had taught them a lesson. For it happened that Noah, who possessed a vineyard, had made himself a very pleasant wine, and when he had partaken thereof, more than was wise, he became drunken, and behaved after the fashion of such people.

THE RAINBOW

Two of his sons felt sorry for their old father, and were quite decent about it. But the third one, called Ham, thought it a great joke and laughed loudly, and was not nice at all.

When Noah woke up from his sleep, he was exceedingly angry and he drove Ham away from his house, and the Jews

THE TOWER OF BABEL

believed that he went to Africa and became the first ancestor of the Negro race, for which they felt a great and most unjust contempt.

Thereafter, we don't hear much about Noah. One of his descendants, called Nimrod, achieved fame as a hunter, but the Bible does not tell what became of Shem and Japheth.

Their sons, however, did something which greatly displeased

Jehovah. For a while, so it seems, they moved into the valley of the Euphrates, where afterwards the city of Babylon was built. They liked to live in this fertile region and they decided to build a very high tower which should serve as a rallying point to all the tribes of their own race. They baked bricks and they laid the foundations for a huge structure.

But Jehovah did not want them to remain for ever in one spot. The whole world had to be populated, not just one little valley.

While the people were busy as bees upon their Babylonian tower, Jehovah suddenly made them all speak different dialects. They forgot their own common tongue and a babble of voices arose on the scaffolding.

You cannot build a house when the workmen and the foremen and the architects suddenly begin to speak Chinese and Dutch and Russian and Polynesian. So the people gave up the idea of a single nation, clustered around the feet of a single tower, and within a short time they had spread to the uttermost corners of the earth.

This, in a few words, is the story of the beginning of the world. From now on, however, we shall only relate the adventures of the race men called the Jews.

THE PIONEERS

CHAPTER III

THE EGYPTIAN PYRAMIDS WERE AGES OLD WHEN THE JEWS, UNDER THE LEADERSHIP OF ABRAHAM, VENTURED FORTH FROM THE OUTSKIRTS OF THE STONY DESERT OF ARABIA AND WENT WESTWARD TO FIND NEW PASTURAGE FOR THEIR FLOCKS

BRAHAM was a pioneer.

He died many thousand years ago, but the story of his life reminds us of the brave men and women who conquered the plains and the mountains of our own west during the first half of the nineteenth century.

The family of Abraham came from the land of Ur which was situated on the western bank of the river Euphrates.

They had all been shepherds ever since their great-grandfather Shem had left the Ark. They had done well in this world, and Abraham himself was a rich farmer who owned thousands of sheep. He employed more than three hundred men and boys to look after his flocks.

They were very loyal to their master and would give their lives for him at a moment's notice. They formed a small private army and they were of great use when Abraham had to fight for new pastures in the hostile land near the Mediterranean shore.

When Abraham was seventy-five years old, he heard the voice of Jehovah, who bade him move away from his father's house and find a new home in Canaan, which was the old name for Palestine.

Abraham was glad to go. The Chaldeans, among whom he then lived, were forever at war with their neighbours, and this wise old Jew was a man of peace, and saw little good in all this useless strife.

He ordered his tents to be taken down. His men rounded up his sheep. The women packed the sleeping rugs and put up food for the trip through the desert. And so began the first great migration of the Jewish people.

Abraham was married. The name of his wife was Sarah. Unfortunately, she had no children. And so Abraham took Lot, his nephew, to be second-lieutenant of the expedition. Then he gave the sign for departure, and followed a path which led him straight towards the setting sun.

His caravan did not enter the great Babylonian valley, but kept close to the outskirts of the desert of Arabia, where the soldiers of the ferocious Assyrian army could not find the Jews and steal their sheep and perhaps their women. Without mishap, they all reached the pastures of western Asia.

There they halted near the village of Shechem, where Abraham built an altar to Jehovah near an oak, called Moreh. Afterwards, he moved on towards Bethel, where he rested for a while to decide upon his future plans. For alas! the land of Canaan was not as rich as he had expected.

When Abraham and Lot so suddenly appeared with all their flocks, the grass of the hillsides was soon eaten up. Then the shepherds of Abraham and Lot began to fight among each other to see who should get the best pastures, and soon the expedition threatened to end in a general riot.

ABRAHAM BUILDS AN ALTAR

This was entirely contrary to the nature of Abraham. He called his nephew into his tent and he spoke to him and proposed that they divide the country and live in peace, as good relatives should always do.

Lot, too, was a sensible young man, and so he and his uncle came to terms without any difficulty.

The nephew preferred to remain in the valley of the river Jordan, and Abraham took the rest of the country, which is now generally called Palestine. He had spent the greater part of his life under the scorching sun of the desert. No wonder that he hastened to find a place which should offer him the cool shade of mighty trees.

ABRAHAM AND LOT REACH RIVER JORDAN

He pitched his tent among the oaks of Mamre, near the old city of Hebron, and there he built another new altar to show his gratitude that Jehovah had safely guided him into this happy new home.

But he was not allowed to live in peace very long. His nephew was already in trouble with his neighbours and Abraham was forced to go to war to protect his family.

The most dangerous of the native rulers was the mighty King of Elam. He was so powerful that he could hold his own against the rulers of Assyria. Just then he was trying to levy tribute from the cities of Sodom and Gomorrah. When they refused to pay, the King of Elam marched against them with his army.

Unfortunately, the fighting took place in the valley which Lot had occupied. Soldiers, when they get excited, do not always stop to ask questions. When they rounded up the men and women from Sodom and Gomorrah, to carry them away as prisoners, they also took Lot and his family.

Abraham heard of this through a neighbour who had managed to run away. He called together all his shepherds. He himself rode at the head of his troop. In the middle of the night he reached the camp of the King of Elam. He attacked the sleepy Elamites at once and before the sleepy guards knew what had happened, Abraham had set Lot free and was on his way back to the river Jordan.

Of course, this made him a great man in the eyes of the neighbouring tribes.

The King of Sodom, who had escaped the slaughter, came forward to meet him. He was accompanied by Melchizedek, who was King of Salem, or Jerusalem, a very ancient city in the land of Canaan which had existed hundreds of years before the Jews had moved westward.

Melchizedek and Abraham became fast friends, for they both recognised Jehovah as the ruler of all the world, but Abraham did not like the King of Sodom, who worshipped strange heathenish gods, and when the King of Sodom offered Abraham the greater part of the booty which he had recaptured from the Elamites, he refused to take it. His hungry men had eaten a few of the sheep, but all the rest went back to the rightful owners in the city of Sodom.

Alas! they did not make good use of it.

Both the people of Sodom and those of Gomorrah had a very bad reputation in the western part of Asia. They were lazy and indolent and they committed all sorts of wicked crimes and never brought a murderer to justice for his wickedness.

Often they had been warned that this could not go on for ever. They merely laughed and continued to be a general nuisance to all the decent folks of that part of the world.

Now it happened one evening, when the red sun had disappeared beneath the dark blue mountain ridges, that Abraham was sitting in front of his tent. He was contented with life, for now at last the promise of Jehovah, made in the old days in the land of Ur, was about to come true. Abraham, who had never had a son, expected his wife Sarah to give him a baby.

He was thinking of this and of many other things, when three strangers came walking down the road. They were tired and dusty and Abraham bade them enter and rest for a while. Sarah was called and she hastily cooked some dinner and afterwards they all sat and talked underneath the tree where they had eaten.

When it grew late, the strangers said that they must be on their way. Abraham offered to show them the nearest road. Then he learned that they were going to Sodom and Gomorrah. Suddenly he recognised that he had been host to Jehovah and two of his angels.

He could well imagine what their mission was, and forever loyal to his own people, he asked that mercy might be shown to Lot and his wife and children.

This Jehovah promised. He went further than that. He promised that he would spare the two cities if he could find fifty or thirty or even ten decent people in either of them.

He does not seem to have been very successful.

For late that evening, Lot received warning that he must at once take his family and bring them to safety, as both Sodom and Gomorrah were to be burned to ashes before morning. He was told to make all possible haste and that he must not waste his time by looking backwards to see what was happening.

Lot obeyed. He awakened his wife and his children and they walked all night, as fast as they could, that they might get to the village of Zoar before morning.

But ere they reached a place of safety, Lot had lost his wife.

She was just a little bit too curious. The sky was red and she knew that all her neighbours were burning to death.

She peeped just once.

But Jehovah saw it. He changed the woman into a pillar of salt and Lot was left a widower with two young daughters. One of these afterwards became the mother of Moab, after whom the tribe of the Moabites was called, and the name of the son of the other was Ben-Ammi. He founded in turn the well-known tribe of the Ammonites.

LOT'S WIFE IS TURNED INTO A PILLAR OF SALT

The sad experience of Lot had greatly depressed Abraham. He too decided to move away from his present whereabouts and farther away from the blackened ruins of the wicked cities and their vile memory.

He left the forest and the plains of Mamre, and once more went westward until he almost reached the shores of the Mediterranean.

The region along the coast was inhabited by a race of men who had come from the distant island of Crete. Their capital city, Cnossos, had been destroyed by an unknown enemy a thousand years before the days of Abraham. Those who had escaped had tried to get a foothold in Egypt, but they had been driven away by the armies of Pharaoh. They had then sailed eastward, and as they were much better armed than the Canaanites, they had been able to conquer a narrow strip of land along the shore of the big sea.

The Egyptians had called these people Philistines, and they in turn called their own country Philistia, or, as we now say, Palestine.

The Philistines were forever at war with all their neighbours, and they and the Jews never stopped quarrelling until the Romans came and made an end to their independence. Their ancestors had been the most civilised people of the western world, when the Jews were still rough shepherds. They had known how to make iron swords when the peasants of Mesopotamia were killing each other with clubs and stone axes. This will explain to you why a few Philistines could for so many centuries hold their own against thousands and thousands of Canaanites and Jews.

THE PHILISTINES LAND ON THE COAST OF PALESTINE

All the same, Abraham and his army of retainers marched bravely into the land of Philistia, and settled down near Beer-Sheba. There they built an altar to Jehovah. They dug a deep well that they might have fresh water at all hours, and they planted a grove that their children might enjoy the cool shade of the trees.

It was really a pleasant home and here the son of Abraham and Sarah was born. His parents called him Isaac, which means "laughter," for surely it was happiness to have an heir when both the father and the mother had given up all hope.

As a matter of fact, during the years of waiting, when it seemed that there would be no descendants, Abraham had taken unto himself a second wife. This was according to the custom of the time and the country. Even to-day, many people in Asia and Africa, who belong to the Mohammedan religion, are allowed to have two or three wives.

The second wife of Abraham was not a Jewess. She was an Egyptian slave girl, named Hagar. Sarah, quite naturally, did not like her at all, and when Hagar had become the mother of a boy, who was called Ishmael, Sarah began to hate the other woman and tried to destroy her.

ABRAHAM BUILT HIMSELF A HOME IN THE NEW COUNTRY

Of course, it was natural for Ishmael and his half-brother to play together on the farm. Most likely at times they quarrelled, and I have no doubt but that sometimes they engaged in a merry fight.

All this Sarah took with very ill grace.

She was much older and not half as pretty as Hagar. She wanted to get rid of this dangerous rival for her husband's affection for all time, and she wanted to get rid of her right then and there.

She went to Abraham and insisted that he send Hagar and Ishmael away. Abraham refused. After all, Ishmael was his own son and he loved the boy. It would not be fair.

But Sarah was firm, and at last, Jehovah Himself told Abraham that he had better follow his wife's wishes. There was no use arguing.

One very sad morning the patient Abraham, for the sake of peace, bade farewell to the faithful slave-girl and to his child. He told Hagar to return to her own people. But it was a long and dangerous voyage from the land of the Philistines to Egypt. Before a week was over, Hagar and Ishmael had almost perished from thirst. They lost their way completely in the wilderness of Beer-Sheba and they would have died of thirst when Jehovah rescued them at the last moment and showed them where to find fresh water.

HAGAR'S FLIGHT

Eventually Hagar reached the banks of the Nile. She and Ishmael found a welcome home among their relations and when the boy grew up, he became a soldier. As for his father, he never saw Ishmael again, and soon afterwards he almost lost his second son. That, however, came about in a very different way.

Abraham, above all things, had always obeyed the will of Jehovah. He prided himself upon his righteousness and piety. Finally, Jehovah decided to try him once more, and this time, the result was almost deadly.

Suddenly Jehovah appeared to Abraham and told him to

take Isaac into the mountains of Moriah, to kill him, and then burn his body as a sacrifice.

The old pioneer was faithful unto the last. He ordered two of his men to get ready for a short trip. He loaded wood on the back of his donkey. He took water and provisions and pushed into the desert. He had not told his wife what he was going to do. Jehovah had spoken. That was enough.

After three days, Abraham and Isaac, who had played happily by the roadside, reached Mount Moriah.

Then Abraham told his two servants to wait. He himself took Isaac by the hand and climbed to the top of the hill.

By now, Isaac was beginning to be curious. He had often seen his father make an offering. This time, however, something was different. He recognised the stone altar. He saw the wood. His father carried the long-bladed knife that was used to cut the throat of the sacrificial lamb. But where was the lamb? He asked his father.

"Jehovah will provide the lamb when the time comes," Abraham answered.

Then he picked up his son and laid him upon the rough stone of the altar.

Then he took his knife.

He pushed the head of Isaac back, that he might more easily cut the artery of the neck.

And then a voice was heard.

Once more Jehovah spoke.

He now knew that Abraham was the most loyal of all his followers, and he did not insist that the old man give further proof of his devotion.

Isaac was lifted to his feet. A big black ram, who had been caught by his horns in a nearby bush, was caught and sacrificed in his stead.

Three days later, father and son were back with Sarah. But Abraham seems to have taken a dislike to the country where he had experienced so much unhappiness. He left Beer-

ABRAHAM SACRIFICES ISAAC

Sheba where everything reminded him of Hagar and of Ishmael and of the terrible trip to Mount Moriah. He returned to the old plains of Mamre, where he had lived when he first had reached the west, and he built himself a new home.

Sarah was too old to stand the hardships of another trip. She died, and she was buried in the cave of Machpelah, which Abraham had bought for four hundred shekels from a Hittite farmer by the name of Ephron.

Then Abraham felt very lonely.

He had lived an active life. He had travelled and he had

THE BURIAL OF SARAH

worked and he had fought hard, and now he was tired and wanted to rest.

But the future of Isaac troubled him. The boy, of course, would marry. But all the girls of the neighbourhood belonged to the tribe of the Canaanites, and Abraham did not want a daughter-in-law who would teach his grand-children to worship strange gods, of whom he did not approve. He had heard that his brother Nahor, who had remained in the old country when Abraham had gone west, had raised quite a large family. He liked the idea of Isaac marrying one of his cousins. It would keep the family together and there would not be all this bother about foreign women.

And so Abraham called one of his oldest servants (who for many years had been the manager of his estate) and told him what to do. He explained just what sort of girl he wanted for Isaac. She must be well versed in the art of making a home, she must be a help on the farm, and above all things, she must be kindly and generous.

The servant said that he understood.

He took a dozen camels and loaded them heavily with gifts. For Abraham, his master, had done well in the land of Canaan, and the people of the old home must be made to understand the importance of their former fellow citizen.

For many days the servant travelled eastward, following the same route which Abraham had taken almost eighty years before. When he reached the land of Ur, he went more slowly and tried to discover where the family of Nahor might be living.

REBEKAH'S WELL

One evening, when the heat of the day was giving way to the cool of the desert night, he found himself near the town of Haran. The women were just coming out of the city to fill their pitchers with water and prepare for supper.

The messenger made his camels kneel down. He was hot and tired and asked one of the girls to give him a drink. She said, "Yes, certainly," and she was most cheerful about it, and when the man had had enough, she asked him to wait a moment, that she might give some water to his poor camels, and when he asked her whether she knew of a place where he could spend the night, she told him that her father would be only too happy to put him up and feed his camels and let him rest until it was time to continue his voyage. All this seemed too good to be true. Here was the perfect image of the woman whom Abraham had described to his servant, and she was alive and young and beautiful.

One more question remained to be asked. Who was she?

Her name was Rebekah, and she was the daughter of Bethuel, the son of Nahor. She had a brother called Laban, and she had heard of an uncle, called Abraham, who had moved into the land of Canaan, years and years before she was born.

Then the messenger knew that he had found the girl he was looking for. He went to Bethuel and explained his errand. He told the story of his master and how Abraham was one of the richest and most powerful men of the country near the Mediterranean Sea. And when he had duly impressed the people of Ur with a display of the rugs and the silver earrings and the golden goblets, which he had brought from Hebron, he asked that Rebekah might accompany him to become the wife of young Isaac.

Both the father and the brother were more than willing to make such an alliance. In those days, the girls were rarely consulted in such matters. But Bethuel was a reasonable man, who wanted his daughter to be happy, and he asked Rebekah whether she was willing to go to a foreign country and marry her cousin whom she had never seen.

She answered, "I will go," and made ready to leave immediately.

Her old nurse accompanied her. So did many of her maids. And they all rode their camels, wondering what sort of strange new country this might be of which the messenger had painted such a glorious picture.

The first impression was a very happy one.

It was towards evening.

The camels were plodding through the dust of the road. In the distance, a man was seen walking in the fields.

When he heard the tinkling bells, he stopped.

He recognised his own animals. He rushed forward and beheld the veiled face of the woman who was to be his wife.

With a few words the servant told the young master all he had done and how Rebekah was as good as she was beautiful.

Then Isaac considered himself a lucky man (as indeed he was) and he married Rebekah and a short time later Abraham died and was buried by the side of his wife Sarah in the cave of Machpelah. And Isaac and Rebekah inherited all the fields and the flocks and everything that had belonged to Abraham and they were young and happy, and when evening came, they used to sit outside their tents and play with their boys who were twins; and the name of the elder was Esau, which meant the "hairy one," and the name of the younger was Jacob, and they were to have many strange adventures, as we shall now tell you.

For Esau and Jacob were as little alike as any two brothers have ever been.

Esau was a rough and honest young fellow, as brown as a bear. He had strong, hairy arms, and was as swift as a horse. He spent all his time out in the open, hunting and trapping, and living with the beasts and the birds of the fields.

Jacob, on the other hand, rarely strayed far away from home. He was his mother's darling, and Rebekah was very foolish in the way she spoiled him.

Big, noisy Esau, who always smelled of camels and goats, and who was for ever bringing puppies home from the stable into the house, did not please her at all. She thought him a dull fellow, only interested in commonplace things. But Jacob, with his mild ways and his pleasant smile, impressed his mother as a very bright boy. She was sorry that he had not been born ahead of Esau. Then he would have been his father's heir, and now all of Isaac's riches were to go to a country bumpkin, who hated fine rugs and fine furniture, and who was no better than one of the sheepmen of the ranch, and hated the bother of being rich and belonging to a famous family.

But facts were facts, even in those days, and Jacob had to content himself with the humble rôle of a younger son, while big, indifferent Esau was known far and wide as one of the most important men of the country.

The story of the plot between Rebekah and her son Jacob, and how mother and son finally tried to cheat the elder brother out of his inheritance, all this does not make pleasant reading. As it had great influence (to bear) upon the rest of our chronicle, it must be told, although I would gladly spare you the details.

Esau, as we have just said, was a hunter and a farmer and a shepherd, who spent most of his time out in the open. He was easy-going, as such people are apt to be. Life to him was a simple affair of sunshine and wind and flocks of sheep—things that more or less took care of themselves. He was not interested in learned discussions. When he was hungry, he ate— when he was thirsty, he drank—when he was sleepy, he went to bed.

Why worry about anything else?

Jacob, on the other hand, sat for ever at home and brooded. He was greedy. He wanted things. How could he get hold of what really belonged to his elder brother?

One day his chance came.

Esau came home from a hunting trip. He was hungry

as a wolf. Jacob was fussing around in the kitchen, making himself a fine stew of lentils.

"Let me have some, and let me have it right now," Esau begged.

Jacob pretended not to hear him.

"I am starving," Esau said; "give me a plate of your lentils."

"What will you give me in return?" his brother asked.

"Anything," Esau answered, for just then he wanted to eat, and he found it very difficult to think of two things at the same time.

"Will you give me all your rights as the eldest son?"

"Certainly. What good are they to me when I must sit here and die of starvation? Let me have a plate of your stew, and keep all the old rights."

"You swear to it?"

"I will swear to anything! Give me some of those lentils."

Unfortunately, the Jews of those early days were very formal. Other people might have thought that such talk between young men amounted to no more than a jest—a hungry fellow who promises everything he has for a square meal.

A promise, however, in Jacob's eyes, was a promise.

He told his mother of what had happened. Esau had voluntarily, and in consideration of a bowl of stew, surrendered his birthright. Now they must discover some way in which they could obtain Isaac's official consent, and then the contract would be formal.

The occasion offered itself very soon.

Isaac was suffering from a complaint which is quite common among the people of the desert. He was losing his eyesight. Besides, he had just passed through a very difficult period.

There had been a prolonged drought in the plains of Mamre, and Isaac had been obliged to move his flocks further westward into the heart of the land of the Philistines.

Of course, the Philistines had tried to keep him out. They had filled up the wells which Abraham, a generation before, had dug in the wilderness of Beer-Sheba. The journey had been weary and the hardships had aged Isaac, who longed for the familiar sight of the old homestead.

ESAU HAS LOST HIS
BIRTHRIGHT

Now at last he was back in the land of Hebron. He felt that he did not have much longer to live and wished to order his affairs that he might die in peace. And so he sent for Esau, his eldest son, and asked him to go out into the woods and shoot a deer and make him a roast, such as he loved to eat. Then he would bless him and would bestow his goods upon him as was according to the law.

Esau said "Yes," he would do this. He fetched his trusted bow and arrows and left the house. But Rebekah had overheard the conversation and she now hastened to tell Jacob.

"Quick!" she whispered, "the time has come. Your father is feeling very badly to-day. He fears that he is going to die and he wants to bless Esau before he goes to bed to-night. But I want you to disguise yourself and make the old man believe that you are Esau. Then he will give you everything he has, and that is what we both want."

Jacob did not like the idea. The plan seemed too risky.

How could he, with his smooth skin and his high-pitched voice, pretend to be the hairy Esau? Rebekah, however, had thought it all out.

"It is simple," she told him. "I will show you."

She hastily killed two young goats and she roasted the meat as Esau used to do. Then she took the skins of the dead animals and tied them around the hands and arms of Jacob. She put an old, sweaty coat, which belonged to Esau, across Jacob's shoulders, and she bade him speak in a gruff tone, and behave just as Esau did upon such occasions.

Isaac was completely deceived. He heard the familiar voice. He noticed the smell of the fields which was for ever in Esau's coat. He felt the strong, hairy arms of his eldest born. And when he had eaten, he made the impostor kneel down and he blessed him and made him heir to all he possessed.

But as soon as Jacob had left his father's room, behold! Esau returned. Then there was a terrible scene. The blessing had been given and Isaac could not go back on his word. He told Esau of his great love, but the evil had been done. Jacob was a thief. He had stolen everything that belonged to his elder brother.

As for Esau, he went storming about and vowed that he would kill Jacob as soon as he had a chance. This frightened Rebekah, who knew that her own spoiled darling was no match for this angry man, made stronger by his righteous wrath.

She told Jacob to flee and go east to the land where her brother Laban lived. And he had better stay there until things had quieted down a little at home. Meanwhile, he might marry one of his cousins and settle down among his uncle's people.

Jacob, who was no hero, did what his mother told him.

But his bad conscience went with him and he had to pass

through several strange adventures, before he dared to return home and face the brother whom he had so cruelly wronged.

He found the country of his uncle without much difficulty, but on the journey he had a strange dream. He had fallen asleep in the desert, near a place called Bethel. Suddenly, so he said afterwards, the sky opened. He had seen a ladder which reached from the earth to the Heavens. On the ladder were many of the angels of Jehovah. At the top of the ladder stood Jehovah himself and Jehovah had spoken and had promised that he would be a friend to the fugitive and would help him during his exile.

JACOB FLEES WHEN ESAU
RETURNS HOME

But whether this is really true, that I do not know and I rather believe that Jacob afterwards told the story to ease the knowledge of his own guilt and make people believe that he was not really as bad as they might think since he had retained the friendship of so powerful a god.

As for the help which was to come to him from Heaven, of that we notice very little. For when Jacob reached the land of Ur, he found his uncle willing to give him a home, but when he asked for the hand of his cousin Rachel, who was young and beautiful, Laban first made his nephew work for him for nothing for seven years, and then gave him his oldest daughter, Leah, whom Jacob did not like and did not want. But when he said so, his uncle told him it was the custom of the country to give the older daughter in marriage before the younger left home, and if Jacob wanted Rachel too, he must promise to work another seven years. In that case, he could have her also.

What could Jacob do? At home, Esau was waiting for him with a club. He had no place which he could call his own. Besides, he loved Rachel, and he felt that he must have her if he was to be happy. He tended his uncle's sheep faithfully for another seven years, and then felt that he had fulfilled his contract.

Even then, he was at the mercy of his mother's relatives. He had no flocks of his own and could not set up a household of his own. Once more, he made an agreement with Laban. He would work for seven more years. Then he would receive all the black lambs and the spotted and the speckled goats which happened to be found on Laban's lands. This would give him a fair start towards independence.

JACOB'S DREAM

It was a curious bargain. Laban knew that black lambs are quite as rare as spotted and speckled goats. He therefore did not expect to lose many, and to protect himself still further, he took all the male and female goats that were spotted and striped and sent them to another pasture, where they were tended by his own sons, who saw to it that none fell into the hands of Jacob.

It was a game of wits between uncle and nephew, but in the end, the nephew proved to be the sharper of the two.

Jacob really was a very good shepherd. He understood his business and had learned a good many tricks. He knew how to change the food and the water of his flocks, so as to increase the number of certain strangely coloured goats and sheep.

Laban, on the other hand, who left most of the farm work to his sons and to his slaves, was not familiar with these new methods of husbandry. Before he knew what was happening, Jacob had gained possession of most of his herds. Then he grew very angry, but it was too late. Jacob had gone. He had taken all his black lambs with him and all his spotted and speckled goats and his two wives and his eleven children. For good measure, he had forced his way into the deserted house of Laban, and had stolen the household goods which belonged to his father-in-law.

It is true that it never came to open warfare between Laban and Jacob. It would have been a sort of civil war, anyway. But Jacob left the land of Ur for ever, and as he had nowhere else to go, he decided to take a risk and return to Canaan. Perhaps Esau would forgive him, and besides there was the inheritance in case of Isaac's death.

Once more, if we are to believe the story of Jacob, his journey through the desert was accompanied by strange dreams. Upon one occasion, so Jacob vowed, he actually wrestled with an angel of Jehovah, who broke his thigh when he threw him, and who told him that his name henceforth would be Israel, and that he would be a mighty prince in the land of his birth.

But when he came near Mamre, he did not feel so sure of himself, and when he heard that Esau was coming forward with many men and many camels, he greatly feared that the day of reckoning had come.

He did his very best to gain the good will of his brother. He offered to give him everything he had. He divided his flocks into three parts, and sent one ahead every day, as a present to Esau. But Esau was as kindly as he was rough. He did not want anything that belonged to Jacob. He had forgiven him long ago and when he met Jacob, he tenderly embraced him and bade bygones be bygones. Their father, so he told him, was still alive, although very old, and he would be glad to see his new grandchildren.

There were eleven of these when Jacob reached Hebron, but before he got back to the family farm there were twelve.

For a long time there had been bitter hatred between Rachel and Leah. Leah, the homely wife whom Jacob did not love, had ten sons and daughters. But poor Rachel had only one, who was called Joseph. And now she died when she gave birth to her second boy, who was called Benjamin.

This was a sad home coming. Rachel was buried at Bethlehem, and then Jacob drove his flocks westward until he reached Hebron.

Isaac was still strong enough to greet his long lost son. Soon afterwards, however, he died and was buried with his father Abraham and his mother Sarah in the cave of Machpelah.

And Jacob, who now called himself Israel, inherited his father's estate, and settled down to enjoy the fruits of a career that had been based entirely upon fraud and upon theft. Such a life, however, is rarely a success. Before very long, Jacob was once more forced to leave his old home. He spent the last years of his life in the distant land of Egypt, and far away from the graves of his ancestors.

But of this, I must tell you in the next chapter.

FURTHER WESTWARD

CHAPTER IV

AFTER MANY YEARS OF WANDERING, THE JEWS FOUND A NEW HOME IN THE LAND OF EGYPT, WHERE THEIR KINSMAN JOSEPH HELD A HIGH POLITICAL POSITION

YOU must remember that the Old Testament is really a collection of short and unrelated histories which were put together into one book when the founders of the Jewish nation had been dead for almost a thousand years. Abraham and Isaac and Jacob had been the original heroes of this chronicle. They had dared to push forth into the wilderness and they resembled our own Pilgrim Fathers in their courage and in their perseverance and in their loyalty to their ideals.

But they lived in an age when the Jewish people had not yet learned the use of letters. The account of their adventures was told from father to son, and each new generation added a few details to the greater glory of their ancestors.

It is not always easy to keep to the main line in this record of events. One thing, however, strikes us with great force.

50

The Jews of thirty centuries ago were obliged to face a problem which is familiar to all students of American history. They were shepherds, and as such they were for ever in search of new grazing lands. Abraham left his home and travelled westward to find pastures for his increasing flocks. Often he thought that he had found a home that would support him. Then we see him building a house, digging wells, clearing the ground for a few small farms. But alas! after a few years, there would be a period of drought. Abraham would break up camp and once more be a wanderer on the face of western Asia.

During the life of Isaac, the land of Canaan was regarded more and more as the definite dwelling place of the Jewish tribes. But this era of peace and prosperity did not last long. Jacob himself never remained for very long in one spot. When he was quite an old man, the prolonged dry seasons had made Palestine almost uninhabitable, and the Jews were forced to leave Asia and move over into Africa. This time, the absence from the land of their choice was of very long duration. But they never lost sight of the old home and returned at the earliest possible opportunity.

And this was the way the story was told when the old men gathered around the city walls of the little Jewish towns and spoke of the mighty deeds of their grandfathers.

Jacob, you will remember, had married two sisters. The name of the elder one was Leah, and she had ten sons. The name of the younger one was Rachel and she had only two sons, Benjamin and Joseph.

Now it happened that Jacob was very fond of Rachel, but did not care much for Leah. Quite naturally he loved the children of Rachel more tenderly than those of Leah, and it seems that he showed his preference quite openly when all the children were together at the dinner table or out in the fields.

This was not very wise. It is not good for little boys to know that their father likes them better than their brothers. It is apt to spoil them.

As Joseph was a particularly bright child, much cleverer than his half-brothers, he soon became a great nuisance around the house. He knew that he would not be punished, whatever

JOSEPH'S FIRST DREAM OF THE SHEAVES

he said or did, and he made the best of his opportunities. For example, one morning at breakfast, he announced that he had had a wonderful dream.

"What was it about?" the others asked.

"Oh, nothing much," he answered. "I happened to dream that we were all out in the field, binding sheaves, and my own sheaf was standing right in the middle. But your sheaves were standing all around in a large circle, bowing very low to my sheaf. That was all."

The brothers may not have been very bright, but they understood what Joseph meant and they did not like him any better for it.

A few days later Joseph tried again, but this time he went too far, for he even annoyed his father, and as a rule, Jacob

JOSEPH'S SECOND DREAM OF THE STARS

thought that everything Joseph said or did was quite funny and only another sign of his cleverness.

"I have had another dream," Joseph said.

"What was it this time?" the other members of the family asked, a trifle wearied. "Something more about sheaves?"

"Oh, no. This time it was about the stars. There were eleven stars in the Heavens and they and the sun and the moon all bowed to me."

The eleven brothers did not feel flattered. Neither did the

father, who thought of Joseph's dead mother. He warned his young son that a little more modesty would not be amiss.

But he could not help spoiling the boy, for soon afterwards he bought him a lovely coat of many colours, and of course,

JOSEPH IS PROUD IN HIS NEW COAT

Joseph must put this on and walk about in it to show the other brothers what a very superior sort of person he really was.

Well, you can easily understand what happened in the end.

At first, the brothers merely laughed at Joseph. Then they got annoyed. Finally, they hated him, and one day, when they were all out in the fields near Shechem, and when the father was far away, they took Joseph, stripped his fine coat off his back, and threw him, howling and fighting, into an empty pit.

Then they sat down to think. After all, they could not very well kill their brother. That would be going a little too far.

Neither did they want him around the house.

But Judah had a bright idea.

The Jews lived near the high-road which led from the valley

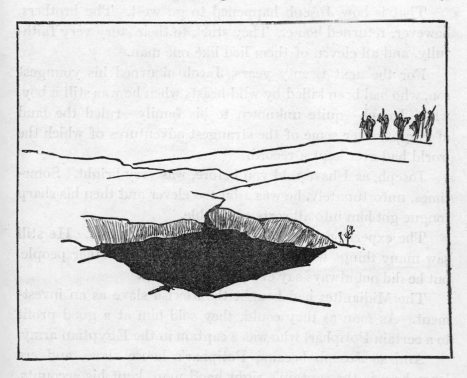

THE BRETHREN THREW JOSEPH INTO A DEEP DARK PIT

of the Nile to the valley of Mesopotamia. Caravans were passing through their country all the time.

"Let us sell Joseph," Judah suggested, "and then we take his coat and tear it up and smear some blood over it and we tell our father that a lion or a tiger came and ate Joseph up, and we divide the money, and no one is any the wiser."

A short time later, a caravan of Midianites came by on

their way from Gilead to Egypt, carrying spice and myrrh for the embalmers of the Nile.

The brothers told them that they had a young slave for sale. After some bargaining, they sold their brother for twenty pieces of silver.

That is how Joseph happened to go west. The brothers, however, returned home. They stuck to their story very faithfully, and all eleven of them lied like one man.

For the next twenty years, Jacob mourned his youngest son, who had been killed by wild beasts when he was still a boy, while Joseph—quite unknown to his family—ruled the land of Egypt, after some of the strangest adventures of which the world had ever kept a record.

Joseph, as I have told you before, was very bright. Sometimes, unfortunately, he was a bit too clever and then his sharp tongue got him into all sorts of trouble.

The experience at Shechem taught him a lesson. He still saw many things which escaped the attention of other people, but he did not always say everything he knew.

The Midianites had bought the Jewish slave as an investment. As soon as they could, they sold him at a good profit to a certain Potiphar, who was a captain in the Egyptian army.

And so Joseph became Potiphar's house slave, and ere long, he was the captain's right hand man, kept his accounts, and was overseer of all the other workmen on the estate.

Unfortunately, Potiphar's wife thought the handsome, black-haired boy much better company than her own dull Egyptian husband. But Joseph, who knew that too great familiarity between masters and servants invariably leads to trouble, kept at a respectful distance.

Well, the wife of Captain Potiphar was no better than she should have been. Her vanity had been hurt, and soon she was telling her husband that his new foreman was a very insolent young fellow, and as for his honesty—well, she had her doubts, and so on—and so forth.

In ancient Egypt, a slave was a slave. Potiphar did not bother to investigate these accusations. He sent for the police and Joseph was taken to prison and locked up, although no charges were preferred against him. But there again his good spirits and his pleasant manner stood him in good stead.

The keeper of the prison was only too happy to let his establishment be run for him by a faithful trusty. Joseph was given the freedom of the jail, so to speak. Provided he did not leave the front door, he was at liberty to do whatever he liked, and

JOSEPH, ALTHOUGH INNOCENT, THROWN INTO PRISON

out of sheer boredom, he spent a good deal of his time with his fellow sufferers.

Among these, two prisoners interested him most of all. One had been the chief-steward of the royal palace and the other had been Pharaoh's baker. In some way or other, both had displeased His Majesty, and that, of course, was a grave offence in a day when a king was regarded as a god. The Egyptians especially had such a tremendous respect for their ruler that they never referred to him by name. They called him Pharaoh, which really meant the "Big House," just as we often say "the White House" when we really mean the President of the United States.

The two men were both servants of the "Big House," and they were awaiting their sentence. They had nothing to do and they whiled away the weary hours as best they could. One of their favourite practices was to tell each other their dreams. The ancient people had great respect for dreams. A man who could explain them was in their eyes a person of importance.

Joseph now made a virtue of his old cleverness. When the baker and the steward came and told him their visions, he readily agreed to explain them.

"This is what I saw," the steward said. "I was standing near a vine, and suddenly three branches grew on that vine and they were full of grapes and I plucked the grapes and pressed them into Pharaoh's drinking cup and placed the cup in my master's hand."

Joseph thought a moment and then he answered: "That is very simple. Within three days, you shall be set free and reinstated in your old office."

Eagerly the baker interrupted him. "Listen to my dream, for I too saw many strange things. I was going to the palace with three baskets filled with bread on my head. But suddenly a number of birds swooped down from high Heaven and ate all my bread. What does it mean?"

"That, too, is simple," Joseph answered. "You will be hanged inside of three days."

And behold! on the third day, Pharaoh celebrated his birthday and gave a great feast to all his servants. He then remembered the baker and the steward, who were still incarcerated. He ordered that the baker be hanged, which was done, and that the steward be set free and be brought back to the palace.

Of course, the steward was very happy. When he left his cell, he promised golden mountains to Joseph, who had foretold him his luck. He was going to speak to Pharaoh and to all the officials, so that Joseph should receive justice and be set free, and he would always remember Joseph's good service. But as soon as he was back in his official uniform, standing behind the King's chair, ready to fill the royal cup at his master's request, the good butler forgot all about the Jewish boy who had been his companion for so many months, and he never mentioned him with a single word.

It was rather hard on Joseph. He was obliged to stay in prison for two more years, and he might have died there if Pharaoh had not had a dream which greatly upset him.

When the King dreamed, it was a great and solemn occasion. All the people talked about it and every one tried to guess what the gods had tried to reveal to the royal slumberer. It was something like a Presidential message in our own day.

The contents of the royal nightmare were as follows: Pharaoh had seen seven ears of good corn, growing on one stalk. Suddenly they had been devoured by seven bad ears. Next, seven lean and miserable-looking cows had suddenly rushed forth upon seven fat cows, who were peacefully grazing along the banks of the Nile, and had gobbled them up, without leaving a trace of skin or bone.

That was all, but it was enough to upset the peace of mind of His Majesty. He asked all the wise people of the land for an explanation, but alas! they were at a loss to tell him. Then the butler remembered the Jewish boy who had been so clever at explaining such things, and he suggested to his master that Joseph be sent for. They found him still in jail and so they had him washed and shaved and ordered his hair to be cut and gave him a new suit of clothes, and brought him to the palace.

The boredom of prison life had not dulled the quickness

of Joseph's mind. He explained the dream with the greatest ease. This was his verdict.

"There will be seven years of plentiful harvests. These were represented by the seven fat cows and the seven ears of corn, growing on one stalk. They will be followed by seven years of starvation and hunger and the seven lean years will exhaust the grain that was grown during the seven good years. Let Your Majesty therefore appoint a wise man to administer the food supply of the country, for great will be the need when the time of famine comes."

JOSEPH IS TAKEN BEFORE
PHARAOH

Pharaoh was greatly impressed. The young man seemed to have spoken with good sense. It was a time for quick action.

Then and there Pharaoh appointed the young foreigner to be his minister of agriculture.

As time went by, the powers of this office were greatly increased. At the end of seven years, the son of Jacob was the dictator of Egypt and ruled supreme in the land. He proved a faithful servant to his royal master. He built enormous granaries and filled them with extra corn against the coming of the evil days.

When at last, famine stalked through the land, Joseph was fully prepared.

JOSEPH EXPLAINS PHARAOH'S DREAM

The Egyptian peasants, who had lived from hand to mouth since the beginning of time, had never saved anything. To get food for themselves and their families, they were now obliged to give Pharaoh first their houses and then their cattle and finally they were forced to surrender their land.

At the end of the seven years, they had lost everything, and the King had got all the land from the coast of the Mediterranean to the Mountains of the Moon.

JOSEPH BUILDS VAST STOREHOUSES FOR GRAIN THAT IS PLENTIFUL

In this way, the old race of Egyptian freemen came to an end. It was the beginning of a slavery which lasted for almost forty centuries and which eventually caused more misery than a dozen famines. On the other hand, it kept the people alive, and it made Egypt the commercial centre of the civilised world. For the famine was international and Egypt was the only country that was prepared.

Babylonia and Assyria and the land of Canaan, they all suffered equally from drought and the grasshoppers and other insect pests. Everywhere the people were dying by the thousands. Whole regions were depopulated and children were sold into slavery to keep the parents alive.

Old Jacob, too, with his sons and all their families, soon felt the pangs of hunger. Until at last, in their despair, they decided to send some one to Egypt for a small supply of grain. Benjamin, the brother of Joseph, remained at home. The other ten sons took their donkeys and their empty sacks and went westward in search of help.

They crossed the desert of Sinai and at last they reached the banks of the Nile. There the Egyptian officials stopped them and took them before the viceroy.

Joseph immediately recognised the bedraggled wanderers as his brothers. But he did not betray his secret. He pre-

FAMINE STALKED THROUGH THE LAND OF EGYPT

tended he did not know the Jewish language. He told his interpreter to ask the newcomers who they were.

"Peaceful shepherds from the land of Canaan, in search of food for their old father," was the answer.

"They were quite sure they were not spies sent out to learn about the defences of Egypt, so that a foreign invader might force his way into the country?"

They swore that they were quite innocent. They were just what they said. They belonged to a family of peaceful shepherds, twelve brothers who lived with their old father in the land of Canaan.

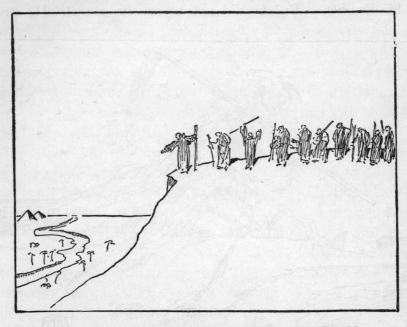

JOSEPH'S BRETHREN TRAVELLED TO EGYPT TO
ASK FOR GRAIN

"Where were the other two?"

"One, alas! was dead. The other had remained at home to look after the father."

Joseph pretended that he was not convinced. They had better all go back whence they came and bring that other brother to prove their words. For the Governor of Egypt had his doubts about the truth of their story. In some way or other, it did not sound quite right.

Then the ten were in great distress. They stood around Joseph's tent and talked rapidly in Hebrew. Their old crime was heavy on their minds. It was a terrible thing to have sold their brother Joseph to the foreign slave-trader. Now, apparently, they were about to lose their second brother. What would their father Jacob say when he heard of this?

They implored Joseph to be merciful. But he refused. He had overheard their conversation. He was greatly pleased at their repentance. The last thirty years seemed to have taught his brothers a stern lesson. But he was not yet certain. He must try them once more before he could forgive them for what they had done unto him when he was young.

And so it was decided that Simeon should stay behind as a hostage, while the others went back to get Benjamin.

This proved no easy task. Jacob was heart-broken. But his family was hungry, his servants were dying, and there was no seed-grain for next year. And so he was forced to give in. Benjamin and the other brothers returned to Egypt and Jacob remained alone.

The last time, they had been arrested as soon as they had crossed the frontier. Now, however, all the officials were most polite. The brothers were straightway taken to the palace of the Governor. There they were given rooms and were entertained in royal fashion.

They did not quite like this.

After all, they were not exactly beggars. They were poor, but they had come prepared to pay for whatever they got. They did not want charity. But when they offered their gold in exchange for grain, they were told that they could have all they wanted for nothing and when they insisted upon paying they found that the money had been returned to them and had been hidden in their sacks.

They were talking about this strange occurrence that night when they were resting after the heat of the day's journey.

Suddenly there were loud voices and out of the darkness there came a group of Egyptian soldiers. They had been sent out to overtake the Jews and to arrest them.

The brothers asked what they had done and protested their innocence. The Egyptian captain, however, had his orders. The drinking-cup of the viceroy had been stolen. No one had been near him that day except a few Jewish visitors. All foreigners must therefore be searched. The brothers submitted to the inevitable. One after another, they opened their packs. And behold! at the bottom of the grain sack which was carried by Benjamin, and which was unpacked last of all, there lay the drinking cup of Joseph!

JACOB WAS LAID TO REST IN THE ANCESTRAL CAVE OF MACHPELAH

The evidence was overwhelming. As prisoners, the Jews returned to Egypt, and were taken into the presence of the viceroy. In utter despair, they tried to explain something that seemed wholly inexplicable. They swore that they were not guilty, but Joseph remained stern and frowning and accused them of ingratitude. At last, they broke down. They told Joseph everything that had happened and how they had once done a very wicked thing, and how they would now give everything they had, could they but undo their crime. Until Joseph could not hold his feelings in check any longer, and he explained how the cup had been placed in Benjamin's sack at his own command.

He ordered all Egyptians to leave the room and when they

were all gone, he came down from his throne and then he embraced Benjamin, and to the terrified sons of Jacob, there stood the mightiest man in all Egypt revealed as their own brother, whom they had sought to kill, and whom they had sold out of greed to the Midianite slave-traders.

Of course, so strange a story appealed to all the people from the highest to the lowest. The King gave a number of his own chariots to bring Jacob to Egypt and Joseph took some of the newly acquired farm lands (which were in a province called Goshen) and he gave them to his own family.

In this way, the Jews happened to leave Canaan and move into Egypt. But in their hearts, they remained faithful to the old home, for when Jacob was dying, he asked that his body be taken to the cave of Machpelah, where his father and his mother and his grandparents lay buried.

This was done. Joseph himself carried the body back to Canaan. Then he returned to Egypt and he lived for many years more, and his people loved him, for he had been as good as he had been generous.

A HOME IN EGYPT

CHAPTER V

BUT THE JEWS WERE ORIGINALLY A SIMPLE PEOPLE OF SHEPHERDS, AND CITY LIFE IN A FOREIGN LAND WAS NOT GOOD FOR THEM. RAPIDLY THEY BECAME EGYPTIANISED AND INSTEAD OF BEING FREE AND INDEPENDENT MEN AND WOMEN, THEY BECAME COMMON LABOURERS WHO WORKED FOR THE KING OF EGYPT AND WHO WERE TREATED AS SLAVES

 NTIL a hundred years ago, we could not read the language of the Egyptians. As soon as the key to their hieroglyphics (or sacred script) had been discovered, a vast new store-house of historical information was opened up to us. Now we no longer depend upon the accounts of the Old Testament for our exclusive knowledge of this period.

In the fifteenth century before the birth of Christ, it seems that Egypt had been conquered by a tribe of Arabian shepherds, who were called the Hyksos. They were of the same Semitic stock to which the Jews themselves belong. As soon as the Hyksos were the masters of the entire land, they built a new capital, many hundred miles away from the old Egyptian centre of Thebes. Then they settled down to enjoy themselves. For almost three hundred years, they remained the undisputed masters of the valley of the Nile.

Joseph came to Egypt when Apepa was Pharaoh. But this king was the last ruler of the Hyksos dynasty. After many unsuccessful attempts, the Egyptians finally succeeded in getting rid of their oppressors. Under a king of their own, called Ashmes (a native of the former capital of Thebes), they drove away the Hyksos and once more regained control of their own country. This, of course, made the position of the Jews a very difficult one. They had been the close friends of the foreign conquerors. Joseph had been a conspicuous figure in the court life of the Shepherd Kings. He had been a high state official and he had shown great favour to his own relatives, at the expense of the natives. All this the Egyptians remembered long after they had forgotten how Joseph had saved their grandfathers from starvation. And of course, they showed it in their conduct towards the Jews, whom they treated with hatred and with contempt.

As for the descendants of Abraham, the long sojourn in the pleasant valley of the Nile had proved a very mixed blessing.

The Jews thus far had been shepherds, accustomed to the simple life of the open fields. Now they had come into contact with a people who preferred to live in cities. They saw the luxury and the comfort of the palaces of Thebes and Memphis and Sais. Soon they began to despise the rude tents in which their ancestors had lived contentedly for so many centuries.

They sold their flocks, they left their farms in the land of Goshen, and they moved to the towns.

But the towns were already overcrowded.

The newcomers were not wanted. The Egyptians regarded them as people who had come to take the bread out of their own mouths.

Soon there was bad feeling between Jews and Egyptians. Ere long, this showed itself in unpleasant race riots.

THE JEWS CAME TO LIKE THE BUSY LUXURY OF THE BIG CITIES

The Jews were given the choice of becoming Egyptians or of leaving the country.

Of course, they tried to compromise, as every one would have done under the circumstances. This was even worse. The situation was becoming intolerable for both sides.

A famine had originally brought the brothers of Joseph to Egypt. Their descendants often talked of a possible return to the land of Canaan. But the journey was long and difficult.

The fleshpots of Egypt were well filled. Life in the desert would be terrible. Life in the cities, on the other hand, was very pleasant.

The Jews found it very difficult to make up their minds.

They feared the uncertainty of the future more than the perils of the present. And so they did nothing. For the moment, they remained where they were, in the slums of the Egyptian cities.

But the moments grew into days and the days grew into years, and the years grew into centuries, and everything remained as before.

Then a great leader arose. He gathered the different Jewish tribes into one nation. He took them away from the too fertile fields of Egypt, where life was made for ease (but where ease did not make for strength of character), and he guided them back to the land of Canaan, which Abraham and Isaac and Jacob had regarded as their true home.

THE ESCAPE FROM SLAVERY

CHAPTER VI

THE SITUATION GREW WORSE AND WORSE AND THERE
SEEMED LITTLE HOPE THAT THINGS WOULD IM-
PROVE, WHEN MOSES, A VERY WISE LEADER, DECIDED
TO TAKE HIS PEOPLE AWAY FROM A LAND WHERE
THEY WERE MERELY "FOREIGNERS" AND TO LEAD
THEM TO A NEW HOME WHERE THEY COULD FOUND
A STATE OF THEIR OWN

N the fourteenth century before the
birth of Christ, when Rameses the
Great ruled in the valley of the Nile,
the relations between the Egyptians
and the Jews had reached a point
where an open conflict could no longer
be avoided.

The welcome guests of a few hun-
dred years before were now being degraded in every possible
way. The kings of Egypt had always been fond of construct-
ing large palaces and public buildings. Pyramids were no
longer in fashion. The last one had been built two thousand
years before. But there were roads and barracks and dykes

to be made and there was a constant demand for workmen on the royal estates. This labour was not very well paid. The Egyptians therefore shunned it as much as possible. Rather than exert themselves, they forced the Jews to do the disagreeable jobs.

Even so, a good many Jews, who were engaged in trade, managed to maintain themselves in the cities. This was a cause of great envy to the Egyptian inhabitants because they could not compete with the foreigners. They went to the King and asked that all the Jews be exterminated. This could not very well be done. But Pharaoh, in his love for his subjects, tried to solve the problem in a different way.

He gave orders that all Jewish babies who happened to be boys should be killed. It was a simple remedy, but a very cruel one.

Now it happened that a man, called Amram, and his wife (whose name was Jochebed) had two children. One was a boy, by the name of Aaron, and the other was a girl, Miriam. When a third child (a boy) was born to them, they decided to save it at all cost.

For three months they hid little Moses in their house with such care that officers of the King could not find him.

But then the neighbours began to talk, and some one had heard the baby cry, and it was no longer safe to have the child in the house.

So Jochebed took her son and she went to the banks of the Nile and she wove a little basket, and she made the sides watertight with clay and she placed the boy inside this crude cradle and let him go forth into the wide world, all alone.

The improvised vessel did not go very far. There was little current. The stream was shallow, and soon the tender raft was caught by the reeds which grew along the shores in such great quantities. By great good luck, the daughter of the King had come to this exact spot to take a swim. Her ladies-in-waiting found the strange bundle and fished it out of the water. A child of four months is usually very appealing. Pharaoh's daughter decided to keep it. But as she knew very little about babies, she asked that a nurse be sent for.

THE CHILD MOSES WAS LEFT TO THE MERCIES OF THE RIVER

Miriam, the sister, had watched this episode from nearby. She now came forward, and said that she knew just the right nurse for a boy of that age. She ran home and got her mother.

In this way, one Jewish child at least escaped the general massacre and was educated in splendour in the royal palace under the secret guardianship of his own mother.

This indeed was a strange fate for one who had been condemned to die. While his older brother had to work in th brickyard, and was beaten by the foreman if he slackened in his labours, Moses went about in fine garments and lived like a young gentleman.

But way down deep in his heart, he felt himself a Jew. And one day, when an Egyptian was beating up a harmless old man who belonged to the tribe of Abraham, Moses interfered. He went further. He hit the Egyptian and he hit him just a trifle too hard. The Egyptian fell down dead and Moses ran the risk of immediate execution if the deed should become known.

It did not remain a secret for very long.

Shortly afterwards, when Moses went out into the streets, he found two Jews quarrelling with each other. He told them to stop. One of them jeered at the peacemaker. "Who made you our master?" he asked. "Do you want to kill us too, as you killed that Egyptian the other day?"

The news travelled fast. Orders were given by Pharaoh that Moses be taken prisoner and hanged.

Moses was warned. He was a wise young man. He fled.

Afterwards, this proved an excellent thing. If Moses had stayed in Egypt, even if he had escaped prison, he might have become completely Egyptianised. Instead, the boy who had been the adopted son of the King's daughter was now a poor exile—a fugitive from justice in a foreign land.

He wandered through the desert which surrounds the Red Sea until he came to a well. Just then the daughters of Jethro, a priest who lived nearby, were bringing their flocks to be watered. At night, all shepherds tried to give their animals to drink at the same time. As a result, they often came to blows. This particular evening, one of the shepherds tried to push himself ahead of the daughters of Jethro. Moses, with his usual courage, came to the assistance of the girls. They, in turn, invited him for supper at their father's house.

In this way, Moses met Jethro and became a shepherd, as Abraham, Isaac and Jacob had been before him. He married Zipporah, one of the daughters of Jethro, and he lived the simple life of all the other desert folk.

In the solitude of the sandy waste, he recognised his true mission in life. His people had strayed away from the true principles which had guarded their ancestors through so

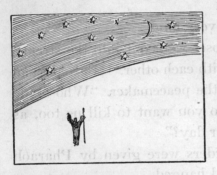

IN THE SOLITUDE OF THE OLD DESERT MOSES FOUND HIS SOUL

many dangers. They had forgotten Jehovah — their God. They were fast losing that belief in a great national future which had inspired their fathers and grandfathers. In short, they had reached a point where city life and luxury (together with ever greater poverty) were threatening to destroy them as an individual and independent race of men.

Moses decided to be the saviour of his own people. He came back to a belief in the almighty power of Jehovah.

He declared himself the humble follower of a great and guiding will. And when he felt thoroughly convinced of his own mission, when he knew that he had heard the voice of Jehovah, speaking from a burning bush, he returned to Egypt and began the gigantic task of moving an entire people from one country to another, through the endless tracts of the desert of Sinai.

But there were other difficulties. King Rameses was dead, and his successor, Mineptah, had probably never heard of the killing of the Egyptian. Moses could therefore safely return to Egypt, as far as the police were concerned. But now the Jews (his own people) were unwilling to believe in him.

Slavery is a bad thing for the souls of men. It makes them cowards. The Jews had a hard life in Egypt. But they were certain of three meals each day. It was no doubt very pleasant to talk about a glorious and free existence in a new country. But that Promised Land lay many miles away and just then it was in the hands of hostile heathen. There would be fighting and months of wandering through the hot sands of Sinai, and at the end, the success of the expedition was very doubtful. Unfortunately, Moses was not a good talker. He was a man of unbounded courage and endless patience and perseverance. But like many another brave and intelligent leader, he got very impatient when he was trying to convince people who were unwilling to see the reasonableness of his arguments.

And so he wisely left the preliminary discussions to his brother Aaron and himself devoted his attention to many details that had to be arranged before anything definite could be done.

He went boldly to Pharaoh and asked that the Jewish tribes which had come to the country voluntarily during the reign of the great viceroy, Joseph, be allowed to depart in peace.

His request was curtly refused. It reacted most unhappily upon the poor workmen in the royal brick-yards. Henceforth they were treated as prisoners who had tried to escape. (They were carefully watched and their tasks were made harder than before.) Formerly, they had been given the straw that was necessary for the making of their bricks. Now they must provide this themselves, and yet they must turn out as many bricks per man per day as they had done before. This meant additional hours of toil. The new regulation made the Jews very angry with Moses. That is what had come of his meddling. He had better return to the desert whence he had come and leave his fellow-countrymen in peace, lest they all perish before the wrath of great Pharaoh.

Moses at last began to have a clear appreciation of the extreme danger of his position.

He sent his wife and his children, who had accompanied him, back to his father-in-law, in the distant Midian country. Then he began in all seriousness to prepare for the days that were to follow. Time and again (but with very little success) did he tell the Jews what they ought to do. He tried to convince them that it was Jehovah who was speaking to them. They must leave the land of slavery at once if the promise to Abraham, that Israel would be a great nation, was ever to be fulfilled.

The Jews listened. They mumbled to themselves and refused to budge. The years of bondage had broken their faith. They doubted the power of their ancient God. They were willing to be slaves.

Moses understood that neither side would make a move without the use of force. He alone was not strong enough to bring his own people to reason. Neither could he hope to convince Pharaoh. Jehovah alone could do this, and Jehovah did not desert his faithful servant in this hour of need. He told Moses to go once more before the King and warn him of the terrible things that would happen if he refused to heed the warnings of the God of the Jews. For the second time, Moses and Aaron went to the royal palace, and asked that their people be allowed to depart in peace.

Again they were refused.

Then Aaron took his staff and stretched it over the waters

of the Nile. The waters turned red, and the people were forced to dig wells, that they might not die of thirst.

Pharaoh heard the cries of the thirsty people, but he refused to let the Jews go.

That was the first plague.

Then came the next.

Often the banks of the Nile were full of frogs. This time, millions of the slimy beasts crept out of their marshy homes and hopped all over the land. They entered the houses and tumbled into the newly dug wells, and made everybody most uncomfortable. Pharaoh saw the floor of his palace turned into one swarming green mass of live frogs. He hesitated. He asked Moses to take the frogs away. As soon as they were gone, so he promised, the Jews would be allowed to leave Egypt. But when the frogs had all died

THEN THE PLAGUE VISITED THE PEACEFUL VILLAGES OF THE LAND OF EGYPT

at the command of Moses, Pharaoh forgot all about his given word. The Jews were as badly off as before.

Then came the next plague.

Clouds of large, disgusting flies began to buzz all over the country. They carried disease far and wide. The food of the Egyptians was being spoiled. People were beginning to die.

Pharaoh tried to compromise. He suggested to Moses that the Jews be permitted to go to the desert for a short while to sacrifice to their own God after their own fashion. If they promised to come back when the sacrifice had come to an end, they could take a short holiday.

Moses made an end to the pestilent visitation of the flies,

and Pharaoh, glad to be rid of this nightmare, disregarded his promise as soon as the last fly had been shooed out of his dining-room.

Then came the next plague.

All the cattle of the Egyptians fell sick with a mysterious and deadly disease. Soon there was a dearth of fresh meat.

Still Pharaoh refused.

Then came the next plague.

The bodies of all men and women were covered with terrible sores, and no physician knew how to cure them.

Then came the next plague.

A hail storm destroyed the harvest that stood in the fields.

Then came the next plague.

Lightning struck the barns where the flax and the seed grain for the next year had been stored.

Then came the next plague.

A cloudburst of grasshoppers broke over the poor country. Within a single day all the trees and shrubs stood bare. Not a leaf was left.

By now, Pharaoh was thoroughly frightened. He asked that Moses come to see him. He offered to let the Jews go, provided they leave their children behind as hostages.

But Moses refused. His people, so he announced, must go with all their sons and daughters. Otherwise, they would stay.

Then came the next plague.

A terrible sandstorm came up from the desert. For three days, the rays of the sun were obscured by the dust. The land of Egypt lay in complete darkness.

Pharaoh asked Moses to hasten to the palace. "I will let your people go," he swore, "but they must leave me their flocks."

"My people shall go, together with their children and their flocks and all their household goods," Moses said, and departed.

Then came the next plague.

The oldest child of every family that dwelled in the valley of the Nile died.

The Jews escaped this dreadful fate. They had been warned. On the door-sills of their houses they had painted a small red mark, made with the blood of a young lamb. When the Angel of Death (at the bidding of Jehovah) went through the unhappy country, he had stricken the sons and daughters of the Egyptians. But wherever he found the sign of the lamb's blood, he had "passed over" the house that harboured a descendant of Abraham.

Then at last, Pharaoh understood that he had been defeated by a power stronger than himself. No longer did he refuse to let the Jews depart. On the contrary, he begged Moses to take his people away as soon as possible that there might be an end to these terrible visitations.

That evening, the tribes Reuben and Levi and Judah and Simeon and Issachar and Zebulun and Dan and Naphtali and Gad and Asher and Ephraim and Manasseh ate their last meal in the land of Egypt. When night came, they and their flocks were well on their way to the old home on the banks of the river Jordan.

But Pharaoh, thoroughly enraged by the death of his oldest son, once more repented of his given word. He and his army followed the fugitives to bring them back and avenge the sudden death of so many innocent children.

Near the coast of the Red Sea, they caught sight of the Jewish caravan. But a cloud (which Moses believed to be Jehovah himself) hid the camp of the Jews from the eyes of the Egyptian soldiers.

Early in the morning, at the command of Moses, the waters of the sea were divided and the tribes passed from one shore to the other without losing a single man.

Then the cloud lifted and Pharaoh saw his enemies ascend-

A TERRIBLE WAVE DESTROYED PHARAOH AND HIS ARMIES

ing the steep banks of the other shore. At the head of his army, he plunged into the shallow sea. But the waters returned as suddenly as they had departed before. With a great splashing of waves, the King and all his generals and all his captains and all his common soldiers were drowned.

No one returned to tell the tale.

The Jews now entered the desert. They were free, but during forty long years, they were to be wanderers in the wilderness.

WANDERING IN THE WILDERNESS

CHAPTER VII

ONCE AGAIN THE JEWS SPENT MANY YEARS IN THE DESERT. OFTEN THEY LOST HOPE BUT MOSES UPHELD THEIR COURAGE WITH HIS VISION OF A PROMISED LAND. MOSES TAUGHT THEM MANY USEFUL THINGS BUT JUST BEFORE HE BROUGHT THEM TO THE LAND WHERE THEY HOPED TO FIND FREEDOM AND INDEPENDENCE, HE DIED

 EOPLE often ask why the inhabitants of our slums do not leave their miserable homes and move into the open spaces of the great west, where a man can be his own master and can give his children a chance to grow up into healthy and strong human beings. The answer is simple enough.

These poor creatures have become so accustomed to the comparative comforts of the city, that they fear to go forth into an unknown land where they must depend upon themselves for their livelihood.

In a town, all sorts of things are done for us by the unseen hands of the government. Even the poorest citizen can get all the water he needs by turning on a faucet. An immigrant, fresh from Ellis Island, can, if he is hungry and has a few pennies, run to a grocery store and buy himself a certain amount of food, neatly prepared and done up in convenient tin cans.

Out in the wilds, however, of an unsettled country, the pioneer must carry his own water from a nearby river. He must kill his own cattle. He must raise his own corn and potatoes.

Lots of people do not know how to do this. They are afraid to take a chance and learn.

And so they live and they die where they were born, and nothing short of actual starvation can make them move.

Human traits rarely change. The Jews of three thousand years ago were not very different from ourselves. They had been unhappy in Egypt because they had been subjected to horrible slavery. Now they were free, but once more they complained. They hated the desert and the sand and the heat; and soon they were all blaming Moses, who had taken them away from their Egyptian tenements to plunge them into a new life which frightened them more than the whips of the royal task-masters.

The story of the forty years in the desert is an endless chronicle of discontent. If it had not been for the unconquerable energy of Moses, the tribes would have returned to bondage before a year was gone.

Yet, during the first moment of exaltation, when the Jews saw their Egyptian enemies perish before their eyes, they knew a moment of triumph and happiness.

"Who is like Thee, O Jehovah?" they sang. "Who is like Thee among all the gods of the earth in glory and power?"

But when they had spent a few months among the endless hills of Sinai, they no longer thought of their God who had triumphed gloriously and who was their strength and their staff. Nay, they forgot all about him and only asked that they be taken back to the land from which he had just delivered them after such tremendous effort.

They cursed the intolerable wilderness and they openly expressed their disgust with Moses and his foolish plans. When provisions began to run low, they said that they were all surely going to die and they went to their leader and asked: "Give us to eat, or let us return."

Moses, strong in his faith, told them that Jehovah would provide for them in their hour of need.

And behold! the next morning, they found the desert covered with small white flakes which could be beaten into a dough, and which made excellent cakes of a honey-like sweetness. The Egyptians, who knew this plant, had called it "mannu." The Jews called it "manna" and they believed that Jehovah had grown it overnight for their own benefit. They gathered a fresh crop every day, except on the seventh day, when they celebrated the Sabbath and lived on the extra supply which they had laid in during the previous twenty-four hours.

Such signs of divine approval made the Jews more obedient for a short time. This mood, however, never lasted very long. Soon there was a lack of water. Again the heads of the different families went to Moses and asked that they might return to their old homes on the bank of the Nile. Moses then beat the rocks with his staff (as Jehovah had told him to do) and a rich stream of water gushed forth from the hard granite and they filled their pitchers and their bowls and their skillets and drank to their hearts' content.

Then they waited for a fresh cause for complaint. One

fierce tribe of Arabs, called the Amalekites, was forever trying to steal the cattle of the Jews. Of course, they could have resisted these robberies, for they were strong enough to defend their own. But, as I have said often before, they had lived for such a long time behind the sheltering walls of the cities that they were afraid of arrows and swords. They would rather

MOSES STRUCK ON ROCK AND THE WATER
GUSHED FORTH

lose a few sheep and donkeys than go forth to battle. This of course encouraged the Amalekites and they harassed the Jewish caravan until Moses decided that something must be done to make an end to this wholesale theft. He called Joshua to him, whom he knew as a brave young man, and whom he had entrusted with some special mission upon several previous occasions.

"Drive away the Amalekites," Moses told him.

Joshua obeyed orders and left the camp with a few volunteers. As soon as he was gone, Moses lifted up his arms toward Heaven and as long as his arms were stretched out over his troops, Joshua, with the help of Jehovah, was successful. But when Moses grew tired and allowed his arms to drop, then the Amalekites returned and fell upon the Jews and killed many of them.

When they saw this, Aaron and Hur supported the aching arms of their leader, and towards the evening, the Amalekites had been completely defeated and Jehovah had given the victory to his faithful followers.

Soon afterwards the caravan reached the land of Midian, where the father-in-law of Moses lived. The old man was very happy to see his relatives once more. He offered a sacrifice to express his gratitude to Jehovah, whom he too worshipped as the sole ruler of Heaven and earth, and he allowed his son Hobab to join the Jews when they marched northward, that he might act as their guide.

The wandering tribes then left the desert and entered the mountainous region which surrounds the rock called Sinai, after Sin, the Asiatic goddess of the moon. By now, it had become clear to Moses that he would never achieve his purpose unless he could make his followers acknowledge that Jehovah was their only God. Abraham and Isaac and Jacob had known this to be the truth. Their descendants, however, had lived for such a long time among people who worshipped several hundred divinities that they had lost the old sense of a personal relationship with one almighty ruler of both Heaven and earth.

Moses bade his men build a fortified camp at the foot of Sinai. He told them to stay where they were and wait for his return. He would bring them a message of the utmost importance.

Accompanied only by Joshua (Aaron remained behind as

THE JEWS PITCHED CAMP AT THE FOOT OF THE MOUNT
CALLED SINAI

commander-in-chief) Moses began to climb the high rocks of the ancient mountain.

When he neared the top, he asked Joshua to leave him while he alone went forth to hear the message of Jehovah.

Forty days and forty nights he was gone.

All that time, the mountain was hidden from view by a thick veil of clouds.

Then Moses returned and behold! he carried two large tablets of stone and upon these stood engraved the law of Jehovah, which has come to be known to us as the Ten Commandments.

Unfortunately, the Jews had behaved very badly while their leader was gone. Aaron was a weak commander. He could not enforce discipline and soon the camp had been turned into a veritable Egyptian village. The women and the girls

MOSES FOUND THE JEWS WORSHIPPING THE IMAGE
OF A GOLDEN CALF

had stripped themselves of their golden ornaments and out of these they had made an idol which reminded them of the holy cows which since time immemorial had been an object of worship to the people of the Nile. They were actually dancing around their golden calf when Moses entered the camp.

He was in great anger. He had heard the singing and shouting from afar. Now he knew what it meant. In his fury, he threw the stone tablets upon the ground so that they were broken. Then he pulled down the golden image and destroyed it and when this was done, he called for volunteers to stamp out this dangerous rebellion.

Only one of the tribes, that of Levi, rallied to his support. They were the strongest of them all. They fell upon their fellow-travellers and they killed those who refused to acknowledge Jehovah and they showed no mercy to the men who had been the ringleaders of the rebellion against Moses and who had stirred up trouble during his absence.

That night, peace descended upon the camp of the Jewish tribe. Two thousand men lay slain and their unseeing eyes were staring at the top of Mount Sinai where Jehovah had talked to the first of those great prophets who since then have tried to show the human race the folly of cowardice and unrighteousness.

Deeply disappointed by this occurrence, Moses acted for once with great sternness. He recognised that his people needed more than personal leadership. They must have written laws and they must be forced to respect the words of their elders. Otherwise the whole expedition would end in anarchy and there never would be a united race of Jewish men and women.

Once more he went to the top of Mount Sinai. When he returned, his face showed clearly that he had seen things which thus far had remained hidden to all other men. His eyes sent forth beams of light. No one could look at him for a long time.

He carried two new tablets of stone and upon these stood engraved those selfsame laws which had been destroyed when Moses had returned to find his people worshipping the golden calf.

And these are the commandments which Jehovah had given to Moses for the conduct of the Jews:

They must recognise no gods except Jehovah.

They must not make themselves graven images, such as had been used in the land of Egypt.

They must not take the name of Jehovah in vain.

AMIDST THE THUNDER OF MOUNT SINAI'S HIGHEST TOP
MOSES RECEIVED THE SACRED COMMANDMENTS

They must work six days but rest on the seventh day, and use it to worship their God.

They must always honour their fathers and their mothers.

They must not murder.

They must not take another man's wife, and women must not take another woman's husband.

They must not steal.

They must never give false testimony against their neighbours.

They must not be greedy and wish for their neighbour's house, nor his servants, nor his cattle, nor anything that belonged to their neighbour.

The Jews now had their laws. But they needed a place where they could come together to worship Jehovah. Moses therefore ordered a Tabernacle to be built. It was really a church, made out of wooden walls, which were covered with an awning. Years later, when the wanderers once more lived in cities, they reconstructed the original Tabernacle with the help of bricks and marble and granite, and then it became the famous temple of Jerusalem.

Next it was necessary to have priests that the service in the Tabernacle might be conducted according to certain prescribed regulations. Because the men of the tribe of Levi had stood by Moses when he tried to suppress the worship of the golden calf, they were chosen to be priests. As "Levites," we shall hear of them all through Jewish history. As for Moses, he made himself the uncrowned king of the surviving Jews. Acting upon the advice which his father-in-law had given him a long time before, he stated that he alone was allowed to come into the presence of Jehovah, whenever it was necessary that some divine command be imparted to the faithful ones.

Furthermore, he ordained that after his death, this high office should go to his brother Aaron and to his sons and grandchildren until the end of time.

Often during the journey in the desert, Moses had suffered because the men and women of the different families hardly knew whom they should recognise as their own immediate head. Moses therefore divided the people into certain definite groups. Over each one he placed a trusted Elder. Him he called a

Judge, that he might hear all minor complaints and settle all small points of dispute, so that the people might live together as good neighbours.

Only when all this had been done, did he give the sign to break up camp. A high pillar of clouds, which for more than

A HIGH PILLAR OF CLOUDS HAD GUIDED THE JEWS
THROUGH THE DESERT

a year had floated ahead of the wanderers, and which had shown them the path in the desert, now settled down upon the holy chest, or Ark, in which the sacred tablets of the Commandments were carried. The Levites took up their holy burden, which was for ever to stand as the centre of the Temple, and the seven thousand men and women and children who remained, continued their way.

But as they came nearer and nearer to the old land of their fathers, their troubles increased. The wife of Moses, Zipporah,

had died and he had married a woman of the tribe of the Cush-
ites. In the eyes of the other Jews, she was a foreigner. They
hated her and openly showed their dislike. In his difficulties,
Moses was not even supported by his own brother and sister.
He had given them high office in the new state which he had

THE PILLAR OF CLOUD CAME TO REST ON THE ARK

just founded. But they were jealous. They wanted more
honours for themselves. They said so until Moses, in disgust,
took Aaron to the top of Mount Hor and there stripped him
of all his former dignities.

Finally, when they were almost within sight of Canaan,
they suffered terribly from the snakes that infested the country. Moses then made a large snake of copper. He put this

image on a high stake where all the people could see it. Thereafter, the deadly bite became quite harmless.

But the nearer the tribes came to the river Jordan, the more aggressive became the attitude of their enemies. Soon the Jewish camp was full of stories about terribly big men, who

THE SPIES REPORTED THAT THEY HAD FOUND
A MOST FERTILE LAND

were called the sons of Anak and who now occupied the old farms of Abraham, which Moses intended to claim for the sole benefit of his own people.

To make an end to these fairy-tales, Moses chose one man from each of the twelve tribes and sent the twelve forward to spy out the land they were about to conquer. After a short while, Joshua (who was forever in the thick of things) and Caleb (a young man from the tribe of Judah) returned carry-

ing an enormous bunch of grapes. These they had found in a
valley called Eshcol. They reported that the land was very fertile. It abounded in milk and honey. Of course, this country
could not be taken away from the present occupants without
some fighting. But they were quite certain that the Jews could
defeat their enemies and they advised an immediate advance.

AT LAST MOSES WAS ALLOWED TO SEE THE PROMISED LAND

But panic had already swept through the tribes. They had
marched and marched and marched. They had suffered from
hunger and from heat and from thirst and from snakes and
now they were asked to expose themselves to the deadly fury
of the Hittites and the Jebusites and the Amorites and the

Canaanites and the Amalekites. This was too much. Once more they broke into rebellion.

Many hot-heads openly advocated a return to Egypt. There was much shouting and there were many speeches. In vain did Moses and Aaron (who had regained his courage somewhat) and brave Joshua try to persuade their followers that no retreat was possible under the circumstances. The people had lost all reason. They were tired of this eternal journeying. They wanted peace, although it be the peace of bondage.

THE DEAD SEA

Then Jehovah grew angry. His patience had become exhausted. His voice was heard from the dome of the Tabernacle. The Jews, so he said, had persistently disobeyed his will. As punishment for their lack of faith, they were condemned to wander in the desert for forty years.

Even then, a few foolish souls tried to push forward on their own account. They were all killed by the Canaanites and by the Amalekites.

But the others accepted their fate. They turned their backs upon the Promised Land and for forty years they wandered through the desert, and they were shepherds as Abraham and Isaac had been before them.

Gradually their children forgot all about the days which their fathers had spent in Egypt, and driven by circumstances, they returned to the simple ways of their ancestors.

That was what Moses had tried to accomplish from the very

beginning. He had reason to be content. His task had been fulfilled.

As for this great prophet, who had given the children of Jacob certain laws which have survived until this day, he was growing old and very, very weary. When he felt that his end was near, he appointed Joshua as his successor, instead of Aaron, who was too old and weak. Then he climbed to the top of Mount Pisgah, which is on the eastern shore of the Dead Sea. From there he looked down upon the valley of the river Jordan.

He died alone, and no one knows where his body lies.

FINDING NEW PASTURES

CHAPTER VIII

THE WESTERN PART OF ASIA HAD BEEN SETTLED FOR THOUSANDS OF YEARS AND THE JEWS WERE FORCED TO FIGHT MANY WARS BEFORE THEY GOT HOLD OF A PIECE OF LAND WHERE THEY COULD FOUND A NATIONAL STATE AND LIVE UNDER THE LAWS OF THEIR OWN CHOICE AND WORSHIP THEIR OWN GOD AS THEY HAD BEEN TAUGHT TO DO BY MOSES

AND now began the great war for the conquest of a new homeland. The handful of frightened Jewish householders who a generation before had fled from the bondage of Egypt were now united into one formidable army of forty thousand men.

Far and wide, the red glow of their watchfires could be seen against the sky of the night. No wonder that the people who lived on the other side of the Jordan became frightened and began to put their country into a state of defence.

But Joshua, the former lieutenant of Moses, who had succeeded his master as commander-in-chief, was a careful leader. He did not mean to leave anything to chance, and before he crossed the river and entered the territory of the enemy he laid his plans with great deliberation.

He had established his headquarters in the village of Shittim. From there he sent two men to Canaan that they might report upon the general lay of the land.

The spies left the Jewish camp and made for the city of Jericho. This was the most important stronghold in that part of the country. It had to be taken before any further progress could be made.

THE GLOW OF THE JEWISH WATCH-FIRES WAS SEEN FAR AND WIDE

The two Jewish soldiers slipped through the gates and entered Jericho. They spent the entire day talking to people and studying the strength of the walls and listening to stories about the conduct and the spirit of the soldiers. When night came, they went to the home of a woman called Rahab. Rahab was not very particular in the choice of her friends. She gave the strangers a room and asked no questions.

But in one way or another, the presence of the two foreign-looking men had become known to the authorities. Soon the police were on the trail of the intruders. At once suspicion turned against Rahab. She did not enjoy a good reputation, and whenever there was trouble, her house was searched before all others.

Rahab, however, proved more reliable than any one had a reason to expect. When she heard a knock on her door, she hastily took the Jews to the flat roof of her home and there she hid them underneath a pile of flax. As the roofs of all the houses were used for the purpose of drying flax, the policemen noticed nothing out of the ordinary. They left and went to another part of the town. But they did not find a single suspicious character anywhere and they decided that they had been misinformed (as happened quite often). They returned to their barracks, and soon the whole city was peacefully asleep.

Then Rahab returned to the roof. She carried a rope made of fresh hemp. It looked a bright red.

"With this rope," so she told her involuntary prisoners, "I will let you down to the street. You can easily make your escape, for the walls are no longer guarded. Once outside, make for the hills, and there await an opportunity to cross the river. But remember one thing. This day I have saved your lives. When your people take Jericho (as they probably will) I expect safety for myself and for my family and for all my friends. That is a bargain."

Of course, the spies were willing to promise anything.

They told Rahab to fasten the same red rope to the window-sill of her house when the troops of Joshua should enter the city. That would be a token to the soldiers that this was the house of a friend, and that the inhabitants must be spared.

This seemed fair to Rahab. She fastened the rope to one of the beams of the roof and the spies slipped down to the deserted street. How they managed to get outside the city, that I do not know. But as soon as they were in the open, they were once more detected. They ran as fast as they could and reached the hills. Three days later they had a chance to swim across the Jordan.

The rest of their trip offered no difficulties.

Soon they were back among their own people and told their general of their experiences.

When Joshua heard that the people of Jericho were in a

THE SPIES ESCAPE FROM THE HOUSE OF RAHAB

state of fear, he decided to make his attack as soon as he could move his men across the river.

This proved unexpectedly easy. For when the priests, who as usual carried the Ark at the head of the troops, had reached the banks of the Jordan, the waters ceased to flow. The priests and their holy burden then took up a position in the middle of the river-bed and there they stood until all the soldiers had safely reached the other side. A few minutes later the waters of the flood returned and everything was as it had been before. At last the Jews were back in the land that had been the home of their ancestors.

After a short march, the army came to a halt near the village of Gilgal. It was the day of Passover.

Much had happened in those forty years since first they had kept the holy feast amidst the sandy wastes of the great desert of Sinai. There was cause for gratitude and thanksgiving.

But much remained to be done. Beyond those pleasant fields where the soldiers enjoyed their holiday lay Jericho. To capture such a town without a prolonged siege seemed well-nigh impossible.

Joshua, the ever careful, knew that he could not rely upon his own strength. He prayed.

He asked Jehovah to help him. And Jehovah sent an angel, who told the Jewish general what to do.

Thereafter, every morning for six days in succession, the army of the invaders marched slowly and solemnly around the walls of Jericho.

At the head of the procession went seven priests. High upon their shoulders they carried the Ark and all the while they blew upon trumpets, made out of the curved horns of the ram.

On the seventh day, they walked around the town seven times.

Suddenly they all stopped.

The priests blew their trumpets until the veins of their brows threatened to burst and all the soldiers shouted words in praise of their God.

THE FORD ACROSS THE JORDAN

At that moment, Jehovah fulfilled his promise.

The walls of Jericho crumbled down like snow melting before the first hot sun of spring.

The mighty city was at the mercy of the Jews.

They killed all the inhabitants, the men and the women and the children, and the cows and the sheep and the dogs and everything that drew the breath of life, with the exception of Rahab and her friends. Then they took possession of the ruins and prepared for the next campaign, for now it seemed that all the land between themselves and the Mediterranean Sea was at their mercy.

But alas! all was not well within the camp of Joshua. The

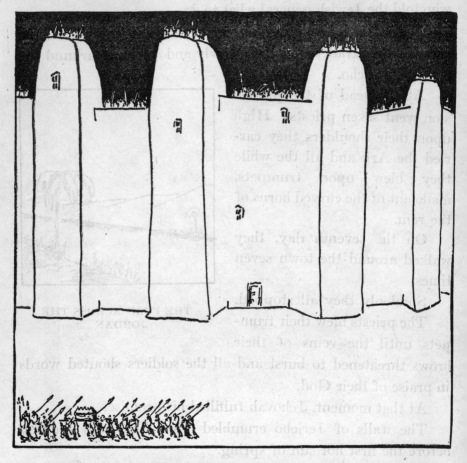

THE JEWISH ARMY MARCHES AROUND THE WALLS OF JERICHO

expedition which had begun so well was suddenly threatened with defeat.

Just before the attack, Joshua had given a few final instructions. He positively forbade the soldiers to take or keep any loot. Everything must be surrendered to the tabernacle.

Most of the men had obeyed these orders, but one private, by the name of Achan, who belonged to the tribe of **Judah,** stole a few hundred pieces of silver and gold and a few bits of clothing and he had hidden them underneath the floor of his tent.

Of course, Joshua could not possibly know this and he

THE WALLS OF JERICHO FALL DOWN

continued his westward march, fully expecting that **Jehovah** would continue to give him victory. But although the people of Ai were much frightened by the horrible things which had just happened to their neighbours of Jericho, they did not surrender. And as soon as the Jews attacked, they made a sally, and they broke through the ranks of the invaders and they forced them to retreat in great disorder and with a severe loss of men.

Then it became clear to Joshua that some one had been unfaithful. He called together all the survivors of the rout and told them what he suspected. He asked the guilty man to confess, that the others might be saved. Achan, however, hoped to lie himself out of his trouble and he did not step forward as he should have done.

After a while, when no one seemed willing to take the blame upon himself, Joshua decided to detect the thief by means of casting lots. The lot pointed to Achan as the thief. He was forced to tell where he had hidden his stolen goods. The gold and silver and the clothes were thrown into the fire.

When this had been done, the soldiers turned upon Achan and killed him.

For a long time afterwards, a small pile of stones in the valley of Achor reminded the passerby of the fate of the first Jewish soldier who had dared to disobey the laws of Jehovah.

Joshua withdrew his troops and then made his plans for a new attack upon the defiant city.

He divided his army into two parts. During the night, thirty thousand men hid themselves in the hills of Bethel, just outside of Ai. Later on, five thousand more were added to their number.

With five thousand others, Joshua boldly marched upon the gates of Ai. The garrison, when they saw this small group of Jews, believed that they had to deal with the remnant of those same forces which they had defeated a few days before. They laughed out loud, and they left the walls of the fortress to punish this recklessness out in the open, where it is easier to kill your enemies.

But Joshua did not wait for them. Followed by his soldiers, he fled away in the direction of the mountains.

Then the men from Ai threw all prudence to the winds and they too ran as fast as they could. Soon they found themselves in a narrow gorge. There Joshua halted.

He waved a piece of cloth on the top of a spear as a sign for the men who were in ambush in the western hills. They rushed out of their trenches and they attacked the Ai-ites in the rear. Caught between two fires, the heathen were entirely at the mercy of the Jews.

A few hours later, they were all dead. And as for Ai, it was captured without any difficulty, as the city gates were still wide open.

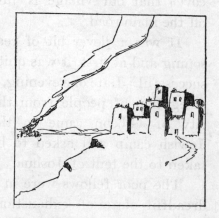

THE PEOPLE OF AI HAD SEEN THE FATE OF JERICHO

The citizens, men, women and children, shared the fate of the people of Jericho. They were all killed and the town was burned down. That evening, the reddened sky of Canaan told for a second time of the arrival of this new and victorious invader, who claimed all Canaan as his own and who showed no mercy to those who dared to oppose themselves against his will.

In their fear, a few of the Canaanite cities tried to escape their ultimate fate by the use of strategy.

One of them almost succeeded. That was the city of Gibeon.

"The Jews," so the Gibeonites argued, "have come to settle here for all time. They are so powerful that we cannot fight them. We shall have to make terms with them as best we can. They will soon be in our neighbourhood. Suppose that we make them believe that our city is really a thousand miles away. In that case, they will perhaps make a treaty with us and they will never dis-cover that our village is just off the main road."

It was a clever bit of rea-soning and at first, it was quite successful. Late one evening, a delegation of people from the city of Gibeon came to the Jewish camp and asked to be taken to the tent of Joshua.

The poor fellows were in a dreadful state of exhaustion. They could hardly walk. Their

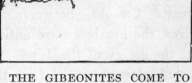

THE GIBEONITES COME TO JOSHUA IN AN EXHAUSTED CONDITION

clothes were covered with mud and they seemed exhausted from lack of water. They carried a little food, but it was mouldy and they explained that it had been spoiled during the days and days and days they had been obliged to march before they had reached the Jewish camp.

Joshua believed this story.

He asked the men whence they came and they answered that they were from the city of Gibeon, which was so far away from the Jewish camp that the envoys had almost perished along the road.

Then they told the Jewish commander how their fellow-citizens wished to live in peace with the new arrivals and would like to conclude a treaty of amity and they pointed out how easy it would be to live in peace with people whose city was a thousand miles away.

It sounded very reasonable and Joshua fell into the trap. Too late did he discover that Gibeon was right on the route which he proposed to follow. He had promised to spare the lives of the Gibeonites. He could not break his sacred word, but in his anger he condemned the Gibeonites to be the slaves of the Jews for all time.

And so, although the Gibeonites and their children were spared, they became hewers of wood and drawers of water and had to work for the benefit of the Jews without receiving any wages. This was a sad fate, but worse was to follow as soon as the other tribes of Canaan heard what had happened.

These others were no cowards and were willing to fight for their own. Jericho and Ai had been destroyed and now a powerful city, a possible ally in the war for defence, surrendered without shooting a single arrow. It was perfectly disgraceful and it deserved severe punishment before others followed this cowardly example.

Then and there, under the leadership of Adoni Zedec, the ruler of Jerusalem, five kings made a treaty and promised each other to make common cause against the Jews and against those who should accept their rule. They called together their armies and they marched against Gibeon to punish the city for its treason.

The Gibeonites, caught between two dangers, sent messengers to Joshua and asked him to come to their assistance.

Joshua knew that this was to be the decisive battle. By forced marches he reached the neighbourhood of Gibeon long before the allies were even aware of his presence. He caught them entirely unprepared. There was no battle, for the troops of the five kings ran away. As for the kings themselves, they tried to hide in a cave and hoped that the pursuing Jews would not be in too great a hurry to find them.

But they were discovered.

A few heavy stones were hurriedly rolled against the mouth of the cave. In this way, it was turned into a prison, while the men of Joshua continued the pursuit of their enemies, to deal with the kings at their own leisure.

Meanwhile, however, the allied forces had regained some of their courage. They too, understood that they were engaged in the last great fight for freedom and independence.

They made halt and rendered desperate resistance. If they could only hold out a few hours longer, it would be night and they might be able to escape.

Joshua needed a victory then and there or all might be lost. Once more he called upon Jehovah for help. Immediately Jehovah ordered the sun to stand still upon Gibeon and he ordered the moon to stand still in the valley of Ajalon.

THE KINGS ARE IMPRISONED IN THE CAVE

In this way, it remained bright daylight for another twelve hours. The Jewish troops were able to continue their attacks. They were victorious and when at last the sun went down, the children of Israel were masters of the entire land of Canaan.

Even then they did not rest. They returned to the cave where they had imprisoned the allied leaders. They took the King of Jerusalem and the King of Hebron and the King of Lachish and the King of Eglon and the King of Jarmuth and they killed them all as an example for the thirty-odd other rulers of Canaan who soon afterward surrendered upon such terms as Joshua was willing to grant.

Then Joshua rested upon his laurels.

THE SUN STANDS STILL

At Shiloh, which was situated halfway between Shechem and Gilgal, he built a tabernacle that the town might become the spiritual centre of the new Jewish nation.

As for the conquered territory, it was divided among the

tribes which had shared equally in the hardships of the desert and which were now equally rewarded for their valour and their endurance.

In this way did the Jews at last find a home of their own. After many centuries of city life and after the interminable journey in the desert, they could at last return to the simple ways of their ancestors, as Moses had wanted them to do.

They were no longer forced to live in the slums of Egyptian towns. Once more they were shepherds.

Each man owned a little piece of land and every family possessed a house which was its castle.

And the scattered tribes of a former age now belonged to a strong nation which recognised one common ideal, the worship of Jehovah, the Master of Heaven and of earth, who had led them out of slavery into the free independence of a powerful state.

THE CONQUEST OF CANAAN

CHAPTER IX

UNDER A NUMBER OF ENERGETIC LEADERS, A JEWISH NATION WAS FINALLY ESTABLISHED IN THE COUNTRY WHICH FORMERLY HAD BELONGED TO THE CANAANITES

 HE land had been conquered. The original inhabitants had been killed or had been driven into slavery. But much remained to be done before the Jews were really to become the recognised masters of all Palestine, as we now call the western part of Asia along the shores of the Mediterranean.

Joshua had died the peaceful death of old age. The tribes had buried him with great solemnity. Then they decided not to appoint a successor.

Now that the fighting was over, it seemed quite unnecessary to have a commander-in-chief. The high priest at Shiloh would undoubtedly interpret the laws of Jehovah whenever the occasion arose. Meanwhile, the election of a new military leader would only call forth the old rivalry between the different families of prominence. Besides, there had been so much fighting these last years that people wanted to get away from all things military. They dreamed of peace and talked of ploughshares.

But soon it became clear that a nation (a new nation at that), surrounded on all sides by enemies, could not expect to survive unless there was at least a nominal head.

The little kings of Canaan had been an easy match for the well-trained troops of Moses and Joshua. But beyond the western border there lived the mighty rulers of the Mesopotamian valley, and one of those, the ruler of Babylon, was from the beginning a serious menace to the safety of the young Jewish state.

When he marched against Canaan and took several of the outlying districts, the Jews were forced to reconsider their original decision. They were not quite willing to turn their state into a regular kingdom, but they tacitly accepted the absolute rule of a single leader whom they called their "Judge." (After two or three centuries, the power of the Judges was greatly increased and out of this high office grew the Jewish kingdom of which you shall hear a great deal in the following chapters.)

The first of these Judges was a certain Othniel. He had made a reputation for himself as the officer under whose command the town of Kirjath-Sepher, the capital of the giant Anakim, had been taken. These same Anakim, a generation before, had frightened the followers of Moses by their size and their strength, but now they were all dead or reduced to poverty, and as harmless as our own Indians. Othniel had another claim to distinction. He had married the daughter of Caleb, who forty years before, together with Joshua, had gone to the land of Eshcol to spy it out for Moses.

Othniel succeeded in driving the Babylonian troops back

from Jewish territory, and thereafter he was the uncrowned
king of the nation for almost thirty years.

But when he died, the Jews relapsed into their old habit
of indifference. They married
the daughters of their heathenish neighbours. They took
wives from among the few
survivors of the old inhabitants of Canaan. And the
children of such unions were
apt to learn the language and
worship the gods of their
mothers. In short, the Jews
forgot that Jehovah had been
their leader in the days of their
hardship and that without
Him they were merely a small

THE JEWS FEARED THE
STRONGHOLDS OF THE
MEN OF ANAK

Semitic tribe which was entirely at the mercy of its more
powerful neighbours.

As a result, they soon lost that feeling of a common destiny
which had been the first and most important point in the
nationalistic programme of Moses. They began to quarrel
among themselves and when news of this internal strife reached
their ever watchful neighbours, the people of Moab and the
people of Ammon and the much dreaded Amalekites made
an alliance, and within a short time they reconquered the land
which only a few years before they had lost to Joshua.

The Jewish armies were defeated and there followed a new
period of slavery. It lasted almost twenty years and during
this period, the Hebrew tribes recognised Eglon, the King of
Moab, as their master.

It was a certain Ehud, a member of the tribe of Benjamin, who at last delivered his people from their bondage.

Ehud was left-handed. This gave him an unsuspected advantage. He hid a dagger in the right side of his cloak. Of course, no soldier of Eglon's body-guard would look for a sword on the wrong side of a uniform.

Thus prepared, Ehud asked to be admitted into the presence of Eglon. He said that he was the bearer of some secret information and that he must have a few minutes with His Majesty alone. Eglon, suspicious like all Oriental tyrants, expected to hear news of an impending revolt. He sent away his followers. As soon as the door was closed, Ehud drew his dagger. Eglon jumped from his chair and tried to defend himself. It was too late. Ehud's dagger was in his heart. He fell down dead.

THE TOMB OF THE GIANT ANAKIM

That was the signal for a general uprising against the Moabites. When they had been driven away, Ehud, in recognition of his services, was elected to be the Judge of Israel, and once more his people enjoyed a short period of peace and comparative independence.

In rapid succession the Judges thereafter followed each other. Invariably they were men of strong character who spent their days fighting the heathen along the frontier. If they had lived in those early days, I am certain that Captain John Smith and Daniel Boone would have been among the great Jewish Judges.

Unfortunately, border warfare is apt to be very brutal. Whenever the Philistines burned down one Hebrew village, the Jews retaliated by destroying two Philistine villages. Then the Philistines thought it their duty to plunder three Jewish villages and the Jews, on their side, went further and pillaged four Philistine villages. It was an endless chain of mutual murder, during which very little of importance was accomplished.

But almost every country, during the early period of settlement, passes through such an agony of bloodshed. It would be foolish, therefore, to blame the Jews for certain crimes which the ancestors of all of us have committed and which are in no way typical of one particular race of men.

Because we have studied the Old Testament with such great care, we happen to know more Jewish history than Babylonian or Assyrian or Hittite history. That is the main difference. For certainly those other inhabitants of western Asia were not a whit better than their Hebrew neighbours. And after this little digression, let us return to the records of the sacred Book.

As time went on, the war along the frontier became increasingly violent, and even the women were called upon to do their part. The little cities of Canaan were no longer a menace. One by one they had been conquered and destroyed. One enemy, however, remained as dangerous and as threatening as before. That was Philistia.

We shall often hear the name of the Philistines in the following pages. Unlike the Jews and the other inhabitants of western Asia, the Philistines did not belong to the Semitic race.

They were Cretans and they had left their native island after the destruction of Cnossos, the famous city of antiquity, which for almost a thousand years had been the centre of the civilised world.

How and why and by whom that city had been destroyed, we do not know. The survivors of the tragedy had escaped by sea. First of all they had tried to establish themselves in the delta of the river Nile. The Egyptians, however, had driven them away.

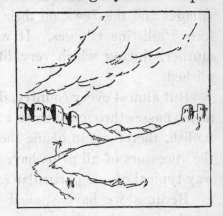

Then they had sailed westward and following the coast of Asia they had occupied a narrow slip of land between the Mediterranean and the hills of western Judæa which had just been conquered by Joshua.

THE FRONTIER BETWEEN THE LANDS OF THE JEWS AND THE PHILISTINES

Of course the Jewish tribes would have liked to possess a few seaports of their own, and the Philistines wanted all the land up to the river Jordan. This led to everlasting warfare between the land-locked Jewish states and their seafaring Philistine neighbours. But as the Cretans were far ahead of their Asiatic neighbours in the arts of peace (and therefore in the art of war) it was not possible for the rude tribes of Israel to make much headway against their enemies of Philistia (or Philistina or Palestine, as we now call that country).

Many of the most famous battles of the Old Testament occurred during eight centuries of strife between the two great competitors for the Mediterranean coast and almost invariably the former Cretans, with their copper shields and their iron swords and their armoured chariots (a sort of ancient tank) were able to defeat the Jews, whose wooden shields and stone-pointed arrows and slingshots only occasionally saved them from defeat.

Once in a while, however, when the Hebrew tribes were conscious of the fact that they were fighting the cause of

THE PHILISTINES LAND IN PHILISTIA OR PALESTINE

Jehovah, they gained a victory and one such triumph occurred during the lifetime of Deborah the Prophetess.

Shamgar the Judge had just died. Immediately the soldiers of King Jabin had marched across the frontier. They had stolen the cattle. They had killed the men. And they had carried away the women and children. The attack called for revenge, but who was to lead the Jews?

The armies of Jabin were commanded by a foreigner named

Sisera. He seems to have been an Egyptian who had come north to make a career. Like most professional soldiers, he was well versed in the most recent methods of warfare. He established a special corps of iron-clad chariots. Those were pulled by horses and they slashed their way through the Jewish ranks with the ease of a knife cutting through butter. It was said that Sisera had not less than nine hundred of these armoured cars. This number was probably somewhat exaggerated, but the Egyptian was powerful enough to threaten the young Jewish state with complete annihilation and great was the fear in the valleys and among the hills on both sides of the river Jordan.

Now it happened at that time that near the village of Bethel there lived a woman by the name of Deborah.

She enjoyed that strange gift which had made Joseph so famous as a child. She could predict the future.

Little wonder that people came from all parts of western Asia to ask her advice before they started upon a voyage or went to war or entered upon new business or got married.

To her the Jews turned and begged that she tell them what to do. Fortunately, Deborah was a woman of courage. She did not advise her fellow countrymen to surrender. On the contrary, she told them to fight.

She sent word to the tribe of Naphtali, and asked that a man by the name of Barak come to see her. Barak had a certain local reputation as a soldier. But when Deborah told him to march boldly against Sisera, he hesitated. "It will end in disaster," he said. "Our troops cannot hold their own against those iron chariots."

Deborah answered that Jehovah would be with the Jewish army as soon as they took the offensive, and would make them invisible. But Barak still had a vision of those nine hundred

armoured cars and he declined the honour of being made commander-in-chief.

In utter despair, Deborah then offered to accompany him,
if this would give him courage. At the same time she warned
him that now the glory of the coming victory would not go to
him but to a woman. Then
at last Barak gave in and ordered his soldiers to leave the
safe fortress of Mount Tabor.

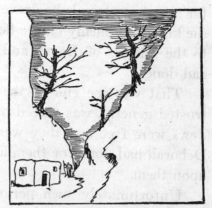

THE LONELY HOUSE
OF DEBORAH
THE PROPHETESS

Sisera had drawn up his
line of chariots in the plains of
Jezreel. There he attacked
the Jews when they came down
from the hills. Jehovah, however, was on the side of the
Jews. The armies of Jabin
fought a desperate battle, but
they were doomed to destruc-
tion. The few survivors fled and even mighty Sisera was
forced to leave his armoured car and to make his escape on foot.

Westward he ran, but unaccustomed to this unusual exercise, he was soon tired out and he entered a house that stood
by the side of the road and asked for food.

It was the house of Heber, the Kenite.

Heber was away, but his wife Jael was at home.

She had heard of the battle. She knew that the man before
her must be Sisera, for he looked like a foreigner and his helmet
was of gold and he ordered the woman about like a man who
is accustomed to give orders. And so Jael gave her unwelcome
guest to eat and to drink, and then, as the man was plainly
exhausted, she told him that he might rest on some rugs on the
floor. Meanwhile, so she promised, she would keep watch and

if any Jewish soldiers came near her house, she would warn the Egyptian that he might escape.

Sisera believed everything Jael said, and soon he was fast asleep.

Then Jael took a large spike (such as was used in those days for a tent-peg) and she drove it through the eye of Sisera and she killed her enemy on the floor of her own home, and she ran to the soldiers of Barak and proudly told them of what she had done.

That was the end of the story. For Jabin, without his trusted general, was forced to make peace and once more the Jews were free and they were very proud of what Jael and Deborah had done for them and they bestowed great honours upon them.

Unfortunately such periods of comparative rest seem to have been very bad for the general morale of the people. The worship of Jehovah, as it had been ordered by Moses, asked for eternal vigilance. But it is not easy to be interested in spiritual affairs when our lives are comfortable and when we do not have a single care in the whole wide world except the problem of how to spend our money as pleasantly as we possibly can.

And those stories which have come down to us from the days following immediately upon the defeat of Sisera show clearly how the great God of the wind-swept desert had been completely forgotten and how His laws were held in contempt by the younger generation, which ate and drank and generally amused itself without a thought for the problems of to-morrow.

Take, as an example, the unpleasant tale of Micah, the only son of a rich widow, who lived in the village of Ephraim. Micah stole money that belonged to his mother, but when she found it out, she not only forgave him, but ordered the gold and the silver to be melted and made into an idol as a present for her darling boy.

Micah liked the shining plaything, and he had a little tabernacle built inside his house and then he hired one of the members of the tribe of Levi (who were the hereditary keepers of the real tabernacle) to become his own private priest and officiate for him, so that he would not have to leave his house when he wanted to go to church.

All this offended horribly against the ancient laws, as they had been revealed to Moses.

It even shocked the other Jews, who by this time were none too pious.

Micah, however, was rich, and did as he pleased.

But one day his house was broken into by some people

MICAH BUILT HIMSELF A TEMPLE WITH A STRANGE IDOL IN IT

from the tribe of Dan, who were travelling westward, looking for fresh pastures for their cattle. They stole Micah's golden idol and carried it to their own village.

As for the Levite who was supposed to be Micah's priest, he ran away as soon as the image was gone, and offered his services to the man who had just robbed his master.

Jehovah certainly had cause to be displeased, and he soon showed his resentment.

He sent the Midianites against the land of Israel. They came every summer with dreadful regularity and stole the barley and the grain that stood in the fields. They spread such terror among the Jewish villages that the inhabitants used to flee to their mountain caves as soon as the first of the Midianite bands appeared and often remained there all winter. At last, in utter despair, they did not even bother to raise further crops. Soon there was famine in the land and people began to die from starvation.

Only here and there a man of stout heart still cultivated his fields, and among those was a certain Joash, who was the father of Gideon. Joash himself was none too faithful to the laws of his country. He, too, worshipped the strange gods who had been dear to the hearts of the original inhabitants of the land. His son, however, who like Deborah and Joseph, could make prophecies, had remained faithful to the old creed.

When his father erected an altar to Baal, young Gideon (encouraged by a dream in which an angel made a rock devour some food which he had placed before it) got up in the middle of the night, knocked down the ugly old idol and on the same spot erected an offering-place to the service of Jehovah.

In the morning when the people of the village in which Joash lived discovered the broken pieces of stone and realised what had happened, they ran to the house of Joash and they shouted that he must punish his boy for his terrible sacrilege.

Fortunately, Joash was a man of some common sense. He said that if Baal were really as powerful as people claimed, he would undoubtedly kill Gideon for what he had just done. But Gideon continued to live quite happily and at the end of a few weeks, when nothing at all had happened, the neighbours changed their mind. In this way, Gideon, who became known far and wide as Jerub-baal (or the Baal-altar-smasher), became a popular hero, whose fame spread to the other cities.

When at last the Midianites became so bold in their attacks that the Jews were forced to take the offensive or perish altogether, it was quite natural that Gideon should be asked to be their leader. He gathered some sort of army together in the ancient plain of Jezreel and tried to drill it into shape for the coming campaign. The spirit of his troops, however, was very bad. They were not really interested in the war. They had grown soft. They wanted to return to their snug caves and preferred hunger to physical hardship.

When Gideon asked them openly whether they would like to go home, the majority shouted, "Yes! the sooner, the better!"

He let them go with the exception of a few thousand who seemed fairly reliable. But even these he could not trust, and he asked Jehovah to give

GIDEON DESTROYS THE ALTAR OF BAAL

him a token of his future approval. He placed some wool upon the ground outside his tent. In the morning, when he picked it up, it was drenched with dew. The grass, however, upon which it had rested had remained dry. This meant that Jehovah would be with Gideon in the coming attack and that he could go ahead with his arrangements.

Gideon took his soldiers out for a long march. When they were quite tired out, he sent them to the river. Only three hundred (out of a total of several thousand) knew enough of the business of war to watch the other bank of the flood while they drank. They also used their hands to carry the water to their mouths. The others leaned forward (like so many thirsty animals) and lapped up the water without further ado.

Gideon kept those three hundred. The others were dismissed. They would have been only a nuisance when it came to fighting.

The three hundred faithful men then received their instructions.

Gideon gave each of them a ram's horn and a torch. The torch was hidden in an earthen-ware jar, so that the rays of the light could not be seen.

THE JEWS WATCHED THE MIDIANITES LEAVING THEIR HOMES

In the middle of the night, Gideon led his men against the Midianites.

While they were running, they all blew their horns, and at a given signal, they broke the earthen jars. The sudden light of so many torches blinded the Midianites. They were thrown into a panic (as happens so often with eastern people) and they fled. Thousands of dead and wounded were left upon the field of battle.

As for Gideon, he was recognised as the uncrowned king of the Jews and he was their Judge for many years.

But after his death there was more trouble. Gideon had been married several times and he left quite a large family. No sooner was he buried than his sons began to quarrel to see who should succeed their father. One of them, by the name of Abimelech, was very ambitious. He wanted to be King of all the Jews and he thought that he had the necessary qualifications. Such young men are rarely appreciated by those who know them best. Abimelech therefore left his home and went to the village of Shechem, where his mother's people came from. In Shechem he began to plot for the throne. He had no funds, but the Shechemites, who could see the advantage of his plan (if he were successful) gave him a loan, and with the money he hired a few professional cut-throats and told them to murder his brothers.

In one single night, all the sons of Gideon were killed, with the exception of the youngest, whose name was Jotham.

Jotham ran away and hid in the mountains.

Abimelech, however, was acclaimed King by the people of Shechem, and there was a great celebration.

During the next four years, Abimelech and his chief lieutenant, Zebul, maintained themselves and forced several other villages and cities to recognise their rule. Once in a while they heard of Jotham. The boy was

THE ATTACK OF GIDEON'S MEN

apt to appear unexpectedly at some market-place, to denounce his wicked brother. Abimelech, however, did not care. Jotham did not have a penny in the world and had no following. His violent denunciations of his bloodthirsty brother were a futile waste of words. They merely amused the crowd.

The glory of Shechem, however, did not last very long. Abimelech was self-willed and stupid. Soon his subjects grew discontented. A man named Gaal made himself the centre of an insurrection. In the fighting which followed, Abimelech and Zebul were victorious. Gaal and his men were driven into a high stone tower.

When Abimelech could not capture this stronghold, he sent his soldiers into the forests for fire-wood. This he heaped up in large piles at the foot of the Tower and Gaal and his followers were all burned to death.

A few years later, however, there was another uprising in the town of Thebez. Again Abimelech defeated the rebels and

ABIMELECH BURNS THE
TOWN OF SHECHEM

for a second time, his enemies barricaded themselves in a tower. But when Abimelech tried to roast them alive (as he had done with the people of Shechem) and stepped proudly forward to set fire to this human funeral pyre, a woman leaned out of one of the upper stories and threw a rock at him. That rock broke his back. Foolish Abimelech, rather than be killed by a woman, told one of his men to put him out of his misery before he should die of his wound.

For a short while afterwards there was an end to these ill-starred efforts to unite the tribes of Israel into a single kingdom. But the border warfare and inter-tribal strife became worse than before. First the Midianites threatened to conquer all the lands on both sides of the Jordan. A few years later the Ammonites tried to do the same thing.

They burned and plundered so many villages that the Jews forgot their own quarrels long enough to fight the common enemy. They chose Jephthah, of the tribe of Manasseh, as their commander-in-chief. Jephthah was a God-fearing man and soon the power of Ammon was broken.

But even in the hour of victory, the old quarrels between the tribes continued with terrible bitterness. Some of the soldiers accused others (who belonged to the tribe of Ephraim) of having been lax in their duties. The Ephraimites, who unfortunately for themselves had arrived upon the field of battle just when the enemy began his retreat, answered that they were sorry but that they could not help being late. They had had to come all the way from the other side of the river and it was a long distance. Jephthah, however, who was a good deal of a fanatic, accepted no apologies, and would not listen to explanations.

He sent guards to all the fords across the Jordan and gave orders that no one be allowed to pass.

Then he rounded up all the men who were suspected of belonging to the treacherous tribe. It was easy to detect them for in their part of the world the common Hebrew word "shibboleth" (which meant river) was pronounced "sibboleth," as the Ephraimites could not make the liquid sound expressed by the letters "sh." Every man who looked as if he might be an Ephraimite was made to say "shibboleth." When he said "sibboleth," he was taken to the gallows and executed.

In this way, so the Old Testament tells us, forty thousand Ephraimites were killed and after this had been done, Jephthah rode home to keep a vow which he had made to Jehovah just before he had broken the ranks of the Ammonites. He had promised that he would sacrifice the first living thing which came to meet him when he reached his home. He had probably thought of a favourite dog, or perhaps a horse. But unfortunately it was his only daughter who rushed forth to greet her father.

Jephthah kept his word.

He took his daughter and he sacrificed her on Jehovah's altar and burned her body and peace reigned once more in the land of Israel.

The story is growing to be monotonous, but ere long, the Philistines and the Jews were once more at each other's throats. The fighting was more ferocious than ever and whole Jewish communities were exterminated.

THE EPHRAIMITES ARE MADE TO PRONOUNCE "SHIBBOLETH"

Then Samson, the great national hero of the Jews, made his appearance. He was as strong as Hercules and as brave as Roland, but not as wise as many of the other great leaders of historical fame.

He was the son of a man called Manoah, and even as a child he was known for his tremendously strong arms.

He was not a nice person to look upon. He never combed his hair, and he let his beard grow wild and he rarely bothered about putting on clean clothes. But he had hands like a pair of hammers and he did not know the meaning of the word "danger."

He gave his parents a great deal of trouble, for when he was eighteen or nineteen, he fell in love with a Philistine woman and insisted upon marrying her. Of course his own people and all the neighbours were horrified at the idea of this marriage with a foreigner. Samson, however, went right ahead and travelled to Thamnata to claim his bride.

On the way west, he was attacked by a lion. With his bare hands he picked the animal up as if it had been a kitten and he killed it and threw the carcass into the bushes by the side of the road. But when he passed the same spot a short while afterwards, he found that bees had made a home in the mouth of the dead animal and were busily gathering honey. Samson took the honey and ate it and continued his journey.

Finally he reached the village where his bride lived and there were many parties given for the happy couple. Samson tried to play the part of the merry groom, al-

JEPHTHAH RETURNS HOME AND IS MET BY HIS DAUGHTER

though he was not very graceful upon such occasions and was more at home in a fight than in a parlour. But he did his best, and one evening, when all the guests were amusing each other with riddles, he offered to tell a little story of his own. He promised thirty suits of clothes to the guests if they could give him the correct answer. They tried but they could not do it.

For this is what Samson had asked: "He who ate was turned into food, and out of the strong, sweetness poured forth. What is it?"

The people of Thamnata guessed and guessed and guessed, but they could not make out what Samson meant. They hated to look foolish before this unkempt stranger who hailed from the hated land of the Jews and they went to Samson's bride and they said: "This man loves you. He will do anything for you. Make him tell you the answer to his riddle."

The woman was not very clever, or she would have foreseen what was about to happen. She made Samson's life miserable until he snapped at her that he had meant the dead lion, whose carcass was now a prey to all animals and whose mouth had been turned into a bee-hive.

Then the Philistines laughed and were happy. They went to Samson and they shouted: "Your question was easy. Of course we know the answer, for what is stronger than a lion and what is sweeter than honey?"

Then Samson knew the trick that had been played upon him. He grew terribly angry and without a further word he left the wedding feast and he left his bride.

He walked to the city of Ashkelon where he came upon a group of harmless Philistines. He killed them all, thirty in number. He took their clothes and sent them to the wedding guests with his compliments as a reward for solving his riddle. Then he returned to the house of his parents and sat and sulked.

For he was deeply in love with this Philistine girl and he could not well keep away from her. He suffered the separation as long as he possibly could and then went back to her in the hope that everything might be set right.

But he came too late. A few days before, the girl had been married to another man of her own tribe. Samson found himself jilted. That was too much for his pride, and he meant to have his revenge.

He went into the mountains and he caught three hundred foxes.

He took them by couples and tied their tails together and

then he fastened a burning torch to the tails of each couple and let them run wild. The poor beasts of course were in dreadful pain. They scattered all over the countryside and in their agony, in order to extinguish the flames, they rolled themselves around in the grain fields that were standing ready for the harvest.

The dry grain caught fire. Next the flames spread to the vineyards and to the olive trees, and in one single night the land of the Philistines was ruined by one enormous conflagration.

The people in their anger did a very foolish thing. They placed all the blame for their misery upon Samson's former bride. They attacked her house and lynched the girl together with her father.

When Samson heard of this, he gathered together all the men who would rally to him and he invaded the land of the Philistines and he slew hundreds of them, from sheer joy of killing.

Just then there happened to be peace along the border and Samson's little private campaign made him very unpopular with certain men of the tribe of Judah who happened to live in that part of the country and who wanted to maintain amicable relations with their Philistine neighbours. They captured Samson and they bound his hands and they carried him to the Philistines. They did not wish to be responsible for the death of a fellow citizen. They therefore decided to leave the actual execution to the Philistines, while they themselves stood by and looked on.

When the Philistines saw the men from Judah and their prisoner come down the road, they were wild with joy. Samson quietly waited until they had almost surrounded him. Then he jerked himself loose, picked up the jaw-bone of a dead donkey that was lying by the side of the road, rushed upon the Philistines and beat them to death, right and left.

From that moment on, the enemies of the great Jewish hero knew that all attempts upon Samson's life were hopeless.

They could not defeat him in open battle.

They must try to destroy him in some underhanded fashion.

This, too, seemed very difficult.

But alas! Samson was his own worst enemy.

He was forever falling in love with this and that and the other woman.

Upon such occasions, he was quite reckless and did not count the cost, but incurred every sort of risk and sacrificed the safety of his country for the sake of his own pleasure.

One evening the Philistines heard that Samson had gone to visit a friend in the town of Gaza.

"At last," said they, "we have caught him!"

They closed the city gates and waited for morning. Samson would be obliged to pass through the gates on his way home and half a hundred well armed men were waiting for him.

Samson must have heard of this plan. He got up in the middle of the night. He left the house. He tore the heavy gates from their hinges. He loaded them upon his back and carried them from Gaza to Hebron. There he left them standing as a warning to all his enemies.

Apparently the man was invulnerable and even the Jews (who did not love his uncouth ways) were forced to recognise his rights as their leader. They made him their Judge and for almost twenty years Samson ruled over Israel. He might have died in the full glory of his fame as a strong man and as a frontier fighter. But when quite an old man, he became involved in another love affair with a Philistine woman and this proved to be fatal.

The girl was called Delilah. She did not care for Samson the least little bit. Her own people, however, had threatened to kill her unless she married Samson and then discovered the source of his incredible strength.

She was promised a thousand Philistine dollars if she would betray her husband, but if she failed (so she was told) she was sure to be stoned to death.

As soon as they were married, she began to flatter her husband because he was so much stronger than other men. One thing, she said, she had always wanted to know. How did her clever husband happen to have such broad shoulders and such powerful arms? Samson merely laughed and told her a foolish

SAMSON CARRIES AWAY
THE GATES

story. His strength, so he answered, would disappear as soon as he was bound with seven fresh twigs.

Delilah believed him. During the night when Samson slept, she allowed her Philistine neighbours to come into the house and they bound her husband with seven green twigs.

The noise they made woke up Samson. He looked around, saw his enemies, shook off the green twigs and went back to bed, while the Philistines fled.

Day after day, this game was repeated. Samson seemed to find enormous amusement in the fact that the Philistines could never capture him. In the reckless mood of a young bridegroom, he told Delilah all sorts of absurdities about the source of his strength.

It would have been better for him had he left this woman who cared more for her own people than for her husband. But he was too much in love to do anything of the sort. He stayed, and of course, in the end, Delilah wore out his patience, and one night, Samson told her the truth and how he would become weak and defenseless if his hair were shaven.

Delilah had won her thousand pieces of silver. She called the Philistines. Quietly they entered the house, and while Samson was lying asleep, Delilah cut his hair.

Suddenly she called her husband.

"Wake up!" she shouted. "Wake up! Here are the Philistines!"

With a smile, Samson got to his feet. He had often heard that cry before and invariably a mere scowl on his part had made his enemies scatter like mice before a cat.

Alas! his strength was gone. His arms hung limp by his sides. He was captured and bound. The Philistines took him and they put out his eyes and threw him into the mill of Gaza to grind corn for the people who had so often trembled at the mere mention of his name.

There in eternal darkness, Samson had time to repent of his reckless bravery and to make his peace with Jehovah.

But while he was in prison, his hair was beginning to grow long again and the Philistines were too much excited by their victory to think of such an unimportant detail.

Now it happened one fine day that they were celebrating a great feast in honour of Dagon, their god.

From far and near the country people had come to town to be present. Suddenly some one remembered the Jewish prisoner in the mill. "Let us bring him here," he shouted.

"Let us bring him here! It will be fine sport. We can laugh at the old man and we can throw mud at him. He used to kill hundreds of our people and now his strength is gone and he is as harmless as a kitten. Let us bring him here!"

Samson was sent for and he was brought to the temple that all the Philistines might see him and revile him to their hearts' content.

By the shouts, he knew what was happening. He asked Jehovah to grant him one final prayer. Let him have his old strength for a single moment.

They placed Samson upon a chair right in the centre of the temple.

SAMSON AT WORK IN THE MILL

There he sat between the two pillars which supported the roof.

Slowly his fingers touched the cold stone.

While the crowd around him went into wild yells of joy, his hands grasped the blocks of granite. With a sudden heaving of his broad shoulders, he pushed the pillars away from him.

They crashed into a hundred pieces.

The roof fell in.

The people in the temple and those on the roof were all killed. And underneath the ruins lay the broken body of a hero who in death had atoned for the foolish mistakes of his youth.

But while all these spectacular events were taking place,

THE DEATH OF SAMSON

other and very subtle influences were at work to change the divided Jewish tribes into a real nation. The people still refused to call their ruler a King. But the power of the Judges was being steadily increased. Indeed, if there had been a man of the strength of character of Moses or Joshua, the Jews would gladly have asked him to be their sovereign.

Eli, however, who had succeeded Samson, was a weak man. As for his two sons, Phineas and Hophni, they were despicable characters. They lived without giving a single thought to Jehovah. They cared only for the pleasures of this world and used their father's high position in the state to do all sorts of wicked things.

It was time for a very different sort of leader, and of course, he was found at the right moment. This was the famous prophet Samuel.

He was born in a little village called Ramah. His father was called Elkanah and the name of his mother was Hannah.

For many years, Hannah had had no children and she used to go every year to the temple in Shiloh to pray that she might be given a son. When the child was born, his happy mother called him Samuel and when he was old enough to walk, she took him to Shiloh and asked Eli to give him some work to do in the temple that he might be ever in the presence of Jehovah.

Eli liked the boy, who was very bright, and because he had given up all hopes that his own sons would amount to anything, he began to train little Samuel as a possible successor.

One night, when Eli was closing the doors of the sacred building, he heard a voice calling Samuel by name. The child, who was asleep on a couch, awoke and said: "Yes, master, I am here. What do you want?"

Eli answered that he did not want anything and that he had not called.

The boy lay down again, but for a second time, the voice called, "Samuel!"

This happened three times in succession. Then Eli understood that it was Jehovah who had spoken. He left Samuel alone and Jehovah thereupon told the boy that the sons of Eli must be killed for their sins because their wickedness threatened to destroy all of the people of Israel.

The next morning, Samuel told Eli what had been revealed to him the night before.

Soon all the people heard of it. Thereafter, they treated Samuel with great respect and they said to each other that the boy would surely grow up to be a great prophet and perhaps their ruler.

But ere that day came, and while Eli was still Judge, the Philistines had once more taken to the warpath.

Now it was the habit of the Jews, whenever they went forth to battle, to carry the Ark with them.

Phineas and Hophni, being the sons of Eli, who was both Judge and high-priest, were ordered to conduct the sacred shrine to the Jewish camp.

This they did, although they had offended against all the laws of the land and had greatly displeased Jehovah.

The Ark, without the presence of the spirit of Jehovah, was just a plain wooden box. Of course it could not avert disaster under such circumstances and the battle which followed ended with a terrible defeat for the Hebrew army. Not only were the depraved sons of Eli killed, but the Ark itself was captured by the enemy. When news of this disaster reached Eli, he gave a great sigh and died and Samuel was elected Judge in his place.

It was one of the worst days in all Jewish history.

The Holy of Holies, which had been carried from Egypt

to the land of Canaan was now reposing in the new temple which the Philistines had erected upon the ruins of the ancient structure destroyed by Samson. It was a war trophy, but still able to influence the fate of nations and the lives of men. For no sooner had the Philistines carried the Ark into the presence of Dagon than the image of their god was struck down by invisible hands and was broken into a thousand pieces.

The Philistines, in great fear, took the Ark away and carried it to the city of Gath. Immediately all the people fell ill. After that there was no end to the ill-luck of poor Philistia. They took the Ark from north

THE ARK IS RETURNED

to south and from east to west, but everywhere disaster followed. Until, in utter despair, the Philistines filled the Ark with gold, hoisted it onto a cart, harnessed two cows in front of the cart, and set the animals free to wander whither they pleased, provided they took this terrible curse away from their country.

The driverless cows started eastward. One beautiful morning, some Jewish farmers who were working in the fields saw the wagon with its holy load standing in the middle of the road. Hastily they built an altar and all the people from the neighbourhood flocked together to worship. Later they brought the Ark to the house of a Levite priest, called Abinadab. There it stood until it was taken to Jerusalem. many years later, when

David was King and dreamed of building that famous temple which was finally constructed by his son Solomon.

The return of the Ark seemed to predict the coming of a better day. But more and more the people grew tired of the loose form of government which had become characteristic of the rule of the Judges. And so they went to Samuel and asked him what they should do in case of his death. Samuel too had two sons, but they were very much like Phineas and Hophni and no one cared to see them as successors to their father.

Samuel asked Jehovah to tell him what measures ought to be taken.

Jehovah spoke of the coming of a king. He was tired of the continued disobedience on the part of his Jewish worshippers. For a long time they had been clamouring for a king of their own. Very well. Jehovah would give them such a king as they deserved. But that king would take the sons of the people to use them as his soldiers and he would take their daughters as his servants and he would take their grain and their oil and their wine to feed his followers and he would take a tenth of everything his subjects possessed and he would rule them with a rod of iron.

When the tribes heard this news, they were actually happy. It was their ambition to become a mighty empire and to rival the glories of Egypt and Babylonia and Assyria. They did not count the cost until it was too late. When they had ceased to be free farmers and shepherds and had become the slaves of a ruler in a distant city, they began to appreciate what they had sacrificed when they asked Jehovah to take away their liberty.

THE STORY OF RUTH

CHAPTER X

THE STORY OF RUTH, WHICH SHOWS US THE SIMPLE CHARM OF THE EARLY LIFE IN PALESTINE

IN the last chapter, which told the story of the Hebrew tribes when the land of Israel was being ruled by the Judges, there was much talk of battle and bloodshed, and we have been forced to describe many cruel and horrible incidents. There was, on the other hand, a different side to Jewish life which was very charming.

Of that we shall now tell you.

There lived a man in the town of Bethlehem who was called Elimelech. The name of his wife was Naomi and they had two sons, Chilion and Mahlon. Elimelech was well-to-do, but when a famine came to the region around Bethlehem, he lost everything he possessed.

He had a rich cousin whose name was Boaz. But Elimelech was too proud to beg. Rather than ask for assistance, he took his wife and his boys and moved into the land of Moab to make a new start.

Soon he was hard at work. But he died quite suddenly and his widow was left with the care of her two sons.

They were decent young fellows. They helped their mother on the farm and when they were old enough, they married girls from a nearby Moabite village and they all expected to end their days among the kindly strangers of their adopted country.

But Chilion and Mahlon, who seemed to have inherited their father's weak constitution, were both stricken with illness and one died within a short time after the other. Their mother, bowed down with grief, decided to go back to the old country, that she might spend the last years of her life among people whom she had known from childhood and who spoke the language with which she was familiar.

RUTH AND NAOMI LEAVE FOR THE OLD HOME

She was very fond of her daughters-in-law, but in all fairness she could not ask the girls to follow her. She told them so, and Orpah, the widow of Chilion, agreed that it would not be wise for her to leave her village. She bade Naomi an affectionate farewell and remained in the land of Moab.

Ruth, however, the widow of Mahlon, refused to leave the old woman, who was now all alone in the world. She had married into the family of Elimelech. She had forsaken her own people for those of her husband. She decided to stay with Naomi. For that, she felt, was her duty. She declared that nothing could ever separate her from the mother of her dead husband and embraced her tenderly.

Together the two women travelled to Bethlehem.

Of course, they were dreadfully poor and they had no money with which to buy bread. But years before, Moses, the wise law-giver who understood the plight of those who sometimes go hungry, had ordained that the gleanings which were left after the harvest must be given to the destitute. The farmer was entitled to all the grain, but the little bits that fell by the way when the reaping was being done belonged by divine right to those who owned no land of their own.

When Naomi and Ruth reached Bethlehem, it was harvest time.

Boaz, the cousin of Elimelech, and his men were out in

RUTH

the fields. And Ruth followed the gleaners that she might get bread for Naomi.

This she did for several days.

As she was a stranger among the Jewish women of Bethlehem, people asked questions about her. Soon every one knew her story and finally it reached the ears of Boaz. He was curious to see what sort of girl this might be and under the pretext of inspecting his fields, he had a talk with her.

When it was time for the noon meal, he invited her to sit down with him and the workmen and he gave her all the bread she needed.

Ruth ate only a little. The rest she took home to Naomi, who was too old to work.

Early the next morning, she was back in the fields. Boaz did not wish to hurt her feelings and yet he wanted to lighten her task. He therefore gave orders to his reapers that they must not be too careful in their labours, but must allow a plentiful supply of grain to remain in the fields.

All day long Ruth worked. At night, when she made

NAOMI BIDS FAREWELL TO RUTH

ready to carry her load home, she discovered that she had gleaned so much that she could hardly lift it.

She told Naomi of what had happened, how she had met Boaz and how she had garnered more grain in a single morning than formerly in a week.

This made Naomi very happy. She felt that she could not live much longer and she now hoped that Boaz might make Ruth his wife. Then she knew that the girl would have a good home for the rest of her days. Yes, it was true that Ruth was a foreigner. But her marriage to a distant cousin of Boaz had almost made her a member of the great Jewish family, and every one liked her.

And so it happened. First Boaz (as was his good right, according to another law of Moses which had been made to protect the farmer against the usurer) bought back the land which had belonged to Elimelech, his cousin. Then he asked Ruth to take him as her husband.

She accepted him and Naomi went to live with her until the day of her death.

But ere she closed her eyes, she had seen the eldest child of Ruth, which was called Obed.

Obed grew to manhood and he had a son called Jesse and a grandson called David. David became king of the Jewish people and he was a direct ancestor of Mary, the wife of Joseph the carpenter of Nazareth.

And in this way did Jesus descend from the gentle Ruth, who had left her people that she might follow the kindly impulse of her heart and tend the woman who had been a good mother to her.

A JEWISH KINGDOM

CHAPTER XI

SAUL AND DAVID WERE KINGS OF AN INSIGNIFICANT TRIBE OF SHEPHERDS BUT WHEN SOLOMON CAME TO THE THRONE THE JEWS HAD GAINED GREAT IMPORTANCE AS TRADERS AND MERCHANTS AND IN LESS THAN A SINGLE CENTURY THE COUNTRY HAD BEEN CHANGED FROM A LOOSE FEDERATION OF TRIBES INTO A STRONG STATE RULED BY AN ORIENTAL DESPOT

 HE Jews had now been living for several centuries in the mountains and in the valleys on both sides of the river Jordan.

After the interminable wars with the original inhabitants of the land of Canaan and with the neighbours of east and west and south and north, the country had at last settled down to a period of comparative peace.

New roads were being opened and caravans, carrying merchandise from Memphis to Babylonia and from Asia Minor to Arabia, began to make use of the highways which ran so conveniently through this western corner of the Asiatic mainland.

This meant a slow but gradual and distinct change in the lives of the people.

The Jewish people had always been fond of city life. Even in the days of Moses, they had preferred the bondage of the Egyptians slums to the liberty of the isolated farms of the Promised Land. With the utmost difficulty had Moses been able to drag his unwilling relatives away from the pleasures and the safety of the high-walled towns.

Now, however, the tribes were their own master. Moses was dead and Joshua, his great successor, was dead and the days of hardship and triumph were beginning to be forgotten.

The life of the farmer and of the shepherd was not an easy one. The hours of work were long and there was little opportunity for pleasure. On the other hand, great profits could be made quite easily in one of the trading-posts along the busy caravan routes.

It was difficult to withstand the temptation. Many people left their villages and returned to the cities. Soon riches increased. But so did poverty. While the cause of national independence and personal liberty began to suffer until it was irretrievably lost.

It is true that the famous Judges who had been in command of the tribal armies during the wars of conquest had often ruled the country with the power of absolute sovereigns.

None, however, had dared to call themselves King.

Their subjects would not have tolerated such a step.

They would have killed the man who tampered with their liberties.

They were willing to obey him as long as the country was in danger. But when peace returned, the Judge was merely the president of a small union of half-independent tribes.

People respected him (just as we respect the Chief Justice of the United States), but it was a far cry from kingship and homage.

As soon as the country ceased to be an agricultural community and became a business office, all this began to change. The majority of the Jews no longer cared to be bothered with affairs of state. They wanted to be left alone that they might devote themselves to their own affairs and might tend to their farms or their businesses. Meanwhile they were quite willing that a few professional military men and a few professional priests should look after the physical and spiritual well-being of the nation.

Of course, they hated to pay taxes. We all do. But provided that those taxes were kept within certain reasonable bounds, the people asked no questions and did not complain. As a result, the country drifted inevitably towards a more and more centralised form of government. Finally it became an absolute kingdom and in less than a century, it grew into a full-fledged, oriental despotism, as we shall tell you in this chapter.

All of this did not come without warning.

In history, as in nature, nothing ever happens suddenly. It often looks that way.

But the underlying secret causes for an abrupt change have been at work for hundreds of years. The final collapse of a mountain or the downfall of an old institution may take a few minutes or seconds. The work of preparation, however, and of slow demolition has been the labour of many generations.

And the Jewish nation just then was passing through such a period of transition, although not one citizen in a hundred thousand seemed to understand what was actually happening.

Perhaps this is a slight exaggeration. Not all the people

were entirely blind to the dangers which threatened the national soul. A few men who could see things more sharply than their neighbours uttered ominous words of warning.

They were called Prophets.

As we shall meet them upon every page of the rest of our story, we ought to tell you something about them.

What was a Prophet?

It is hard to define the word.

Perhaps we shall do best by calling the Prophets the spiritual leaders of the Jewish people.

Many of them were great poets. But they were more than that.

Several of them had the gift of speech. But they were something beyond mere orators.

THE PROPHET BECAME THE CONCRETE EXPRESSION OF THE NATIONAL CONSCIENCE

One thing they all had in common. They dared to stand up for the truth as they saw it.

A good many of them were very narrow-minded and utterly intolerant of any opinion which differed from their own view. But they had the courage of their convictions and sacrificed everything (including their own lives) when it came to a question of principles.

Whenever a King of Israel or a King of Judah committed a wrong, there was a Prophet to tell him so.

Whenever the people left the narrow path of divine righteousness, a Prophet stepped forth to remind them of the error of their ways.

Whenever the nation was guilty of a crime, a Prophet foretold the coming wrath of almighty Jehovah.

Until the voice of the Prophets became the concrete expression of the national conscience.

Centuries afterwards, when the Jewish state lay buried beneath the ruins of its own follies, this national conscience, the work of half a hundred men, remained as the triumphant heritage which the people of Israel and the people of Judah bestowed upon all mankind.

WOE UNTO THE TOWN THAT LISTENED NOT TO THE VOICE OF THE PROPHET

In the coming chapters, we shall have to give an account of an exceedingly complicated period of history.

First of all, a union of semi-independent little wandering tribes becomes a kingdom under David.

That kingdom is immediately turned into an absolute despotism by David's son Solomon.

There is a rebellion against this tyranny and as a result, the Jewish state is divided into two separate kingdoms, which hate each other with a ferocious hatred and fight each other until they are both destroyed by their powerful neighbours of the east.

Then follows an era of foreign domination and of exile.

The faithful ones, however, return to Jerusalem as soon as they can and rebuild the temple.

A short time later, the country is invaded once again. Jewish independence comes definitely to an end, but the genius of the Jewish spirit escapes the narrow nationalistic boundaries of Judah and Israel and conquers the entire western world.

In the coming pages we shall hear long lists of names of

kings and queens and high priests. Rehoboam and Asa and Jeroboam and Baasha and Menahem and Joash and Amaziah and a score of others, ending with the unspeakable Herod, succeed each other with indecent and gory haste.

Their days upon this earth were filled with murder and plunder. They promulgated laws which have been forgotten and they built cities which have disappeared from the face of the earth.

They entered upon wars and they celebrated great victories and they conquered vast territories (and they lost them again) and the very names of their newly acquired provinces have been obliterated by time.

Of all their glory nothing remains but a casual reference in the brick library of a deserted Chaldean palace.

They were like a thousand other kings and the sooner we shall forget them, the better.

Their only claim to fame is an involuntary one. Among their subjects, they counted a few Prophets. And what those men spoke and thought three thousand years ago stands to-day as true and noble as it did when the Chaldeans were at the gates of Jerusalem and when the Assyrians threatened Samaria.

For that reason, and for that reason alone, we should know the history of Israel and that of Judah.

It is the very worldly background for one of the greatest spiritual dramas of all times.

* * * * * * *

When we finished the last chapter, Samuel was still the Judge of the Jewish people.

He had warned his followers that soon they would be the subjects of a king who would take away their sons and their daughters and their goods and their chattels and who would use them for his own pleasure and delectation.

That, however, was exactly what most of the people wanted to happen. They could see the glory of their imaginary empire. They did not think of the cost.

And so Samuel, who was a practical man, set about to look for a suitable candidate for the Jewish throne.

He found him in the village of Gibeah.

The name of the boy was Saul and he was the son of Kish, who belonged to the tribe of Benjamin.

The meeting between the two heroes of the Jewish race was quite accidental. Kish had lost a few of his cows. They had wandered away from the flock and could not be found. Saul was told to bring them back. He went from one village to the next, and everywhere he asked whether the people had seen his father's cows, but not a trace of them was discovered.

In his despair, Saul then went to Samuel to ask him for advice. Samuel looked at Saul and knew at once that this youngster was called to be the ruler of the Jews.

He told him so, and Saul got frightened. It seemed too great an honour for a shy young fellow.

When the time came for him to be anointed and to be shown to his new subjects, he had to be dragged from among the donkeys which carried his father's luggage. He had hidden himself behind the trunks and would gladly have escaped if he had been given a chance.

Samuel, however, was a stern master and Saul accepted his fate and henceforth allowed himself to be trained for his high office.

First of all, he was made commander-in-chief of the army, and as such he fought a great many battles against the inevitable Philistines and against the Ammonites and against the

Amalekites and other Canaanite tribes which had never been fully conquered.

He still had much to learn.

The idea of absolute and unquestioning obedience to the will of Jehovah, upon which Samuel insisted at all times, was not agreeable to a brilliant young fellow who loved his own freedom of action. Furthermore, he began to enjoy the many advantages of his new position and he remembered that one passes through this life only once.

Often when the army was victorious there was a great deal of booty. Samuel insisted that the greater part of this be given to the service of the Tabernacle. Saul on the other hand preferred to keep a little for himself and for his soldiers.

In the end, the inevitable happened. Saul, who was out in the field, and who rubbed up against all sorts and conditions of men, became more and more worldly in his views.

While Samuel, who was very old and who sat forever in his own room with his books and his thoughts, insisted that every one follow his own rigid example and spend all his waking hours in some form of divine worship.

Saul was not negligent in his religious duties, but he was what we now call a little too "practical."

After he beat Agag, the King of the Amalekites, he decided that the army needed a suitable reward. And so he quietly kept the herds which had belonged to the king and did not surrender them to the priests, as he ought to have done. And to make matters worse, he spared the life of Agag, whereas, according to the Jewish law of that time, he ought to have killed all his captives.

When Samuel heard of this, he scolded Saul for his disobedience to the will of Jehovah.

Saul did not confess his crime, but tried to excuse himself.

He said that the cows and the oxen and the sheep had beer kept back that they might be fattened before they were finally slaughtered and sacrificed.

Samuel knew that he had intended to do nothing of the sort and he told him so. He accused Saul of double dealing and of dishonesty and warned him against the consequences of such deplorable conduct, which made him unfiit to be King of the Jewish people.

Saul did not argue the point.

He returned to his home in Gibeah.

But he felt dreadfully hurt and he soon showed his anger.

It was commonly said and eagerly believed that Samuel could predict the future and was a fortune-teller and sooth-sayer of no mean ability.

Saul of course knew this too and he gave orders that within his realm all fortune-tellers should be either killed or should be forced into exile.

Samuel from his side did not remain idle.

He was angry and he intended to keep his threat. He began to look for a more suitable occupant of the throne. This time he meant to find a candidate who was willing to listen to the wise council of an old man, who would be less independent in his actions than Saul had been.

He asked for information about different young people and some one spoke to him about a certain David, who was the son of Jesse of Bethlehem, and a grandson of Ruth and Boaz.

The boy was a shepherd and he had quite a reputation among the people of his own village for his courage.

On one occasion his sheep had been attacked by a lion and another time, they had been attacked by a bear, and in both cases David had killed the brute and had saved his flocks without calling for help.

Furthermore, David was an excellent musician. Not only could he sing, but he also had taught himself to play the harp and during the long and lonely hours when he followed his sheep he used to make up bits of verse which he sang afterwards to melodies which he had composed himself. He was quite famous for his "Psalms" (as those songs were called) and people came from far and wide to hear him.

When it became known that David enjoyed the particular favour of Samuel, and was destined by him for a great future, it was everywhere said that it was a most excellent choice and would bring happiness to the whole nation.

Only one man did not share this general enthusiasm about the young harpist.

That was Saul.

His conscience bothered him.

He knew that Samuel had been right when he accused him of having kept the flocks of Agag against the express command of Jehovah.

He now lived in constant fear of David and wished that he could get rid of his unpleasant rival.

But what could he do? The Jewish people were watching the two men very carefully and Saul had to be very careful in whatever he did.

Fortunately, a new war came to his assistance. The Philistines were coming back. They had reorganised their armies and now threatened the eastern valleys of Saul's domain.

They were led by a giant who was called Goliath. He was as big as a house and he wore an enormous coat of mail, the like of which had never been seen by the Jews.

Every morning and every night, he strutted around between

the lines of the Jews and those of the Philistines and dared his enemies to leave their trenches and fight him.

He carried a sword that was seven feet long and he waved it ferociously and he called the Jews cowards and all sorts of horrible names and he jeered at them and generally made himself most detestable.

This went on day after day and week after week and nothing happened. The soldiers, ashamed of their own fear, looked for some one whom they could hold responsible for this humiliating situation.

Saul as commander-in-chief, became their scapegoat.

Why did he not go forth himself and fight a duel with the big Philistine?

For the simple reason that he was ill. He suffered from a terrible mood of depression which soon began to affect his mind. He sat in his tent and brooded and brooded and brooded, day after day and week after week. Finally his generals began to worry.

It seemed that Saul was losing his reason. He spoke to no one and hardly answered when he was asked a question. Something had to be done and it had to be done at once.

The wonderful curative power of music was known to the ancients. It was suggested that Saul be distracted by the pleasant songs of David. This seemed an excellent idea and David was sent for. The boy came and played so well that Saul wept bitter tears and for a short while forgot some of his troubles, and said that he felt much better.

But even then he did not stir from his tent and the army remained inactive and Goliath continued to abuse the Jews, and every day at a certain hour the Philistines left their fortifications and stood about and laughed until their sides ached.

This might have gone on indefinitely, when David happened to return to the Jewish camp.

He was one of a family of eight, and three of his brothers were in the army.

The Jewish soldiers were supposed to be their own cooks and quartermasters, and the sons of Jesse had sent word to their father that they needed fresh supplies. Jesse had ordered David to take a sack of corn and carry it to the front. When David with his burden reached the camp, he heard every one talking about the terrible giant, who quite alone seemed to hold an entire army at bay.

David did not quite understand such a feeling of panic before the name of a mortal man. Like most people who lead a solitary life he had thought a great deal upon religious subjects. He had an implicit faith in the power of Jehovah. Nothing could happen to the righteous man who was assured of the support of the great Jewish God.

He volunteered to go forth by himself and to kill this enemy of his people without the help of a single soldier.

The men of the army told him that he was both reckless and foolish, but David insisted. When his comrades saw that he meant to do what he said, they tried to prepare him for the combat. From the King down, they offered him their armour.

But David answered "No." He did not need swords and spears and shields.

He needed the moral support of Jehovah. That was all.

He went to the banks of the river and he picked up a handful of shining, round pebbles. Then he took his sling and left the trench.

When the Philistines saw that a mere child was going to fight a man twice his size, they called for their hero and bade

him make an example of the boy.   Goliath needed no urging.
Swinging his terrible sword, he rushed at David.

But a small pebble from David's sling hit him right in the
eye.   Stunned by the blow, Goliath stumbled and fell and
dropped his weapon.

Quick as lightning, David was upon him.

DAVID BRINGS BACK GOLIATH'S HEAD

He grabbed the giant's sword.

He hacked at him with unexpected violence.

With a single blow he cut off the monstrous head.

He picked it up and carried it back to the jubilant soldiers.

The Philistines fled and David was hailed as the Saviour
of the Country.

After such an exploit, even Saul was forced to take some
public notice of the national hero.   He asked David to come
and visit him, but he never could overcome his old suspicion.
His dislike grew into open hatred when he noticed the friend-

ship which sprang up between his son Jonathan and the shepherd from Bethlehem as soon as the two had met.

To make matters worse, his daughter Michal fell in love
with the handsome red-haired David. Saul told David that
he might marry her if he first destroyed a hundred Philistines.
A hundred, of course, was a very large number and Saul no
doubt counted upon David being killed before he had accomplished his task.

But David was successful in this as in all other things and
so he married Michal and the two rival kings were now in
the relation of father-in-law and son-in-law.

It is no wonder that Saul's old fits of melancholia returned
worse than before and when his doctors were at their wits' end,
they once more suggested a concert. This time, however, the
performance was almost fatal to the unfortunate harpist.

As soon as he had struck a few chords, Saul fell into a violent rage.

He took his spear and he threw it at David. David saved
himself by jumping out of the room. He did not care to meet
the King again. He left the royal tents and ran away.

Then Saul's wrath turned against Jonathan and he tried
to kill his own son. But his followers held his hands and pre-
vented the murder. Jonathan felt terribly upset by what had
just happened and felt that he ought to speak to David and
explain things. When they met for the last time, the two
friends bade each other an affectionate farewell and David fled
into the desert, where he established himself in a cave, called
Adullam.

Soon, however, the soldiers of Saul discovered where he was
hiding himself. But David had been warned and had escaped
further into the wilderness. The cave was empty. The victim
was gone.

Life in the desert was very dull and to while away the tedious hours of the endless day, David wrote several more poems. A few of these you will find in a special chapter of the Old Testament, called the Psalms. I shall not print them in my story. Centuries ago they were translated into such perfect English that it would be very foolish for me to try to repeat them in my own words. Besides, I am only trying to give an account of the adventures of the Jewish people and the Psalms have very little to do with actual history. But they are a magnificent expression of the old poetic spirit of the Jewish race and they contain more beauty and more wisdom than many of the purely historical books of the Old Testament which are devoted to the endless recital of foreign war and domestic upheaval.

But to return to David. He now passed through the strangest adventures of his long and very checkered career. He was in a very difficult and awkward position. Theoretically, he was the King of the Jews, for Samuel had deposed Saul after his disobedience in the Agag campaign and had thereupon anointed David as his successor.

The mass of the people, however, had not been able to follow such a rapid political change. They still vaguely recognised Saul as their King and if the word were not a little too colloquial, we would say that they regarded David as a sort of official understudy, a crown-prince, who at any moment might be called upon to act as regent.

Unfortunately in those days (as now) possession was nine points of the law.

Saul, whatever his actual status, continued to live in the royal tents. He was surrounded by his body-guards and by his attendants and he was the commander of a full-fledged army, ready to do his bidding.

David, on the other hand, was no better than a fugitive before the law. He lived in a cave in the wilderness and he could not show himself in any of the nearby cities or villages without running the risk of being arrested.

Afterwards, when he himself was the undisputed ruler of the Jewish people, this period of David's exile needed a good deal of explaining. At times, our hero seems to have been little better than the leader of a band of brigands. Finally, he even went so far as to take service with the Philistines.

But we must not judge him too severely. David had been treated most unfairly by Saul. It was greatly to his credit that he continued to treat his enemy with the utmost courtesy and generosity.

Saul, judging him by our modern standards, was going stark mad. In restless haste, he was forever travelling from one part of the country to another.

One day, on his trip through the desert, he was overtaken by darkness and went into a cave to spend the night. It happened to be the same cave in which David had made his home after his flight from the residence. David saw his unwelcome guest as he entered, but he hid himself and waited.

In the middle of the night, he crept toward the sleeping man and cut off a piece of his coat. The next morning when Saul departed, David ran after him and called him by name and showed him the piece of cloth.

"Look at this," he said, "and think what I might have done to you, and what I have not done. You were in my power. I might have killed you quite easily. And yet I spared you, although you continue to persecute me."

Saul of course could not fail to see that David was right. But he hated this one particular person with the unreasoning resentment of a madman, and although he mumbled an apology and called his soldiers back, he did not ask David to return to his Court.

A short while afterward, Samuel died.

At the funeral, David and Saul met, but the two men were not reconciled.

And so things continued for a long time.

SAUL ENTERS THE CAVE OF DAVID

Then it happened during one of Saul's endless peregrinations that he found himself for a second time at the mercy of his hated rival.

Saul, to the end of his days, remained at heart a simple Jewish farmer. He hated cities and refused to live in a house. Whenever he could, he spent his days in the desert. Once more he left his village to enjoy the peace and quiet of the wilderness. During the afternoon when it was very hot he had fallen asleep underneath a high rock, which was often used by David when he wanted to listen to the voice of the sun and the wind, that they might tell him those strange secrets which afterwards he repeated in his songs.

Abner, a cousin of Saul and commander-in-chief of his armies, slept by his master's side.

David had seen the two men when they approached. Noiselessly he climbed down the steep path which led to the foot of the rock. He took Abner's sword and spear, and returned whence he had come.

Then he shouted: "Oh, Abner! Abner!"

When the soldier awoke, David upbraided him for his neglect of duty. The man who was called upon to protect the King allowed a casual stranger to steal his arms. He was a faithful servant indeed! And more words to that effect.

Even Saul, in the tortured agony of his stricken soul, was forced to recognise the generosity of David's heart. For a second time, David had spared his life. He now told David that he was sorry for the cruel way in which he had treated him and asked him to come back.

And so David gathered up his few belongings and returned to the court, but not for long.

Saul was steadily growing worse. After a few weeks, everything was as it had been before and it was no longer safe for David to be seen around the royal buildings.

Of course, he could have insisted upon his rights as the only truly anointed ruler of the Jews. But he knew that the days of Saul were numbered and he did not force the issue.

He went away and never saw his old enemy again.

After a while he settled down in the village of Ziklag. It belonged to Achish, the King of Gath, and was situated on the border.

Here David's position was far from pleasant.

He had a way of attracting men. He was forever surrounded by adventurous young fellows who hoped to make
their fortune as his soldiers and servants.

It had been that way in the wilderness where David at one
time had commanded no less than four hundred volunteers.
It does not sound like a very large number to us, because we
are accustomed to armies of millions, but in the eleventh century before our era, four hundred men were a formidable army,
and David had been the undisputed ruler of almost an entire
province and many stories of his strange exploits have survived
until this day.

David seems to have hired himself out to the farmers of
that neighbourhood as a sort of private policeman to protect
them against robbers. At least, we know of one occasion when
a certain Nabal, the Sheik of Carmel, had refused to pay him
for his services. David, according to the story, was so angry
at this injustice that he gathered all his men and was about to
kill the entire Nabal tribe, when Abigail, the wife of Nabal,
rushed forth to meet him and appeased the wrath of the great
Philistine fighter with presents and fine promises.

Incidentally, when Abigail returned home, she found that
her husband was in such a state of drunkenness that he could
not be told of the events of that afternoon. The next morning,
when he was told of the danger which he had just escaped, he
had a fit, of which he died ten days later.

This left Abigail a widow. During her short interview, she
made a deep impression upon David. When he heard of her
husband's death, he asked her to become his wife, and she
accepted.

He had apparently grown tired of Michal (Saul's daughter) for he gave her to a friend who lived in the village of

Gallim, and then he married Abigail and took her to Hebron, and there a son was born to them who was called Chileab.

This new marriage, however, did not in any way settle David's other difficulties. He still had a faithful band of followers, but there was no police work to be done and it was hard to make both ends meet. And finally, the same man who a few years before had been the scourge of the Philistines was almost forced to enter their service.

It happened this way. King Achish, his host, informed him suddenly that the Philistines were going to make war upon the Jews. He, Achish, was bound by treaty to offer his help and as David enjoyed his hospitality, he expected him (David) to take part in the campaign on the side of his country's enemies.

David was at his wit's end. He gave an ambiguous answer, and sparred for time. As nothing happened, he finally marched to the Philistine camp. The Philistine commander, however, had wisely decided that help from such a source would be of very doubtful quality. He quietly allowed David to return to Ziklag and did not bother him.

When he got back he found that during his absence the village had been plundered by the Amalekites. He followed the robbers, attacked them, defeated them, killed them all (with the exception of four hundred) and once more returned to the peaceful ways of a Simeonite village.

The Philistine campaign took place as it had been planned.

It had a very unexpected result. When Saul was told of the approaching danger of a new invasion, he fell into an abysmal gloom.

He felt that the end of all things had come.

He was so desperate about the future of himself and his family, that he decided to consult a sorcerer. But all the magicians either were dead or had left the country. They had been driven away from the country by Saul's own edict.

At last, however, the King was told that there was an old witch who lived in Endor, the village near which Sisera had been murdered by Jael.

In the middle of the night (for he felt ashamed of what he was doing) Saul went to see the witch. The woman, however, was afraid to receive him. She knew the terrible punishment for sorcery and refused to open her door to the King.

Saul reassured her.

He promised her that she would be richly rewarded if she made it possible for him to speak to the soul of one who had been dead for several years.

The witch asked him what he meant.

Saul answered that he wanted to speak to his old master Samuel

Then out of the ground there arose the dark figure of an old man, wrapped in a long black cloak.

It was the ghost of Samuel.

Once more Saul, the living King, and Samuel, the dead Judge, were face to face and there Samuel told Saul of the terrible fate which awaited him at the hands of the Philistines.

When Samuel ceased to speak, Saul had fainted.

But he had a brave soul, this old frontiersman.

Early the next day, he attacked the Philistines.

Before noon his army had been annihilated. His sons, Jonathan and Malchishua and Abinadab, had all been killed and Saul himself lay dead with his own sword through his heart. He had remembered the fate of Samson and he had killed himself rather than fall into the hands of his enemies.

His body was found by the Philistines.

They cut off the head and sent it throughout the land that it might carry the glad tidings of victory to all the people.

They took the shield and the spear and the armour and placed these in the heathenish temple of Ashtaroth among the other trophies of their endless wars.

They then fastened the headless corpse of Saul and those of the three royal princes to the walls of Beth-shean.

When the people of Jabesh-gilead heard of this, they decided to rescue the remains of the man who had once saved their city from siege. In the dark of night they stole into Beth-shean and they took the bones of their royal master and his three sons and they buried them secretly underneath the sacred tamarisk tree of their own village.

The news of this terrible national tragedy reached David in a curious way. One of the Philistines, hoping to gain favour in the eyes of the new Jewish King, rode at great speed to the village of Ziklag and informed David that Saul was dead.

He also explained how it happened that Saul had been slain together with so many of his sons.

"I came upon them suddenly near the mountain called Gilboa," he lied, "and I killed them all because I knew that they were your enemies."

He did not receive the reward which he had expected.

David ordered that he be hanged and when this had been done, he went into deep mourning for his former master and for his dearly beloved friend, Jonathan.

As usual, he found sure relief in music and in poetry and he composed that noble song which begins: "The beauty of Israel is slain. How are the mighty fallen," which you will find in the first chapter of the second Book of Samuel.

Then he fasted for a long time and when he had expressed his sense of mourning in such a way that all the people should know the deep sincerity of his grief, he made ready to claim his kingdom.

He asked Jehovah whither he should go at first and Jehovah told him to travel to Mount Hebron.

There all the men of the tribe of Judah met their new sovereign and David was officially anointed as the successor of Saul.

THE BURIAL OF SAUL

For almost forty years David was king of the greater part of the Jewish lands.

He was a man of great executive ability. Otherwise he would have failed in a task which was well-nigh hopeless.

In the first place, there were the Philistines. Centuries of war had not enabled the Jews to shake off this constant menace. Time and again we read that the power of the Philistines had been broken for good. But a few years later, there would be fresh trouble, and until the end of their national independence, the Jews were forced to pay an annual tribute to the much-hated neighbours, whose superior skill in war made them invincible whenever the armies met in pitched battle.

In the second place (and this was almost worse) David had to contend with interminable quarrels among the Jewish tribes themselves. The different clans were as jealous of each other as only the people of small villages can be.

They wanted a King.

But just as soon as they had a King they began to resent his power.

And even David, with his tremendous prestige, was not strong enough to overcome prejudice and assert himself when he was called upon to punish a popular soldier who had broken the law.

For example, when Joab, his own nephew, who held a high position in the army, murdered Abner, the faithful servant of Saul, David did not dare to execute Joab. He gave Abner a magnificent funeral, but that was all.

Joab was never brought to trial and David was to regret the day that he had spared his life.

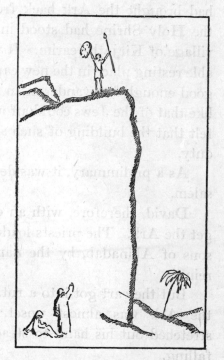

Very slowly and only by using all his intelligence and all the strength of his indomitable will, he made himself the absolute master of the land.

A short time later, when the servants of one of Saul's remaining sons killed their master, David was ready for them. He hanged the murderers and announced that a

DAVID TAKES THE SHIELD
AND SPEAR OF ABNER

similar fate awaited all those who were going to take the law into their own hands.

This at last put the fear of Jehovah into the hearts of the Jews, and then David took a further step which was to be of great benefit to the new kingdom.

He moved the capital of the country to the city of Jerusalem, which was conveniently situated upon the highroads from Africa to Mesopotamia.

There he built himself a palace.

When that was done, he began to talk of plans for a Temple which was to replace the Tabernacle.

Ever since that memorable day when the driverless cows had brought the Ark back from the land of the Philistines, the Holy Shrine had stood in the house of Abinadab in the village of Kirjath-jearim. It was time that it be given a suitable resting place in the new capital. The Tabernacle had been good enough for wanderers in the desert, but a powerful state like that of the Jews could afford a real Temple and the people felt that the building of such an edifice had become a national duty.

As a preliminary, it was decided to bring the Ark to Jerusalem.

David, therefore, with an entire army-corps, went east to get the Ark. The priests loaded it upon a cart and one of the sons of Abinadab, by the name of Uzzah, took hold of the reins.

But the cart got into a rut, one of the oxen stumbled, and the Ark was almost upset. Uzzah, quite unconsciously, stretched out his hand to steady the shrine and keep it from falling.

At once he was struck dead.

According to old Jewish law, no layman had the right to touch the Ark. That was the exclusive business of the priests.

The happy procession, with David at its head, came to a sudden halt.

Uzzah was buried, and the Ark was carried into the house of a Gittite by the name of Obed-edom.

There it stood for three months.

Then David returned with all his soldiers. Once more the Ark was hoisted upon a wagon.

This time it safely reached Jerusalem and it was placed in a new Tabernacle which Solomon, the successor of David, was afterwards to change into the well-known Temple.

From that moment on, Jerusalem was not only the capital of the Jewish states but it also became the religious centre for all those who claimed descent from Abraham. There were other holy places in Palestine, but these were all surpassed by the splendours of the house of offering of Jerusalem.

Furthermore, the Levite families, who had a monopoly of the Jewish priest-craft were clever men. They tolerated no rivals and they were staunch supporters of the King. He in turn showed his favour by ordering that all the other shrines in the land be closed and by forcing the worshippers to come to his own capital.

When the religious side of life had been attended to, David turned his mind to affairs of a military nature.

First he rounded out the frontiers of his kingdom.

Next he defeated the Ammonites in such a decisive way that they ceased to trouble the Jews.

In the third place, he made a truce with the Philistines, who thereafter left him in peace.

From a worldly point of view, the kingdom of David was a great success.

But all was not well with the man who stood at the head of the nation.

The unlimited power of his exalted position was beginning to spoil him.

Like Samuel, David was in many respects a very weak man. He was kindly and wise and very good-natured, even to his enemies. He had been very generous to the only living grandson of Saul, who happened to be the son of his bosom friend, Jonathan.

This poor boy, who was lame in both feet, was adopted by David as his own child, and until the day of his death, lived with him in the palace of Jerusalem.

But when his own pleasure was involved, David could be as mean and cruel as the worst of his subjects.

One evening, while taking the air on the roof of his palace (as was the custom of the Jewish people during summer when the weather was hot) David saw in the distance a woman.

He liked her looks, and he said that he wanted her for his wife.

But when he made inquiries about her, he discovered that she was already married to a Hittite by the name of Uriah, who was an officer then serving at the front under Joab, the same general who (as you will remember) had never been punished for the murder of Abner.

Of course, David ought to have forgotten the woman at once, but he did nothing of the sort.

Instead, he invited her husband to his palace.

He treated him most kindly and gave him presents and then he sent him back to the army with a letter to Joab in which he told Joab to place Uriah in the front line and to leave him there, that he might be killed by the enemy.

Joab, who was no better than a common criminal, was just the sort of man to arrange such a cold-blooded murder. He did not warn Uriah of his danger. On the contrary, he flattered the poor fellow and told him that he was to be entrusted with a place in the line of danger in recognition of his bravery. Uriah believed all this and cheerfully assumed command of the vanguard.

When the attack was made, the plan of David was carried out with scrupulous regard to detail.

Uriah rushed forward.

At a word of command by Joab, the other soldiers retreated.

Uriah was left alone and he was killed.

This made his wife, Bathsheba, a widow, and soon afterwards, David married her.

David, however, was mistaken when he thought that his evil deed had not become known to the people of Jerusalem.

The soldiers at the front (who always know a good many things) had told their relatives. News travels fast in a small country and soon all the Jews knew how their King, desiring the wife of another man, had first ordered the husband to be killed and had then married the widow.

But of course the King was the King and even then there were many people who thought that David could do no wrong.

As for the others, they feared to speak their mind lest they be thrown into prison and get hanged for their trouble.

That was one of those great moments in Jewish history which we mentioned in the beginning pages of this chapter.

When all the Jews were silent, the national conscience spoke up.

Nathan the Prophet went to the palace of David the King. He had just heard a little story which he wanted to repeat to David.

David bade him go ahead.

"Once upon a time," so Nathan began, "there was a rich man and a poor man and the two were neighbours. The rich man had many sheep but the poor man had but a single little lamb. He was very fond of his pet and treated it as if it had been one of his own children and when he did not have much to eat, he shared his bread and his milk with his beloved lamb and when it was cold, he hid the lamb within the folds of his cloak so that it should not freeze.

"One day the rich man was obliged to entertain a friend. He could easily have killed one of his own sheep. But no, he must go and steal the little lamb from his poor neighbour and have it served at his dinner-table for the amusement of his guest."

When David heard this, he was terribly angry. He said to Nathan that it was the most dastardly crime he had ever heard.

He promised to inflict a severe punishment.

The poor shepherd whose lamb had been stolen would receive a seven-fold compensation.

As for the wretch who was guilty of the crime, he would be killed at once.

Then Nathan the Prophet stood up and said: "O King, you are the man. It is you who have killed Uriah because you wanted his wife. And therefore Jehovah shall bring grief upon you and upon your family, and the son of yourself and of Bathsheba shall die a violent death to atone for the terrible sin of his father and his mother."

David was stricken with fear and remorse. A short while later, his youngest child fell ill. That was part of the prophecy. David put ashes upon his head and humiliated himself before Jehovah in every possible way. For seven days and seven nights he did not eat nor drink. On the eighth day, the child died and the words of Nathan had come true.

From that moment on, David regarded himself as the murderer of his own boy. He confessed unto Jehovah that he had been utterly wrong in his treatment of Uriah. He offered to do penance. He begged and prayed and beseeched that he might be forgiven. Apparently this show of grief impressed

Jehovah with its sincerity and for a short while David suffered no further punishment.

Soon afterwards Bathsheba had another son. He was called Solomon, and David, in his joy, promised the mother that he would make that boy his successor to the exclusion of all his other children.

This, of course, was very unpleasant news to the rightful heirs, whose names were Absalom and Adonijah.

Adonijah was not very energetic and did not care much what happened. Absalom, however, whose mother had been born in the hot Syrian desert, was a reckless youth, and he began to plot against his father.

He went out of his way to make himself popular with the people of Jerusalem. He was a good-looking young man with long blond hair which he wore down his neck. For ever he was to be seen where there was a crowd. He loved to pose as the defender of the poor against the oppressions of the rich. As David was becoming more and more of a despot, and as taxes were going higher all the time, there were plenty of people with grievances. They eagerly brought their complaints before this crown-prince who so suddenly had lost his claim to the throne.

After four years of such agitation, when Absalom thought that he could count upon a sufficient number of followers, he left Jerusalem and went to Hebron, on the pretext of there making a sacrifice to Jehovah, but really to start his campaign against his father.

It was a terrible blow to David.

He had loved Absalom better than all his other children and felt that he had not been quite fair to him. He could not bear the idea of making war upon his own flesh and blood. He left his palace and he fled across the river Jordan and went to live in the village of Mahanaim.

As a result of his flight there followed a period of civil war. But in this hour of defeat and humiliation, the people remembered David the glorious leader against the Philistines who had slain Goliath, while they forgot David the King who had stolen another man's wife.

They rallied to their master with the greatest loyalty.

Soon the entire country was divided into two parts. One of these supported David and the other was faithful to Absalom. But the majority was on the side of the King.

A battle took place in the forest of Ephraim, east of the river Jordan. Before the fighting commenced, David begged his soldiers to deal kindly with Absalom. Even then he cared more for the boy than he was willing to confess after his scandalous and rebellious conduct.

All day long the partisans of the King and those of his son fought. Many men were killed but when evening came, the followers of David got the better of their adversaries and Absalom was forced to retreat.

He trotted away on his mule as fast as he could. But the stout branch of a tree caught his long hair. The animal which he was riding got frightened and ran away and Absalom was left hanging in the air.

One of David's soldiers found him. He knew that the King had asked mercy for the rebels and he refused to kill the boy.

He ran back and told Joab.

This gruff sinner had no such scruples. He took three spears and went to the place where the helpless Absalom was suspended between the heaven and the earth, and he killed him and threw the corpse into a grave underneath the oak tree and he called a negro slave and ordered him to go and tell David what had just happened.

The negro went to the King's camp and cheerfully informed the old ruler how his enemies had been defeated and how his son had been killed. David did not rejoice. He was broken-hearted.

He remembered his own crimes and the curse of Nathan the Prophet.

Now that he was victorious, all the rebellious tribes hastened

THE DEATH OF ABSALOM

to make their peace, but this could not bring back poor Absalom, for whom David wailed from one end of his palace to the other.

And now there followed another succession of misfortunes. The King was growing weak and his days were numbered. He could no longer lead his armies and soon there was another invasion on the part of the Philistines.

Then Adonijah, the brother of Absalom, began a revolution.

This aroused David to his last great act.

He ordered Solomon to be crowned King of the Jews.

Adonijah, who knew that Solomon was far brighter than he was himself, thereupon surrendered and made his peace with his brother, who forgave him.

But of all these events, David took no notice. He sat in a dark corner of his palace and mumbled words of affection for his son Absalom, who had been slain when he dared to make war upon his father.

Until merciful death made an end to his suffering and gave him that peace which he had not been able to find since he had broken the commands of the God of Moses and Joshua.

And now Solomon was King of all the Jews and many things had changed since the first of the pioneers had left the desert lands of Ur to settle down amidst the hills and the valleys across "the River," which in those days was the common West-Asiatic appellation for the Euphrates.

When Abraham desired to entertain a guest, he told his servants to kill a single lamb.

Solomon lived on a different scale. The daily provisions necessary for his table were as follows: Thirty measures of flour, seventy measures of meal, ten fat oxen, twenty lean oxen and dozens of deer, roebucks, chickens and other game.

When Abraham moved into a new territory, he built himself a simple tent and slept on a few old rugs.

Solomon, on the other hand, spent twenty years building himself a new palace and ate from dishes made of solid gold.

It makes interesting reading, but it cost a terrible lot of money. Many hundred years afterwards when the Jews lived in exile in Babylon and wrote down the records of the past, they loved to dwell upon the glories of the reign of Solomon who according to them had been the undisputed master of all the land between the Euphrates and the Mediterranean Sea.

But the subjects of the mighty monarch who were obliged to do forced labour on all public works and who were forced to pay annual levies for the maintenance of the royal palace, the national temple, the terraced fortress of Millo, the walls of Jerusalem and the three new frontier cities which Solomon rebuilt and fortified, they were less enthusiastic and (truth to tell) they were for ever on the verge of rebellion.

Fortunately Solomon was a shrewd man and he kept the expenditures of his court within certain limits.

Like Joseph and several other great Jewish leaders, Solomon was very apt to have visions when he was asleep. Shortly after his accession to the throne, he dreamed that Jehovah asked him what gift he desired above all others.

Solomon answered that he chose wisdom. The word "wisdom" in the old Hebrew sense could be translated by either "wisdom" or "shrewdness."

Solomon had his share of both. He was exceedingly bright but not rash.

As King of the Jews he also was the chief-justice of the nation. One of the first cases that were brought before him was a quarrel between two women who both claimed a small child as their own. Solomon ordered one of his life-guards to take the baby and hack it in two and give half of it to each of the women. What he had expected, actually happened.

The real mother begged the soldier to spare the child's life. "For it is better," so she argued, "that the wrong mother keep the child than it should suffer death in this terrible way."

Such a quick and penetrating decision greatly pleased the multitude. It made Solomon popular. Not even the follies of his old age could quite deprive him of the affection of his subjects.

So he ruled for forty years, from 943 B.C. to 903 B.C.

And all that time, he spent money like water.

First of all he constructed the royal palace. It was an enormous building consisting of many halls and courtyards, all of them leading up to the Temple. Inside the high enclosure there was an armoury, a room where the King gave audiences and listened to cases of law. There were extensive living quarters for his Majesty and for all his attendants and there was a harem where the royal wives were kept far away from the gaze of the curious crowd.

Everything was built of stone and finished in cypress wood. It took twenty years to build.

Then came the temple. Of course, an ancient temple was something quite different from a modern church. It was a holy place where people came to make sacrifices to the gods, or in this case, to only one God, who was called Jehovah. No sermons were ever preached and the worshippers kept coming and going all the time.

It was not necessary that the building should be very large and Solomon's temple measured only ninety-five by thirty feet, which is the size of the average village church.

All the same, the edifice cost untold millions. The Jews were farmers and merchants and had little skill as artisans. The necessary stone-cutters and wood-carvers and goldsmiths had to be imported from abroad. Most of them came from Phœnicia which was the greatest commercial centre of the world of three thousand years ago.

To-day, Tyre and Sidon are forlorn little fishing villages, but in the days of Solomon they were ports which impressed a visitor from the land-locked Jewish state as New York is apt to overawe a man who comes from a little city in the heart of the prairies.

David had already made a treaty with the ruler of Tyre. Solomon now concluded an alliance with the King of Sidon.

In return for an annual supply of grain, King Hiram placed a number of his ships at the disposal of the Jewish sovereign and promised to provide him with the necessary skilled labourers for his Temple.

The ships which Solomon chartered visited all the harbours of the Mediterranean as far as Tarshish (which the Romans called Tartessus) in Spain and they gathered gold and precious stones and costly woods for Solomon's holy shrine.

But the world of the Mediterranean was too small to supply all the needs of the great monarch. He decided to establish a trade-route into the Indies. He engaged Phœnician ship-builders to settle down on the shore of the Gulf of Akabah, an eastern branch

THE ALTAR OF BURNED OFFERING STOOD OUT IN THE OPEN

of the Red Sea. There they built a ship-yard near the town of Ezion-geber (which the Jews had visited six centuries before when they were wanderers in the desert) and their vessels travelled as far as Ophir (which was either on the eastern coast of Africa or on the western coast of India) and then returned with sandalwood and with ivory and with incense, which caravans then carried to Jerusalem.

Compared to the pyramids (which were then almost three thousand years old) and to the temples in Thebes and in Memphis and in Nineveh and in Babylon, the temple of Solomon was not a very imposing building.

But it was the first time that one of the many small Semitic tribes of western Asia had ventured forth upon such an ambitious building plan. Even the rich Queen of Sheba, the famous gold land of Arabia, was driven by curiosity to visit the new capital of her northern neighbours and honoured Solomon with a visit, and expressed her admiration for what he had accomplished.

Unfortunately we have no foreign account of the Temple and the Book of Kings which gives a minute description was written several centuries later. By that time it was commonly believed and said that the Temple had cost 108,000 talents of gold and 1,017,000 talents of silver, or 2,450 million of our modern dollars. But this was about fifty times the total gold-supply of the whole ancient world, and the amount is probably somewhat exaggerated. As hardly a single stone remains of the original building, and as the site of the temple now lies buried underneath one hundred and twenty feet of accumulated rubbish, it will be difficult to form a correct modern estimate.

We know, however, that the old hill of Moriah (originally occupied by the farm of Araunah the Jebusite) was gradually covered with a complex system of buildings the fame of which has come down to us through the centuries. They were begun in the four hundred and eightieth year after the flight from Egypt (the first positive date in the Old Testament) and they were finished in the four hundred and eighty-seventh year.

All the preparatory work of cutting the stones and hewing the wood into the proper shape was done far away from the hill of Moriah so that the actual work of construction should be done with a minimum amount of noise.

The Jews, who even then rarely lived in stone houses, did not like bare walls. Solomon therefore covered all the floors and the walls and the ceilings of the holy edifice with boards of cypress and of cedar and these again he overlaid with a thin layer of gold.

The heart of the temple, the Holy of Holies, was a square little room, thirty feet long and wide and thirty feet high. Inside there stood the carved figures of two large angels. Underneath their outspread wings rested the Ark, the plain wooden box which had now followed the Jews on their peregrinations for almost five centuries. It contained the two pieces of stone upon which Jehovah had engraved his Holy Laws, when he appeared to Moses amidst the clouds of Mount Sinai.

Inside of the small room there reigned eternal silence. Only once each year the High Priest was allowed to enter into the presence of the Divine Spirit. That was on the Day of Atonement.

Upon that occasion the High Priest laid aside his official garments and dressed himself in pure white linen.

In his hand he held a censer containing some coals for the altar.

In the other he carried a golden bowl with the blood of a sacrificed bullock. This he sprinkled upon the floor as a sign of atonement.

Then he retired. The golden doors, decorated with the pictures of flowers and palm trees, were closed and once more the silent figures stood guard over the Ark which rested underneath their outspread wings.

The Sanctuary, however, which was separated from the Holy of Holies by a partition of cedar boards, was the real, busy part of the Temple. There stood the Altar of Incense and the law required that all those who wished to make an offering should pour the blood of one sacrificial animal before this famous shrine.

From morning till late in the evening, the room was filled with the noise of both men and beasts.

THE HOLY OF HOLIES

The Jewish law of sacrifice was intricate and complicated. The priests, who made a great deal of money out of these offerings, were forever making changes in the regulations which had originally been laid down by Moses. There was a special form of sacrifice for every sort of sin and crime.

Very poor people were allowed make an offering of unleavened bread or of roasted grain.

But those who could afford to do so were supposed to buy a bullock or a sheep or a goat, and bring these to the temple that they might be surrendered to the priest for further treatment.

For the sake of convenience, such animals were held for sale near the temple entrance and all day long the air was filled with the loud noise of bleating sheep and mooing cows. In the beginning, the person who brought the offering was supposed to kill his own victim. Gradually, however, this work was taken over by the priests and the offering lost much of its personal character.

The animal was first of all killed and cut into pieces. The blood was either smeared upon the altar of incense, or was poured down before it. The rest of the animal (or a part of it containing the fat) was then allowed to be consumed by the coals of the Altar of Offering, which was made of brass and which stood outside of the temple in the so-called Court of the Priests, where the smoke could easily rise toward Heaven.

Whatever remained after the offering was then eaten by the people who made the sacrifice, or it was given to the priests, who together with their families, occupied three entire tiers of rooms which were conveniently built against the sides of the temple.

When the temple had been finished and was ready to open its doors to the faithful, Solomon dedicated the holy edifice with great and solemn festivities.

He invited all the leaders of the Jewish people to come to Jerusalem.

Together they first walked from Jerusalem to Zion to fetch the Ark.

Zion was the name of one of the hills on which the original village of Jerusalem had been situated. It had been a fortress which had belonged to the Jebusites, some of the original inhabitants of the land of Canaan. Their king had been killed by Joshua but they had maintained their independence for several centuries longer.

Finally David had captured Zion.

He had called it the City of David and had made it the nucleus for his future capital.

When he had brought back the Ark from Kirjath-jearim, it had been placed in a temporary tabernacle which had been constructed inside the old royal palace.

From there the priests now carried the Ark to its final resting place inside the Holy of Holies.

As soon as this had been done, a cloud filled the Temple, to show that the spirit of Jehovah was present. Then Solomon knelt down and prayed for his people and a bolt of fire descended from Heaven and it consumed the offering which had been placed upon the altar and the King and all his subjects knew that Jehovah was well pleased with his new home.

The feast which followed lasted two full weeks.

Solomon slaughtered twenty-two thousand oxen and one-hundred-and-twenty thousand sheep and the other people made offerings to the best of their ability.

All this greatly increased the fame of the King of the Jews.

For the first time in history, his country attracted international attention. There were visitors from many lands. Trade became more brisk than it had been before. Many of the Jewish merchants established offices of their own in the cities of Egypt and in those that were situated along the shores of the Mediterranean and the banks of the Euphrates and the Tigris.

It was the beginning of a great era of prosperity.

But the money did not prove an unmixed blessing. Solomon now rarely left his palace. He increased his body-guard and he was the first of the Jewish rulers to maintain separate regiments of cavalry. As he grew older, he withdrew completely from all business of state. He ceased to regard himself as the king of a few simple tribes of shepherds. He became undisputed ruler of a powerful oriental nation.

For reasons of state he had married the daughters of several of his more powerful neighbours.

Each of these women, whether Egyptian, Moabite, Hittite, Edomite, Ammonite or Phœnician, had of course remained faithful to the religion of her own country, and within the enclosure of the royal palace there might be found altars to Isis and to Baal and to the other heathenish gods of Africa and Asia.

Sometimes, to please a favourite wife, Solomon had allowed her to build a little temple of her own that she might worship her own gods as she had done when she was a child in the valley of the Nile or among the hills of Aram. It showed that the King was still a man of large and liberal views. But it did not increase his popularity among the masses who were strict followers of the only true God.

They had slaved and they had laboured and they had suffered untold hardships that the Temple might be built.

And now their King (of all people) deserted the House of Jehovah that he might sit in the dim splendours of some heathenish sanctuary.

It caused a great deal of discontent.

It kindled the spirit of revolt which was to break out into open rebellion as soon as Solomon should have passed away.

We know very little about his last years. They were

minutely described in the "Acts of Solomon," but the book has unfortunately been lost.

Solomon died peacefully and was buried with his fathers in the family vault in the City of David.

He might have laid the foundations for a strong Jewish state. His personal love of luxury and his spiritual indifference had made this impossible.

As soon as he was dead, the storm broke.

CIVIL WAR

CHAPTER XII

A WISE LEADER MIGHT HAVE SAVED THIS NATION FROM THE FATE OF ALL EMPIRES. THE IMMEDIATE SUCCESSOR OF SOLOMON, HOWEVER, WAS INDOLENT AND IGNORANT AND SURROUNDED BY EVIL ADVISORS. HE FORCED THE TEN NORTHERN TRIBES TO RISE UP IN REBELLION AGAINST HIS MISRULE. THEY CHOSE A KING OF THEIR OWN AND FORMED A NEW STATE, CALLED ISRAEL. THE SOUTHERN PART OF THE COUNTRY REMAINED FAITHFUL TO THE LEGITIMATE SOVEREIGN AND IT BECAME KNOWN AS JUDAH AND JERUSALEM WAS ITS CAPITAL

 EHOBOAM, who succeeded his father, was the son of Solomon and Naamah, a woman who belonged to the tribe of Ammon.

He was dull, ignorant and narrow-minded.

But it is not quite fair to blame him for all the evils which befell his country immediately after his accession to the throne and for the final division of the people of Israel into two small and hostile kingdoms.

There were other reasons besides the universal unpopularity of the sovereign.

From the very beginning of Jewish history there had been jealousy and bad feeling between the tribe of Judah, which lived to the south of the valley of Achor, and the tribe of Israel, which lived to the north.

It is very difficult to follow those ancient rivalries back to their origin. The first eleven books of the Old Testament (which are our only source for this entire period) contain many legends but little accurate history. The men who wrote these chronicles were often people with a personal bias who were trying to prove a favourite point. Not infrequently they added little bits of irrelevant gossip which had nothing to do with the real story of the Jewish nation.

Furthermore, during all these centuries, the territory which the Jews had occupied was in a continual process of transition.

Many of the original inhabitants had been killed or had accepted the Jewish rule and had gone over to the Jewish religion.

But here and there a village or a small city had maintained a semi-independent existence for a number of centuries and it is quite impossible to say when Palestine had really become a definitely Jewish country. Let me try to make this clear by a comparison with modern times.

When you study the history of our own great west, you will discover how difficult (almost impossible) it is to state in which year a certain part of the west ceased to be a wilderness and became a civilised community. Often we know the date on which the first pioneers moved their herds and their families into the plains across the Alleghanies. We know when the earliest houses were built in cities like St. Louis and Chicago. But exactly when did Missouri and Illinois drop the habit

of a "frontier country" and when did they assume the outward
and inner aspects of the older states along the Atlantic seaboard?

It is impossible to give a more specific answer than "sometime during the first half of the nineteenth century."

In this respect, Jewish history greatly resembled that of
our own country.

But there are other puzzles and parallels in this chapter
which will make it necessary for you to read it with great care.

There is the question of the names of "Judah" and "Israel"
which occur on every page of the books of the Old Testament.
They are used in a most irregular fashion.

The authors of the books of Joshua and Judges and Kings
often wrote Israel or Judah when they really meant "all of
the land that had been won from the Canaanites and the Ammonites and the Jebusites." Sometimes they were even more
careless and called Israel Judah, and vice versa.

To make this point clear, let me give you one more modern
example.

Suppose that a writer three thousand years hence discovers
a number of books dealing with the history of our country,
which have been hidden in a deserted cellar in the ruins of
Boston. He reads them with the help of an ancient English
grammar which he had found in a museum and he finds continual references to "America," to the "United States," and
to "The States."

How is he going to know what the historians of the year
1923 actually meant when they used those terms so indis-
criminately?

"America" is the name of a continent which stretches from
the North Pole to the South Pole.

But common usage had also given the same name to a

small part of that continent, situated between Canada and Mexico. How does the future author know that in this case "America" actually meant the "United States of America" and not the entire continent? Again, when he reads "The United States," how will he be able to decide positively whether this referred to "The United States of Brazil" or the "United States of Venezuela" in the southern hemisphere or to "The United States of America" in the northern?

And when he comes across a reference to "The States" how is he going to be certain whether the name was in this instance given to the country as a whole or to the individual states of the east or the north or the south or the west?

To the Jewish scribe of two thousand years ago such a term as "Judah" or "Israel" meant a very definite region and there was no chance for misunderstanding. But that world now lies buried underneath twenty centuries of accumulated historical rubbish and it is not easy for us to decide what the particular "city" and "river" were to which the Prophets so often refer when they naïvely state that "the men from across the river destroyed the city." Most likely the "men from across the river" were the Babylonians who lived on the other side of the river Euphrates. In nine cases out of ten "the city" was the city of Jerusalem. By the application of a little intelligence we can often guess at such things with a very great degree of accuracy. But we are never quite certain and further explorations in Mesopotamia may show us that we are wrong after all.

You will now understand that we can make only the most general historical assertions in the chapters which are to follow and that we are none too certain of our arguments in the present chapter, which endeavours to explain why the Jewish kingdom was predestined to go to pieces before it had even acquired the outward characteristics of a regular empire.

Whether the men of Israel (the direct descendants of Jacob) were more energetic than those of Judah (who claimed their descent from Jacob through his fourth son and a native woman of the village of Adullam), we do not know.

Whether living among the wide and pleasant valleys of the northland, with its many villages and cities, had made the Israelites different from the Judæans, who dwelt amidst the dark rocks of a high and arid plateau and retained the habits of the patriarchal shepherds much longer than their neighbours, we could not tell you with any degree of accuracy.

But the fact remains that almost all the leaders of the Jewish people, from the days of Joshua and Gideon and Samuel and Saul, to those of John the Baptist and Jesus, were born in the north.

Indeed, with the single exception of David, the south produced almost no men of great prominence.

It is an open question whether it would not have been better for the Jewish people if the consolidation of the tribes into a single state had been undertaken by a northerner.

But such historical speculations are of little value. Germany to-day would undoubtedly be a much pleasanter country if Bismarck had been a Bavarian.

But he was a Prussian, just as David happened to be a Judæan, and nothing can change those facts or their influence upon all future historical development.

This much is certain. Once David had escaped the wrath of Saul (who was probably prejudiced against his rival on the general ground of his being a "southerner") and had been made King of the Jews, he followed a very wise policy of conciliation.

In his eagerness to placate the prejudices of the north, he often went so far that he incurred the hostility of his own tribesmen. But his kingdom was based upon the firm foundation of moderation and compromise and it easily weathered the revolutions which took place when the sovereign himself was too old to take the field.

Solomon, during the first half of his reign, tried to follow the same policy. He was, however, less truthful and less generous than David.

Those who threatened to be dangerous to the safety of the state were ruthlessly persecuted and killed.

In the field of foreign politics, however, he was more successful than his father. By a series of successful wars (fought by his generals, for the King himself had no love for the hardships of camp life) he protected his frontiers against all enemies and he assured peace and prosperity to his own subjects.

Within a short time he had made himself as popular in the north as he already was in the south. But when Solomon reached middle-age, he began to commit those errors which finally brought about the downfall of the Empire, as we shall now tell you.

Probably for reasons of strategy, Jerusalem had been made the capital of the entire country. It is true that the Israelites would have liked to see the royal palace and the temple built within their own northern domains, but they accepted the decision of Solomon with good grace and travelled many hundreds of miles whenever they wanted to make a sacrifice to Jehovah.

Then Solomon commenced to build.

Of course, other monarchs have driven their subjects into bankruptcy by the glorious ambition of their architectural dreams. But few countries have ever been so completely drained of their gold and silver supply as both Israel and Judah were drained by the exactions of the "Peaceable Monarch."

In the beginning, the Israelites did not object. They felt that they were working for the glory of Jehovah and were willing to make great sacrifices. But when Jerusalem was turned into a gaudy, barbaric capital, and when the King himself began to waste the royal revenue upon temples to Moloch and to Chemosh and to a dozen other strange heathenish gods, there was a murmur of discontent among the masses.

Finally when they were being driven into practical slavery and serfdom, that Solomon might order further cargoes of gold from Ophir and more shiploads of silver from Tarshish, they threatened rebellion.

But before they took to arms, a Prophet had already given utterance to the national grievance.

One of Solomon's officials, by the name of Nebat (of the tribe of Ephraim) had a son who was called Jeroboam. He was a foreman and worked on the temple. One day as he was going to his job, he met the Prophet Ahijah who had moved to Jerusalem from the village of Shiloh. The Prophet was wearing a new coat. That in itself was a very strange sight. Prophets were usually too poor to wear anything but an old camel's hair shirt.

As soon as Ahijah saw Jeroboam, he took off his fine garment, cut it deliberately into twelve pieces and handed ten of them to Jeroboam. It was a token that Jehovah intended Jeroboam to be ruler over ten of the tribes of Israel.

Solomon, who was well served by his secret agents, heard what had happened and gave orders that Jeroboam be killed. News, however, travelled fast in such a small town as Jerusalem and Jeroboam was warned. He escaped and fled to Egypt where Shishak, a Pharaoh of the twenty-second dynasty, gave him an asylum.

Shishak was a clever statesman who regarded the growth

of a strong Jewish empire on the east of his own frontiers with serious misgivings.

No doubt he hoped to use Jeroboam as a rival candidate for the Jewish throne as soon as Solomon should have died. This is exactly what happened. As soon as the Pharaoh heard that Rehoboam had succeeded his father, he gave Jeroboam money enough to finance his return trip to Jerusalem and offer himself as a rival candidate. For almost two generations, now, the Jewish state had been a hereditary monarchy. But certain forms of "election" survived from the old days of the Judges. Therefore, whenever the ruler died, there was to be a meeting of the tribes to "elect" the new sovereign.

When the representatives from all parts of the land had come together, they discussed the political situation. They were willing to acknowledge Rehoboam as their King, but before they acclaimed him they insisted on some sort of "Magna Charta," or "Constitution" (as we would say today), that they might be protected against a too harsh execution of the tax-laws.

Rehoboam, who had been educated in the harem of the royal palace and had rarely come into contact with his subjects, sent for a number of ancient councillors who had served under his father.

What would they advise him to do?

The old men told him that the country was groaning underneath an unbearable burden and that the King ought to grant the wishes of his national council.

Rehoboam, however, who loved his ease, did not like to hear people talk about a decrease in the royal budget.

He turned to the young gentlemen of the court who were his boon companions and asked them what they thought of this popular demand for "economy."

They expressed deep contempt for the rabble and gave him courage for the foolish answer which has survived throughout the ages, and which is forever connected with his name.

"My father," so Rehoboam spoke, "has put a heavy yoke upon you. Very well. I, your new King, intend to add to that yoke. My father chastised you with whips, but I will chastise you with scourges."

This was the proverbial last straw.

Ten of the tribes refused to recognise Rehoboam and elected Jeroboam as their King.

Only the tribes of Judah and Benjamin remained faithful to the son of Solomon.

In this way the Jewish nation was divided into two parts, which were never to be reunited.

The chance for a strong, centralised kingdom was gone for ever. But the world at large gained by the failure of the Jewish imperial ambitions. Together, Judah and Israel (comparable in size to the modern kingdom of Belgium) might have grown into the most important state of western Asia.

Divided, the two little countries were too weak to maintain themselves against their mighty neighbours of the east.

First of all (in the year 722 B.C.) Israel was overrun and conquered by the Assyrians.

A century later, Judah suffered a similar fate at the hands of the Chaldeans.

The Jews were driven into exile.

Far away from the Temple and their homes, the priests remained scrupulously faithful to the letter of the ancient laws.

They forgot nothing, and they learned nothing.

But the Prophets made good use of this unexpected chance to widen their view of both men and affairs and to study their own people in relation to the rest of the world. It gave them an opportunity to revise their spiritual ideas.

The cruel and implacable Jehovah, who had been worshipped by Moses and by Joshua and by David, had been the tribal god of a small community of farmers and shepherds, who lived in a forgotten corner of western Asia.

Because of the courage and vision of the exiled Prophets, the old Hebrew deity now developed into that universal and eternal concept of the Divine Spirit which is accepted by the people of the modern world as the highest expression of Truth and Love.

THE WARNING OF THE PROPHETS

CHAPTER XIII

**THE TWO LITTLE JEWISH KINGDOMS MADE WAR
UPON EACH OTHER ALMOST INCESSANTLY AND THIS
FRATERNAL STRIFE SO WEAKENED THEM THAT
THEY WERE FOREVER AT THE MERCY OF THEIR
NEIGHBOURS. THEIR FINAL MISFORTUNES, HOW-
EVER, DID NOT COME WITHOUT A WARNING. WHILE
KINGS AND POLITICIANS AND PRIESTS WERE NEG-
LECTING THEIR DUTIES, A NUMBER OF COURAGEOUS
MEN, KNOWN AS THE PROPHETS, STEPPED FORWARD
IN A VAIN ATTEMPT TO LEAD THE PEOPLE BACK
TO THE TRUE WORSHIP OF JEHOVAH**

HE work of the Judges and that of
David and Solomon stood undone.
Their dream of a great Jewish empire
had come to grief. A strong line of
fortifications, running all the way from
Gilgal near the river Jordan (once the
headquarters of Joshua), to the city of
Gezer on the Philistine border, divided
the Jewish lands into a northern and a southern part.

United, they would have been able to maintain their com-
non independence.

Divided, they were at the mercy of their powerful neighbours.

We are about to tell you the unhappy story of an unhappy people. Centuries of civil war and anarchy will be followed by two hundred years of exile and slavery. It will be a record of dark deeds—of sudden murder and futile ambition. But it will provide us with the proper background for the most interesting spiritual struggle of ancient days.

We must know the main events of this complicated period if we are to understand the life of the greatest of all the Prophets, who was born long after the last remnant of Jewish independence had been destroyed by the armies of Pompey.

Solomon the Magnificent died sometime between the years 940 and 930 B.C.

Five years later, the division of his empire had become an accomplished and generally accepted fact.

It was then possible to compare the strength of the two new nations. Israel was three times as large as Judah, and had twice as many inhabitants. Her pastures were incomparably richer than those of Judah where three-fourths of the land was barren wilderness. This did not mean that Israel was twice as strong or three times as rich as her southern neighbour. On the contrary, the very extent of her territory was a disadvantage to Israel. Judah, small and compact, enjoyed a more centralised form of government and was better prepared to resist invasion.

On the east, the rocky wilderness of the Dead Sea, sweltering in the salty heat of a valley situated 1200 feet below the level of the Mediterranean Sea, presented an almost insurpassable barrier against the aggressions of Moab and Ammon.

On the south, there was the desert, which stretched as far as Arabia.

The western frontier touched the land of the Philistines. These old Cretan fugitives had lost much of their former ferocity. They had settled down to the peaceful life of the farm and the workshop. They now rarely bothered their Judæan neighbours and they protected them against marauding expeditions on the part of the uncivilised barbarians who had just occupied the nearby peninsula of Greece.

Israel, on the other hand, was on all sides exposed to the attacks of her enemies. The river Jordan would have provided the country with a first class natural boundary. But a number of successful wars had extended the Israelitic sphere of influence several hundred miles towards the east. And the Chinese, thus far, are the only people who have ever had the patience to build protective walls across a desert.

Several times the Israelites seem to have been on the point of fortifying this region. The unsettled conditions at home made this impossible. Thereafter the Israelites trusted to luck and were of course defeated by their powerful eastern neighbours, whose faith was firmly based upon the efficiency of their archers and their cavalry.

The kingdom of Israel suffered, however, from another and serious disadvantage. It was composed of ten different tribes. The tribesmen talked much of Union and Co-operation, but they were as jealous of their own rights as the original thirteen colonies of our own country. They could not even decide upon a suitable capital. Shechem, in the land of the Ephraimites, seemed in many ways the right spot for the future centre of the Israelite nation. It was a famous old town. It had been visited by Abraham when he had gone west in search of the Promised Land, and was closely connected with the last ten centuries of Jewish history.

But Jeroboam, who had come to the throne by way of a

successful rebellion (and who was for ever on the defensive against all sorts of real and imaginary enemies), did not think that Shechem offered sufficient safety. He removed his court to Tirzah, which was situated further towards the east.

Fifty years later, Tirzah was given up for the benefit of Samaria which was situated on the top of a hill and commanded a fine view of the surrounding landscape.

The lack of a well-established capital (which has ruined many a strong nation since the beginning of history), did much to retard the normal growth of the little kingdom.

The real underlying cause, however, of Israel's weakness had nothing to do with geographic boundaries or political centres. It was something very different.

From the very beginning, the Jewish state had been a theocracy. A "theocracy" is a country which is being ruled by a "theos" or god. As he cannot reside on this earth, he governs his domains by means of a class of professional priests who give expression to the divine will as it is revealed to them from time to time by dreams or by certain tokens, such as the whispering of the leaves of sacred trees or the signs which come from Heaven when an offering is being made.

The "theos" (whether he be Jehovah or Jupiter) must of course remain invisible to the mass of the people. His priests, therefore, become his representatives on this earth and the executers of his commands. Their power is not unlike that of the viceroy of India, who rules hundreds of millions of people in the name of a distant and mysterious Emperor who resides in Buckingham Palace in London, and who is never seen by the inhabitants of Calcutta or Bombay.

Almost every country, at one time or another, has passed through that particular stage of political development. We find it in the valley of the Nile and in Babylonia. We hear of it in Greece and in Rome. The idea was strong enough to survive the chaos of the Middle Ages. It made the King of England the "Defender of the Faith." It gave the Czar of Russia the opportunity to establish himself as the semi-divine head of both his Church and his State. Even to-day we are able to discover slight traces of the theocratic idea in the meetings of our Senate and our House of Representatives and all our state assemblies, where the proceedings are opened with an invocation (given by a member of the clergy) acknowledging the fact that no wise conclusions can be reached without the guidance of the divine spirit.

It is quite natural that primitive man, at the mercy of all the forces of nature, should have appealed to those holy priests who alone could protect him from the wrath of their gods. It is equally natural that such a favoured position in the state should have given one class of society unlimited power which was never relinquished willingly, and which gave rise to those terrible wars which accompany the change from a theocratic to a purely monarchical form of government.

Among the Jews (almost alone of all peoples) the idea of a theocracy had taken such a firm hold upon the imagination of the people that it could never be broken.

Moses, from the very beginning, had insisted upon a strictly theocratic form of government. The Ten Commandments were really the constitution of his new state. The High Priest, by his command, became the chief executive of the people. The Tabernacle was in a sense the national capital.

The struggle for the conquest of the land of Canaan had temporarily weakened the power of the church, and had given certain great advantages to the military leaders. Even so, many of the Judges were also priests and exercised a double influence upon the life of the country.

During the reign of David and Solomon, it seemed that the kings were about to establish an absolute monarchy in which the High Priest was to execute the will of his worldly master rather than that of Jehovah.

The revolution of Jeroboam, however, and the division of the state into two separate kingdoms gave new strength to the priesthood, and gave these shrewd men a chance to regain much of their old prestige.

Adversity has its advantages.

Rehoboam, the king of Judah, had lost two-thirds of his subjects and three-quarters of his territory, but he had retained Jerusalem, and this city, as the religious centre of the Jewish people, was worth more than half a dozen Samarias and Shechems. This will become clear to you if you will remember that in the tenth century B. C. the temple of Jerusalem had a practical monopoly of all divine worship in the land of the Jews.

It is not easy to imagine such a state of affairs. Nowadays we belong to a large number of denominations. We are Methodists or Catholics or Jews or Christian Scientists or Baptists or Lutherans. But we all live in the peaceful harmony of decent neighbours, and on Sunday (or whenever we please) we go to the church of our preference and worship according to the dictates of our conscience.

The ancient Jews, however, had no such choice. They had to make their offering before the altar of the Temple of Jerusalem or neglect their religious duties.

As the country was very small, this meant no great physical hardship. Most of the Jews, anyway, did not visit the Temple more than twice or three times in all their lives, and then only upon very solemn occasions. They did not mind the few days' travel necessary to reach the Holy of Holies. But it gave Jerusalem a tremendous hold upon the people.

During the Middle Ages, it was said that all roads led to Rome. In old Palestine, all roads led to the Temple of Solomon.

When the kings of Israel built the barrier which was to keep their own subjects separate from their hated Judæan neighbours, Jerusalem acquired an unexpected dignity. It assumed the rôle of a sacred martyr. The priests of the temple made common cause with the kings of Judah. They refused to recognise the "unlawful" rulers of Israel. They denounced the "rebels" of the north, who had refused to accept the "legitimate" candidate to the throne, and thereby had disobeyed the will of Jehovah. They practically excommunicated all Israelites, and cursed them for their wickedness. And when the poor kingdom of the north fell a victim to the political greed of Assyria, the guardians of the Judæan shrine were jubilant in their joy.

Jehovah, so they claimed, had punished his unfaithful children, and all was well with the world.

Alas! a hundred years later, they were to suffer a similar fate. And succeeding centuries of exile taught them the hard lessons of tolerance and mercy.

It is not easy for a child of our modern times to get a clear idea of such a situation. If his parents (for one reason or another) do not like their minister, they quietly go to another church, and do not feel conscious of having committed a sin. But an Israelite of the tenth century was as faithful a servant of Jehovah as his Judæan contemporaries. He rejected the idea of his being a "heretic" as a citizen of our country would reject the idea of his being a political outcast because he had not voted the same ticket as the majority of his neighbours and fellow townsmen. He wanted to keep in contact with the Temple. But the Temple stood in Jerusalem, and Jerusalem was the capital of a rival and hostile country. Much against his will he was forced to establish a few holy places of his own.

That, however, did not improve matters.

On the contrary, it made things worse. It put him into the same uncomfortable position as those Europeans of the fourteenth century who dared to elect a pope of their own in competition with the recognised head of the Church, who was supposed to reside in Rome.

We are sorry to have dragged so many historical explanations into this chapter. That, however, is the only way in which we can hope to give our readers a clear picture of the complicated and unfortunate relations between Israel and Judah.

Israel enjoyed all the worldly advantages.

Judah maintained her one great religious advantage, and in the end it was Judah which proved the stronger of the two.

And now we must give a very brief account of the political developments in the two kingdoms from the time of the division until the era of exile.

The quarrel between Israel and Judah was rudely interrupted by an invasion from the east. Shishak, an Asiatic adventurer, who had made himself master of Egypt, and had established a new dynasty in that country, had followed the affairs of the Jewish nation with close attention. He had, as you may remember, offered his hospitality and his friendship to Jeroboam, when the latter had fled before the anger of Solomon, and he had encouraged his guest to return to Jerusalem, and begin that revolution which had deprived the house of David of the greater part of their possessions.

Now that the tribes of the old kingdom were engaged in civil war, Shishak made the best of his opportunity. He invaded Israel, he took Jerusalem, and he allowed his soldiers to destroy the Temple. Then he marched northward, captured and destroyed one-hundred-and-thirty-three cities and villages of Israel, and returned to Egypt, loaded heavily with the plunder of the Jewish nation.

Israel recovered easily, but Judah suffered an almost irreparable loss. The wealth of the country had been carried away. The Temple was rebuilt, but the exhausted treasury did not allow a display of the former luxury. Iron and bronze took the place of gold and silver. The old splendour was gone. There were no more visits from the curious Queen of Sheba.

Shortly after this last invasion, Jeroboam died, and was succeeded by his son Nadab.

This young man did what so many of his wise predecessors had done. He went to war with the Philistines.

When the town of Gibbethon refused to surrender to him, he laid siege to the city. Before he had made any impression upon this stronghold, he was murdered by Baasha, of the tribe of Issachar, who seems to have been one of his own generals.

Baasha then made himself King of Israel, killed all the relatives of Nadab, and went to live in Tirzah.

He continued the siege of Gibbethon, but in addition, he declared war upon Judah.

There Rehoboam had died, and had been followed by Abijam. Abijam had ruled only three years, and upon his death had left the throne to Asa, one of his forty-two children.

Asa was a better King than any of his predecessors. He strengthened the position of the priests of the temple by destroying all foreign altars which were found within his domains.

The forty-one years of his reign, however, were not easy. First of all, he had been forced to defend his country against an attack of several Ethiopian tribes. When these had been beaten back, the war with Israel had commenced. Baasha had begun a regular blockade of Judah. He had fortified the town of Ramah which commanded the highroad from the north to the south. This meant that Judah was cut off from all communication with Damascus and Phœnicia.

Asa, who feared that his country would be strangled to death by the economic policy of Israel, looked for help. He sent a diplomatic mission to the court of Benhadad, the King of Aram (often called Syria) who ruled in the plain which stretches from the mountains of Lebanon to the banks of the River Euphrates.

The Jews offered the Aramean monarch a large bribe if he would attack their Israelite kinsmen in the rear.

Benhadad was agreeable to this plan.

It was true that he had just concluded a treaty of friendship with Baasha, but in those days, people did not take treaties very seriously.

Benhadad gathered his armies, left Damascus (his capital), and marched southward.

He captured the northern fortress of Dan and conquered all the Israelite lands as far as the Sea of Galilee. Baasha was forced to sue for peace. Judah was saved and the road to Damascus was open to the Judæan trade once more.

Asa no doubt had done what seemed to be best for his own country. But he and all the people who came after him lived to regret the day when they had first dragged a foreigner into their domestic quarrels. From that time on, whenever the potentates of the east were hard up for money, they let themselves be "invited" to come to the assistance of either Israel or Judah and plundered the countries individually or collectively to reimburse themselves for the expense of their "Relief Expedition."

As for Baasha, he ruled twenty-nine years and spent most of that time fighting with the Prophet Jehu.

The continued worship of heathen idols was the cause of this dispute.

While Judah was a fairly compact nation, there still lived a large number of foreign tribes within the realm of Israel. Some of these made sacrifices to Baal, the god of the sun. Others worshipped the Golden Bull, which to many people of Asia and Africa had always seemed the embodiment of all that was strong and dignified.

It was very difficult for the kings of Israel to make an end to this most regrettable state of affairs. After all these centuries, the Israelites still formed a racial minority in the country which Joshua had conquered. They could not afford to interfere with the private opinions of the original natives, without the risk of causing a revolt. To-day in India there are many religious sects of which the British people do not approve, but the government wisely refuses to interfere. There had been one great rebellion, due to a misunderstanding of certain religious prejudices of certain native troops, and that lesson has not been forgotten. The government keeps aloof from the native temples.

Baasha had been faced with similar difficulties. There were a score of unheeding fanatics in his country who regarded all tolerance as a sign of moral weakness. They were for ever urging him (and all the other kings) to exterminate the pagan gods and the pagan priests, and those who refused to recognise Jehovah as the only true God. When the rulers (for practical reasons of state) refused to follow this program and commit political suicide, these same zealots denounced them as enemies of all righteousness who were unworthy to occupy the throne.

Baasha, who had come to his high position over the dead

body of his murdered sovereign, was in no position to take any risks. He was forced to be very lenient towards those who made their offerings before a golden calf, if in turn they promised him their support against his enemies. He listened politely to Jehu, whenever the Prophet felt compelled to deliver his message, but he refused to take any steps whatsoever against the much despised heathen, and when he died, there were more temples of Baal in Israel than there had ever been before. Jehu, in his wrath, prophesied all sorts of terrible things which would happen to the Baasha dynasty as a punishment for their indifference.

These predictions came true with alarming quickness.

Baasha had been dead only a short time when his son Elah was murdered. This young man was no better than his father. At a very disreputable party which he gave in Tirzah, he got into a quarrel with Zimri, the commander of his war-chariots. Zimri took his dagger and stabbed Elah. Then he proclaimed himself King of Israel and took possession of the royal palace.

This brazen act of violence was too much for the people, accustomed as they were to murder and bloodshed. They sent messengers to Omri, the commander-in-chief of the army, who was finishing the siege of Gibbethon and asked him to return to the capital and establish order. When Zimri heard that the army was marching against Tirzah, he lost courage. He set fire to his palace and to the city and less than a week after his accession to the throne, he perished amidst the flames of his own capital.

As Zimri had assassinated all the brothers of Elah during the six days of his reign, there was no legitimate candidate for the throne. Omri, as the only logical candidate, was made King. He decided to leave the ruins of Tirzah, and he began to look for a suitable location for his own capital.

This he found further towards the west on the top of a hill which belonged to a farmer by the name of Shemer. Omri bought the hill for two talents (or about 3,000 dollars) and there built a city which was called the town of Shemer, or Samaria.

Among the many rulers who succeeded each other in such rapid succession to the throne of Israel, Omri was by far the most important. Whatever his failings, he could at least fight. He spent twelve years of his reign making war upon Ben-hadad. It was a very uneven struggle, but Omri held his own, and even added small bits of territory to his old possessions.

When he died, he left a greatly increased kingdom to his son Ahab.

With Ahab, the real troubles of Israel began.

For Ahab was weak, but his wife Jezebel was strong.

Soon the woman was the real ruler of Israel and all the people were made aware of this fact.

Jezebel was the daughter of Ethbaal, the king of the Phœnician city of Sidon. The Phœnicians were sun-worshippers and Jezebel was a devout adherent of the Baal faith. As a rule, queens adopt the religion of the country of their husbands. Jezebel, however, did nothing of the sort. When she came to Samaria, she brought her own priests with her and as soon as she had established herself in Ahab's palace, she began to erect a temple to Baal in the very heart of the Israelite capital.

The people were shocked and the prophets cried out to high Heaven. But Jezebel did not care and ere long, she began a regular campaign against those who had remained faithful to Jehovah and inaugurated a reign of religious terror which lasted until she was overthrown by the revolution of Jehu.

Fortunately for the persecuted followers of Jehovah, the

kingdom of the south just then was ruled by a very wise and intelligent king who was called Jehoshaphat. He was the son of Asa. He had been carefully trained for his high office, and was a diplomat and strategist of no mean ability.

Jehoshaphat knew that his own kingdom was inferior to that of Israel when it came to a contest of arms.

He therefore established a truce between the two countries. First of all, his son married Athaliah, the daughter of Ahab and Jezebel, and next he concluded an offensive and defensive treaty with his new father-in-law. When in this way he had obtained a guarantee of safety for his northern frontier, he attacked the Ammonites and Moabites who lived across the Dead Sea and conquered their territory. This brought him great fame, but it did not placate the anger of the old Prophet Jehu, who upbraided him for his friendly attitude towards the wicked Jezebel, and who denounced the treaty with Israel as a direct insult to Jehovah.

Notwithstanding these accusations of lukewarm faith, Jehoshaphat continued to be successful in everything he undertook and he died, much regretted by his subjects, in the year 850 B. C. and was buried with his fathers in the family vault in the city of David.

So much for the history of Judah during the first half of the ninth century. In Israel we shall see a very different picture.

In that poor country, everything was going to rack and ruin.

Jezebel had established a veritable inquisition which punished with death or exile all those who refused to worship the sun-god. Nothing seemed to be able to stop this wholesale and enforced conversion of an entire nation.

But as always before, in the hour of need, the national conscience was stirred into action.

The Prophet Elijah stepped forward and saved the people from utter degradation.

We know very little about the early years of this remarkable man. He may have been a native of the land of Galilee (the home of so many of the great prophets) but this is not certain. The greater part of his younger years he spent in the wilderness of Gilead on the eastern bank of the river Jordan and his life was influenced by his physical surroundings. He was essentially a man of the old school. He accepted Jehovah as his master without reasoning, without arguing and without questioning.

He preferred the simple and uncomfortable ways of the desert to the ease of the cities. Indeed, he abhorred all cities. To him they were the hotbed of luxury and religious indifference. They tolerated and even welcomed strange gods brought thither from Phœnicia and from Egypt and from Nineveh. They were the breeding place of heresy and ought to be wiped from the face of this earth, together with most of their inhabitants.

From the point of view of Ahab and Jezebel, the Prophet Elijah was an exceedingly dangerous man.

He had a sublime confidence in the righteousness of the cause which he had espoused.

He was as brave as a lion.

He was without a single worldly ambition.

He despised personal possessions.

A rough coat, made of the hairy skin of a camel, was his only garment.

He ate whatever charitable people gave him.

In case of extreme need, he was fed (so people told each other) by the ravens.

In short, he was absolutely invulnerable, for there were no ties which bound him to this world, and death, however violent, meant nothing to a man whose whole being was dedicated to the service of his God.

No wonder that such a teacher made a deep impression upon his contemporaries.

Elijah led a very restless life, and he had a strong sense of the dramatic. Suddenly he would appear in the market place of a distant city. He would utter ominous words of warning. Before the people had a chance to recover from their surprise, the Prophet was gone again.

A few days later, he would be seen in a different part of the country and again he would disappear as mysteriously as he had come.

Until the people believed that he was possessed of some strange power, and could make himself invisible at will.

Ever since the beginning of time, people have loved to exaggerate the virtues of their heroes. As time went by (and as the stories were repeated from father to son) Elijah assumed more and more the character of a great magician. His words of wisdom were forgotten. But his miracles were remembered and hundreds of years after his death, the Jewish mothers used to tell their children of a wonderful man who could reverse all the laws of nature, who could stop the flow of rivers by a gesture of his hand, who could turn one bushel of corn into a dozen, who upon many an occasion had cured the sick, and who sometimes had raised the dead with equal facility.

This tremendous figure, feared and yet revered by all his contemporaries, now became one of the leading actors in the great religious drama of his time.

Like a bolt of lightning from high Heaven, the Prophet fell upon the unsuspecting Ahab. The king had just made some further concessions to Baal. He was to hear his punishment.

"There will be a drought in the land," so Elijah spoke, "and there will be famine and there will be pestilence, for Jehovah will not tolerate the sin of idolatry."

The next moment he was gone. The soldiers of Ahab looked for him in vain. He had quickly crossed the high plateau of Israel, and had returned to his beloved desert. A simple hut, on the banks of a deep gorge, called the Brook Cherith, was his home. There he remained until late in the summer when the lack of drinking

ELIJAH APPEARS SUDDENLY
OUTSIDE THE GATE OF
AHAB'S PALACE

water forced him to look for new quarters. He now crossed the country from the east to the west until he reached the village of Zarephath, on the coast of the Mediterranean. This was situated within the jurisdiction of the Phœnician city of Tyre. But Elijah's reputation as a wonder-worker followed him even among the heathen, for we hear stories of how he raised the dead son of his landlady, and how he kept that faithful woman well provided with oil and flour through the many years of hunger which followed in the wake of the ruined crops.

But if Elijah had expected that the misery of his subjects would bring the wicked King to reason, he was mistaken. On

the contrary. This national calamity so greatly incensed Jezebel that she persecuted the followers of Jehovah more unmer-
cifully than ever before. Only a few of the faithful old priests
survived, but they depended for their support upon Obadiah,
the master of the palace of Ahab, who was a good man,
and who hid them in his palace. Before they too should be
killed, Jehovah decided to save them.

THE BROOK CHERITH

He ordered Elijah to return
to Israel and address the King
once more.

Of course, Elijah knew that
he took his life in his hands the
moment he crossed the border
of Israel.

He waited outside the royal
residence until he met Obadiah
(who was looking for grazing
fields for the King's horses),
and he bade this excellent man
prepare Ahab for another solemn visit of Jehovah's messenger.

Once more, the King and the Prophet faced each other.

Ahab, who was in dreadful fear of Elijah's magic power,
listened patiently enough, and did as he was told to do. He
called together all the priests of Baal. He told them to come
to the top of Mount Carmel, which dominated the great plain
of Jezreel, and not to tarry by the way. Unless there was immediate relief from hunger and thirst, there would be a revolution, and this meeting (so Ahab was told) might give him
the opportunity to save his country.

From far and wide the priests of Baal hastened to Mount
Carmel.

The people, hoping to witness an exhibition of Elijah's
strange magic, were present in large numbers.

They saw a lonely old man standing in front in a neglected and half-ruined stone altar which had been erected hundreds of years before when the earliest settlers had taken possession of the land.

When all the Baal priests seemed to be present, Elijah addressed the multitude.

There seemed to be some doubt, so he said, who was mightier, Jehovah or Baal. Very well. That question was to be decided now and for all time. Then he asked for two young bulls. One of these he gave to his enemies, that they might prepare it ready for sacrifice. The other he kept for himself.

When the animals had been killed, the pieces of meat were laid upon the wood of the altars.

"Now we will wait for a miracle," Elijah announced. "Neither of us will use fire to light the wood of our altar, but we will each pray to our god, and then we will see what happens."

ELIJAH'S SACRIFICE

All day long, the heathen threw themselves upon their faces before Baal, asking him to come to their assistance. But their altar remained as cold as the waters of the river Kishon. They shouted and chanted strange incantations, but nothing happened.

Elijah taunted them.

"A wonderful god, this Baal of yours," he cried, forgetting the danger in which he stood, "a noble god, who cannot even come to the rescue of his own people. Perhaps your Baal has gone on a journey. Perhaps he is asleep. Shout a little louder. He may hear you yet."

But nothing happened.

Elijah allowed them until evening.

Then he asked the people to step close and watch him.

He took twelve stones (as a symbol of the twelve tribes of the old Jewish nation) and with these he repaired the altar. Next he dug a trench around it so that it should stand isolated from everybody and everything.

Finally, to impress the crowd, he asked some men to pour out barrels of water over the wood and over the stones.

When this had been done three times, and the whole altar was thoroughly drenched, Elijah called upon the God of Abraham and Isaac and Israel.

Immediately a bolt of fire fell from Heaven.

Amidst the hissing of steam and the crackling of the wet branches, the offering of Elijah went up into smoke.

The power of Jehovah stood revealed before all the people.

Elijah made good use of that moment of victory.

"Destroy these impostors," he shouted, pointing to the prophets of Baal, and the Israelites fell upon the foreign intruders, and they took them to the bank of the river Kishon, and they killed every single one of the four-hundred-and-fifty false priests.

Then Elijah turned once more to Ahab. Jehovah, he now told him, was satisfied. Before evening, the drought would come to an end.

With this promise ringing in his ears, Ahab returned to his residence. Before he had driven half a mile, the sky was darkened by the clouds which suddenly came up from the sea. A few minutes later it began to rain. The rain poured down upon the parched fields. For the first time in three years and six months, the soil of Israel felt the touch of a drop of water.

When Ahab told his wife what had happened that afternoon, the Queen was beside herself with anger. She gave orders that Elijah be taken and be brought to justice for the murder of her friends.

Elijah, however, had disappeared. He knew that this time he could not hope for mercy, and he hid himself with unusual care. He walked clear through Israel and Judah and did not stop until he had reached the village of Beer-Sheba, on the southern frontier of the southern kingdom.

Even there he did not feel quite safe. Soon he pushed further into the desert and for a moment it looked as if he would perish from hunger and thirst.

But an angel of Jehovah brought him food and he ate it and thereupon he was able to wander forty days without a further meal.

At last he reached Mount Horeb, one of the peaks of the peninsula of Sinai. This was holy ground. Here, a thousand years before, Moses had received the laws of Jehovah amidst the crash of thunder.

The experience of Elijah, when he received his divine message, was quite different. First of all there came a terrible gust of wind which almost blew the Prophet down a precipice.

Elijah listened, but did not hear anything.

Then there was heard the rumbling noise of a mighty earthquake. It was followed by a fire.

Once more, Elijah listened, but he heard nothing.

Suddenly the earth and the wind came to rest.

There was the sound of a thin silence.

And Elijah heard the voice of Jehovah.

He was told to return whence he had come that he might ind a worthy successor to continue the task for which he himself was growing too old. His days were numbered, so he was told, and there was much work to be done in the land of Israel.

Elijah obeyed. He left the desert and went back to the hated cities. When he reached the plain of Jezreel where the Judges of ancient days had destroyed the armies of the Amalekites and Midianites, he saw a farmer ploughing peace-fully in the fields of that prosperous country.

ELIJAH IN THE MIDST OF AN
EARTHQUAKE

Jehovah gave him a sign that this boy was to be his disciple. Elijah stopped. He left the road and dropped his mantle across the shoulders of the young man.

Elisha (for that was his name) understood what this ceremony meant. He left his plough. He went to his home, bade farewell to his father and mother and followed his new master, that he might learn the ways of wisdom and godliness and be worthy of this high honour.

When Elijah and Elisha reached Israel, they found the country in a terrible condition. Under the influence of Jezebel, things had gone from bad to worse. Other Baal priests had been sent for from Phœnicia and the country was as full of heathenish superstitions as ever before.

Meanwhile the King in his restlessness had removed his home from Samaria to the town of Jezreel and he was building himself a new palace.

Now it happened that a vineyard which he wanted as part of his own grounds belonged to a citizen by the name of Naboth.

Ahab told Naboth that he wanted to buy this vineyard. Naboth, however, answered that the vineyard had been in his family for many generations and that he did not care to sell it.

Jezebel suggested an easy way out of the difficulty. Ahab was King. Could he not do what he wanted? Why not take the vineyard and kill Naboth? It was all very simple.

Ahab, however, refused to do this. He dreaded another interview with Elijah and to make an end to all further explanations, he pretended that he was sick and took to his bed.

Jezebel made the best of her opportunity. While Ahab was confined to his bed, she accused Naboth of high treason. There was no trial. The poor farmer, together with his sons (who would have been heirs to the much coveted vineyard), were all stoned to death, and their bodies were thrown before the dogs.

ELIJAH HEARS THE VOICE
IN THE DESERT

No sooner had this been done than behold! there stood Elijah before the garden of the palace.

He had arrived in his usual unexpected way.

His message filled Ahab with unspeakable horror. Before another year was gone, the same dogs who had just licked the blood of Naboth, would lick that of the King, and they would eat the torn flesh of Jezebel the Queen after her body had been thrown into the streets of Jezreel.

It seemed impossible and highly improbable. Nevertheless,

Ahab was frightened, and tried to discover a way in which he could escape his fate.

He had so firmly established his tyrannical rule over Israel that he did not fear his own subjects. If he was destined to be killed, death would come to him from the side of his enemies. His enemies, as all people knew, lived in the north. Evidently Ahab must guard himself against a new attack from the side of Aram. Fortunately for him, that country just then was sorely pressed by the King of Assyria. An attack from the south, made simultaneously with that from the east, might put an end to all further Aramean ambitions.

NABOTH'S VINEYARD

Ahab decided to take the initiative and waste no time. He sent fleet messengers to Jehoshaphat, the King of Judah, and proposed that the latter join him in his campaign against Damascus.

Jehoshaphat was willing, and together the two monarchs marched northward.

The priests of Baal predicted a great victory, but Micaiah, one of the few prophets who had remained faithful to Jehovah, repeated the warning that the King would be killed, no matter how hard he tried to escape his fate.

What Ahab did then shows just what sort of man he was. He disguised himself as a common soldier, and at the same time, he encouraged Jehoshaphat to wear his kingly robes.

"For then," so he reasoned, "the Arameans will recognise Jehoshaphat, and they will try so hard to shoot him that they will pay no attention to me."

But when the battle took place, Jehoshaphat in his scarlet mantle remained unharmed. Ahab, on the other hand, in his mean coat, was struck down by a chance arrow and he died of his wound.

His body was brought back to Jezreel. Just before the funeral took place, the royal war-chariot was washed to cleanse it of Ahab's blood. The inevitable dogs which always live in the streets of Oriental villages licked up the mixture of water and blood. In this way, the prophecy of Elijah came true. The war-chariot stood on the ground which once had belonged to Naboth.

The death of Ahab meant more than a change in the succession. It was the beginning of another long period of anarchy.

Ahab was followed by his oldest son, Ahaziah. But shortly after his anointment, the boy fell out of a window of the palace of Samaria and was badly hurt. He sent messengers to the temple of Baal to ask whether he would recover. Elijah intercepted these messengers and answered "No!"

Ahaziah died.

His brother Jehoram was little more fortunate. Mesha, the King of Moab, who was supposed to pay an annual tribute to Israel, rose up in rebellion. Jehoram suggested to Jehoshaphat that they take the land of the Moabites together and divide it.

The King of Judah thought this a very good idea.

This expedition was followed by ill luck from the very beginning. For some unexplained reason, the two monarchs tried to cross the wilderness of the Dead Sea, instead of taking the usual, more convenient route from the north.

They lost their way in the desert and almost perished from thirst.

When they reached Moab, they found that the King had put his capital in such excellent state of defence that it was necessary to lay siege.

The siege dragged on through many weary months. At last, when it seemed that the town must surrender, the King of Moab decided to make a sacrifice. It was to be an occasion which both the gods and men would remember. The King took his oldest son and he killed him on the walls of his capital (in full sight of the enemy), and he burned the body to the greater glory of the Moabite idols.

A LITTLE PILE OF STONES BY ONE SIDE OF THE WALL SHOWED WHERE AHAB WAS BURIED

When they saw this, the Jews were greatly disheartened, for they (the generation of Jehoram and Jehoshaphat), did not place much trust in their own Jehovah.

They feared the wrath of his Moabite rivals, who had just been favoured with such a signal evidence of devotion and worship. They said that it would serve no good purpose to continue the siege under those circumstances and they went home.

It was a most critical moment in the history of the Jewish people. The house of Omri was now almighty in both kingdoms. In the North, Jezebel ruled with the fierce violence of a despot. In the South, her daughter Athaliah managed both her husband and his country according to the wishes of her foreign councillors. Everywhere the reign of Jehovah seemed to have come to an end. Baal seemed to be triumphant. Something must be done and it must be done quickly to save the people from the consequences of their own folly.

It was a moment which demanded immediate and energetic action.

But the man of few words and big deeds was gone.

Elijah no longer dwelled upon this earth. One day while he was walking with Elisha, a fiery wagon had descended from Heaven, and had carried the old Prophet to his reward. At least, so Elisha told the people when he returned alone from the town of Bethel, and they dared not doubt his words. For Elisha had inherited his master's power over the forces of nature and he was a man to be treated with awe and respect.

When naughty little boys from the village of Bethel poked fun at the Prophet's bald head, two bears rushed forth from the bushes and ate up the children as a warning to all others. That, however, was only a detail. There was no end to the things which Elisha could do. Like Elijah, he could make rivers stop at a single word of command. He could make iron float on top of the water and he was for ever curing sick people. Finally, he too possessed the wonderful gift of making himself almost invisible.

All this stood him in good stead when he felt that the time had come to remove Jezebel from the scene of Jewish national life. He deliberately placed himself at the head of a revolutionary movement which planned to overthrow the house of Omri, and to purge both Israel and Judah from the iniquities of the Baal service.

Elisha did not take part in the actual uprising.

He was not a man of the sword, although he was by no means of a peaceful nature when it came to a matter of principle. But the fighting he left to a man called Jehu, one of the most picturesque figures of the Old Testament.

Jehu was a captain in the Israelite army. He was famous for his careless bravery. He could ride faster than any other man and he could shoot straighter and he was absolutely indefatigable in the pursuit of his enemies. He was just the sort of leader to be chosen for the dangerous task of upsetting an old and established dynasty.

Luck was with him. The King of Judah and the King of Israel happened to be staying together. They were closely related and outwardly they maintained a semblance of good feeling.

Jehoram, King of Israel, was the first to discover the danger. When he heard that Jehu was on the war-path, he tried to escape in his armour-clad chariot. It was too late. Jehoram fell dead with an arrow through his heart. His body was left by the side of the road and when the soldiers of the regular army (who followed their master at a distance) found it there, they threw it on the land which Ahab had stolen from Naboth, and there they left it to the mercy of the ever-present dogs.

Ahaziah, warned by the fate of his uncle, did his best to reach his own frontier. Near Ibleam in the land of Manasseh he was overtaken by the rebels, and was mortally wounded. He managed to drag himself to Megiddo, the famous old fortress near the battlefield of Armageddon (where so many kings of the Jews had met a violent death) and there he died.

When this had been successfully accomplished, the wrath of Jehu was turned against Jezebel. The old Queen, when she saw that she was doomed, met her fate with great dignity. With great care she dressed herself in the royal robes. Then she awaited the arrival of the men who were to be her executioners. When Jehu reached the palace, he called to Jezebel's servants and ordered them to fling their mistress out of the window. A couple of eunuchs (the private guardians of the harem) obeyed this order.

Jezebel was thrown into the street. Jehu drove his chariot across her dead body and went his way, without looking backwards.

That night, under cover of darkness, a few faithful retainers of Ahab, remembering better days, left the palace to give their dead ruler the funeral which befitted the daughter of a king.

They could not find Jezebel's body.

The dogs of Jezreel had torn it to pieces.

Next it was the turn of all the descendants of Ahab. Most of these had fled to Samaria. But when they saw how the whole country rallied to Jehu, they understood the

JEHU DRIVES HIS CHARIOT ACROSS THE BODY OF JEZEBEL

uselessness of a defence and they surrendered upon such terms as Jehu was willing to grant. He did not spare a single one. Their heads were placed in two large heaps just outside of the city gate as a warning to those who might try to oppose the will of the rebel chieftain.

A little later, forty-two other princes of the royal house of Judah suffered a similar fate.

There still remained the priests of Baal. Jehu let it be known that he had no quarrel with them and felt rather kindly disposed towards their religion. He therefore asked them to meet him in their temple that they might discuss what ought to be done. They came, believing that he had spoken the truth. As soon as they were all inside the building, the doors were closed. When night came, the Sun-worshippers without exception had all been killed.

With a single blow, Jehu had made an end to the danger of a foreign domination.

The house of Omri had been exterminated.

The Baal priests were gone.

Jehu ruled as King in Israel, and Elisha rejoiced.

The triumph of Jehovah was complete.

But soon it became evident to all the people that this victory, based upon murder and bloodshed, had accomplished very little for the good of the country.

It is true that Jehu was brave and reckless, but he lacked both wisdom and a sense of proportion. He was clay in the hands of a number of religious leaders who now rallied around his throne that they might put into execution their own narrow ideas of a perfect state.

Their fear of everything foreign, both gods and men, was so great that they would not tolerate any one within the country who was not of pure Jewish blood. They erected an imaginary barrier around Israel and Judah which kept away all those who had been born outside the Jewish pale. They frowned upon "entangling alliances" with other powers and declared that treaties with other powers (who did not recognise Jehovah) were odious in the sight of their own God.

But as both Israel and Judah were too weak to survive without the help of a few good friends in the east and in the west, this insistence of the prophets upon a holy separation proved a disastrous innovation, and it came at the very moment when all the professional fighters (the princes of royal blood) had been exterminated and when the army had been deprived of eighty per cent of its higher officers.

In the eyes of the faithful, the great revolution of Jehu had purged Israel and Judah from all barbarian influence. Henceforth the two countries were to be really "holy ground." It was a noble ambition, but it was doomed to failure.

Nothing has ever been accomplished in this world by murder.

Even such pious people as the Prophets Amos and Hosea were to recognise this fact ere very long and were to express their regret at the shedding of so much innocent blood. But when they spoke, it was too late.

Israel had already been conquered by the nations of the east.

In Aram, too, there had been a revolution. There Hazael, a Syrian general, had murdered his master, King Benhadad II, and himself had mounted the throne.

He had increased the strength of Damascus, but when Shalmaneser II, the son of Ashurnasirpal of Assyria, attacked the Aramean domains, there was a sudden end to the glory of Hazael, the usurper. His armies were defeated near Mount Hermon, and Damascus was captured. When news of this disaster reached the coast of the Mediterranean, the rulers of Sidon and of Tyre and of Israel hastened to accept such terms as the Assyrian conqueror would grant. They knew that they had found their master.

We possess certain Assyrian documents of that era which state that the battle of Mount Hermon took place in the year 842 B. C., and that Jehu, the son (which meant the successor) of Omri, himself paid tribute to Assyria. To make up for his losses, Hazael, as soon as Shalmaneser had returned to Nine-

veh, overran the northern part of Israel and consoled himself
with several Jewish districts. He exterminated whole tribes,
killed the men, stole the women, threw the children from the
rocks and repopulated the region with immigrants from Aram.

Jehu, not knowing what to do, called upon Shalmaneser,
whose vassal he now was. But before the Assyrians could
come to his assistance, the Arameans (informed of his treach-
ery) had overrun Israel for a second time, had destroyed the
armies of Judah for good measure, and together with the Moabites and Edomites and Philistines had plundered both countries to their heart's content.

Those who had been spared by the sword of the invader
and had not died of hunger, accepted slavery.

Samaria was the only town which remained in Jewish
hands.

In this hour of disaster, Elisha came to the rescue of his
ruler. Together, the King and the Prophet defended their
city until help could reach them from Assyria.

From a purely patriotic point of view, they were the
saviours of their country. The Assyrians defeated the King
of Aram, took Damascus, and in this way relieved the pressure upon Israel. But when this had been done, they presented their bill for services rendered.

They expected Israel to pay, and pay heavily, and insisted
on an annual retainer which was little more than a bribe for
their continued good will.

The Israelites spent the whole of the next century trying
to get rid of this self-imposed yoke, and sometimes with a fair
degree of success.

Jehoahaz, the son of Jehu, was fortunate in his war for independence. He took Damascus and his troops pushed almost
as far east as the town of Nineveh.

His son, Jehoash, also was lucky as a warrior. He allowed Elisha to guide him and remained a devoted supporter of the great prophet until the latter died. Jehoash was faithful in his religious duties. His respect for Jehovah, however, did not prevent him from plundering the temple of Jerusalem when the opportunity offered itself.

But it remained for Jeroboam, the son of Jehoash, to give Israel a last taste of independence and glory.

To the contemporaries of this great king, it seemed that the wonderful old days of Solomon had returned. Their country, so they flattered themselves, was on the point of resuming its ancient position among the nations of the East.

They were to be sorely disappointed.

That brilliant sky did not proclaim the coming of another day. It was the last red glow which preceded the setting of their national sun.

Undoubtedly the first fifty years of that century were an era of sudden and unexpected prosperity. Overnight, villages were turned into cities. Shepherds left their flocks that they might share the abundance of the nearest market-place. The old trade-routes were restored and caravans once more passed from east to west and from south to north.

But with this return to wealth, came the evils of an economic system which was built upon speculation.

The simple ways of the patriarchs which had survived in many of the remote villages came to an end.

The days of Solomon had returned in the worst sense of the word.

Jehovah was neglected. Soon he was forgotten. With infinite patience and courageous tenacity, Amos and Isaiah and Hosea, the great prophets of the eighth century, laboured to convince their fellow citizens that they were worshipping false ideals and that wealth alone could never make men happy.

Elijah and Elisha had denounced the wickedness of the world amidst the clang of thunder and the flashing strokes of lightning.

Amos, Hosea and Isaiah belonged to a different type of men. They not only preached. They also wrote.

For by this time the Jews had learned the art of writing from their Babylonian neighbours, and they were beginning to make collections of stories from the past and they were copying the words of the prophets that they might teach wisdom to their children and to their grandchildren.

Endlessly Isaiah, Hosea and Amos repeated their warning that the unreasoning accumulation of gold and silver was not the only purpose of life. With untiring energy they tried to persuade the younger generation that pleasure, while not wicked in itself, did not produce that mysterious spiritual contentment without which existence is barren and devoid of true interest.

When they noticed that their talk was in vain and when they began to foresee, with ever increasing clearness, the inevitable loss of their country's independence, they changed the tone of their warning and uttered words of burning shame, the like of which had not been heard in the land since the days of Elijah.

During the greater part of their career, however, they kept away from politics and contented themselves with a discussion of the Truth.

In modern times, we probably would have called them "social reformers."

They admonished the rich to be charitable and the poor to be patient.

They spread a new doctrine of forbearance and cheerful helpfulness.

And drawing a logical conclusion from their original ideas, they finally preached the novel doctrine of a kindly Jehovah who loved all his faithful followers like his own son and who demanded that all his children should do the same unto each other.

Alas! very few people cared to listen to them.

The Jews were so happy with their newly found prosperity; with the conquests of their king, Jeroboam; with the increasing volume of trade and commerce; that they had no time to waste upon a few queer people who stood on the corners of the market-place and talked of coming disasters, just when the whole country was booming with wealth.

When finally they began to suspect that there might be some truth in these words of warning, it was too late.

In the distant city of Nineveh, a soldier of fortune of remarkable ability and great shrewdness, had made himself master of the throne. He called himself Tiglath Pileser, in honour of a national hero who had lived five hundred years before. He dreamed of an empire that would stretch from the Tigris to the Mediterranean.

Sooner than he had expected, the Jews gave him the chance to realise this ambition.

Ahaz, the King of Judah, engaged in one of those obscure quarrels of which we do not know the details, was on the point of war with Aram. Ahaz asked Tiglath Pileser to help him. When this became known, the Prophet Isaiah went to Ahaz to warn him against such an alliance with a heathen. The King of Judah ought to place his confidence in Jehovah and in no one else. Ahaz answered that he did not believe this. He even refused to ask for a token from Heaven. He knew what he was doing. His expedition against Aram simply could not fail.

But Isaiah disagreed with him and foretold the downfall of both Judah and Israel. It would take place very shortly. Before the children then born should have reached the age of manhood, both countries would have lost their independence.

Even then, Ahaz was not convinced. He took all the gold and silver he could find in the temple and sent it to Nineveh as a present for Tiglath Pileser. And when he travelled northward to do homage to his august ally, he even took the brass altar, which had been standing in front of the Holy of Holies ever since the days of Solomon, and had it carried to Damascus, where he offered it to the Assyrian King.

Tiglath Pileser was much pleased.

Whether these gifts changed his mind and made him more friendly towards the Jewish people than the Assyrians had been before, we do not know for death made an end to all the King's plans.

We have good reason, however, to suppose that Tiglath would at least have spared Judah.

His successor, Shalmaneser, who no doubt inherited his foreign policies from his predecessor, was very lenient to the little kingdom, but he showed no mercy towards Israel.

When Hoshea, the last wicked king of Israel, heard that his country was about to be invaded, he tried to make a hasty alliance with Egypt, but before an expeditionary army from the banks of the Nile could reach him, Shalmaneser had crossed the frontier, had defeated the Israelite armies and had sent the king himself back to Nineveh as a prisoner of war.

Then he laid siege to the city of Samaria.

The Samarians defended their last stronghold with the courage of despair.

They held out for more than three years.

Shalmaneser, so it seems, was wounded during a sally and died under the walls of the town.

But Sargon, who followed him, pushed the attack with great vigour, and Samaria was taken.

The last resistance of the Israelites had been broken.

Their kingdom came to an ignominious end.

Then began a period of terrible suffering.

Twenty-seven-thousand two-hundred-and-eighty families (about a hundred thousand people) were driven into exile. The country, terribly devastated by endless years of war, was repopulated with settlers from five Assyrian provinces, together with the remnants of the ten Jewish tribes. These immigrants formed a new race which became known as the Samaritans. At first, they were Assyrian subjects. Afterwards they were ruled by the Babylonians and the Macedonians and the Romans. They never again formed an independent state.

Judah survived her sister nation by a century and a half and only maintained a nominal independence by a most abject servility towards all her neighbours. When Sennacherib came to the throne of Assyria and began his ill-fated expedition against Egypt, Hezekiah, the King of Judah, bought immunity for his country with a gift of thirty talents of gold.

To obtain this amount, the last remnant of gold had to be scraped off the walls of the Temple.

It is curious that even then, the people of Jerusalem did not feel the utter humiliation of their country's position. They ate and drank just as merrily, while foreign officers and soldiers insolently sauntered down the streets of their home city.

Suddenly, however, their indifference was turned into abject fear.

It was rumoured (and upon good grounds) that Sennacherib had repented of his leniency and was about to destroy the Jewish capital to remove the possibility of an attack from the rear.

In the panic which followed this announcement, the Judæans at last turned to one of their prophets.

Their King had failed them, but Jesaiah spoke eager words of encouragement and promised his people the support of Jehovah, if they would only make up their minds that Jerusalem should (and could) be defended until the end.

It seemed that he had foretold the truth. The armies of Assyria were caught in the marshes of the Nile delta. The greater part of the soldiers died from fever and the others, frightened by this mysterious disease (and by an even more mysterious attack of mice, which ate the strings of their bows), refused to continue the war and returned home.

Jesaiah rejoiced, but it was too soon for jubilation. The enemy was making ready for a terrible revenge.

Early in the middle of the sixth century, Zedekiah came to the throne of Judah. He was completely under the influence of several foreigners. His own comfort was his chief interest. The independence of his country meant nothing to him.

Assyria had gone the way of all empires and in turn had been conquered by the Chaldeans (another Semitic tribe) who had founded a new country, of which the old city of Babylon became the capital.

This change in masters made little difference to Zedekiah. Provided that he himself was left in peace, he was willing to pay tribute to a Chaldean as cheerfully as to an Assyrian or an Egyptian. Such cowardly people, however, are apt to be rash, when for once in their lives, they ought to be cautious.

When Nebuchadnezzar, the Chaldean ruler, got into

trouble with Egypt, Zedekiah willingly listened to those of his friends who told him that the time had come for some great deed which should bring everlasting renown to Judah and to her King.

In vain did Jeremiah, now a prophet of woe, raise his voice against such folly.

He appeared before the King and warned him that an attempt at revolution could only end in disaster.

Zedekiah, in his new enthusiasm, refused to listen to all arguments.

In vain Jeremiah reminded the King that he had already served four other Judæan kings and had never been found wanting.

Zedekiah simply grew angry and sent Jeremiah away.

Suddenly he refused to pay the annual tribute to Chaldea and declared himself independent. At once his capital was infested by the soldiers of Nebuchadnezzar.

Jerusalem was not prepared for a long siege.

There was a lack of food and a lack of water, and soon pestilence broke out among the poorer people. Jeremiah alone stood steadfast and would not hear the word "surrender."

The people, weakened by sickness, turned against him. They accused their faithful leader of having been in the pay of the Chaldeans. When he tried to prove his innocence, they threw him into a dungeon.

A kindly negro took pity upon the old man and released him from the dark pit into which he had been cast, and hid him in the guard-house until the end of the siege.

Before the official surrender of the town took place, the last of the Judæan kings had deserted his people.

In the middle of the night, accompanied by a few courtiers,

he had left the gates of his palace and had slipped through the lines of Chaldean sentinels.

When morning came, he was on his way towards the river Jordan.

Nebuchadnezzar, when he heard of this, sent fleet horsemen to intercept the Judæan ruler.

JEREMIAH ON THE WALLS
OF JERUSALEM

Near Jericho, Zedekiah was taken prisoner.

He was taken back to the royal camp and terrible was his punishment.

First, he was forced to witness the execution of his sons. Then he was blinded and he was sent to Babylon, where he was made to march in the triumphal procession of the Chaldean emperor. Shortly afterwards, he died in a Babylonian prison.

As for Jeremiah, the Chaldeans, who were a highly civilised people, spared his life and treated the old man with great honour. They respected his unselfishness and his wisdom and they told him that he might stay right at home, and that no harm would befall him.

Most of the Judæans, however, feared that they would suffer the fate of the Israelites and would be taken to Mesopotamia as captives. They prepared to flee to Egypt. Jeremiah advised them to remain where they were. The Jerusalemites, however, were in a panic and refused to listen to him. They gathered their possessions and trekked eastward. Jeremiah, who was the soul of loyalty, followed his people. He was too old for the hardships of such a voyage. He died in an Egyptian village and was buried by the side of the road.

It was the five-hundred-and-eighty-sixth year before the birth of Christ.

Jerusalem lay in ruins.

A Chaldean governor dwelled in the land of Joshua and David.

The smoke-stained walls of the temple stood dark against the blue sky of Canaan.

The last of the independent Jewish states had come to an end.

Judah had paid the price of its indifference to the will of Jehovah.

DOWNFALL AND EXILE

CHAPTER XIV

THE JEWS REFUSED TO LISTEN UNTIL A LONG PERIOD OF EXILE IN ASSYRIA AND BABYLONIA BROUGHT THEM TO A REALISATION OF WHAT THEY HAD DONE AND WHAT THEY OUGHT TO HAVE DONE. FAR AWAY FROM THE OLD HOME, SCATTERED AMONG THE TOWNS AND VILLAGES OF THE VALLEY OF MESOPOTAMIA, THEY BEGAN THAT CLOSE STUDY OF THE ANCIENT LAWS AND THE EARLY CHRONICLES WHICH IN DUE TIME WAS TO BRING THEM BACK TO A MORE SINCERE AND EAGER WORSHIP OF JEHOVAH

 HE new masters of the Jewish people belonged to a very remarkable race. Ever since the days of Hammurabi, their great law-giver, who lived and wrote a thousand years before Moses, the Babylonians had been regarded as the most civilised people of western Asia.

The capital of their vast empire was a mighty fortress. It was protected by a double row of high walls which surrounded almost a hundred square miles of houses, streets, gardens, temples and market-places.

BABYLON

The town had been laid out very regularly. The streets were both straight and wide.

The houses, built of brick, were spacious and sometimes two or three stories high.

The river Euphrates ran right through the middle of the town and offered direct connection with the Persian Gulf and India.

In the heart of the city, on a low artificial hill, stood the famous palace of Nebuchadnezzar.

With its many terraces, it created the impression of a large park, suspended in mid-air, and gave rise to the strange myth of the hanging gardens.

The town was as cosmopolitan as the modern city of New York.

The Babylonian merchants were excellent business men. They traded with Egypt and with far-away China. They had invented a system of writing, out of which the Phœnicians developed that handy alphabet which we use to-day. They were well versed in mathematics. They gave the world its first notions of scientific astronomy and divided the years into months, and the months into weeks, as we do. They devised that system of weights and measures upon which modern commerce is based.

And they first developed those moral laws which were afterwards incorporated by Moses in his Ten Commandments and which form the corner-stone of our own Church.

They were very efficient organisers and steadily and deliberately increased their domains. Their conquest of the land of Judah, however, was an accident and had nothing to do with their policy of expansion.

It happened that one of their rulers had gone forth to conquer Aram and Egypt. The little independent nation of the Judæans happened to be situated upon the highroad from the north to the south and from the east to the west.

It was occupied as a matter of military precaution.

That was all.

We doubt greatly whether the Babylonians of the age of Nebuchadnezzar were ever conscious of the existence of the Jews. They probably regarded them as we regard the Pueblo Indians. We know that a tribe of aborigines maintains some sort of semi-independent life somewhere in the southwest. We do not know exactly where and we do not greatly care. We take it for granted that some one in the Bureau of Indian Affairs or in the Department of the Interior will look after their interests. But life is full of a number of things. We are busy with our own affairs and cannot bother about a small ethnological group which means nothing to us beyond a name and a few pictures of queer religious dances.

You must get this point clearly fixed in your mind if you wish to understand what is to follow.

There was not a single early indication of the important rôle which the descendants of Abraham and Isaac were to play eventually in the history of mankind.

The earliest authors of world-histories do not mention the Jews with a single word. Take the case of Herodotus. He tried to give a reliable account of everything that had happened since the days of the flood (the Greek flood, and not the flood of Noah, which is part of an ancient Babylonian myth). Like most Athenians, he was both tolerant and curious. He wanted to know everything of importance that his neighbours had ever said or thought or done, that he might put it into his books.

He had no racial prejudices and he travelled far and wide to obtain first-hand information. He tells us several important things about the Egyptians and the Babylonians and many other people of the Mediterranean seaboard, but he has never heard of the Jews and refers to the people of the Palestinian plains very vaguely as an unknown tribe which practiced certain curious hygienic precautions.

As for the Chaldean contemporaries of the Jews, they looked upon the poor exiles as we look upon a group of forlorn Russian or Armenian refugees who happen to cross our city bound for some unknown destination in the west.

Which leaves us the Old Testament as the main source of our information.

But the compilers of that great national history (as we have told you before) were not trained historians. They did not care how they spelled the names of their foreign masters. They were very hazy about their geography. Constantly they refer to places which no one has ever been able to identify with any degree of certainty.

Again, they often deliberately hid the real meaning of their words. They used strange symbols. They referred to a whale, which swallowed a shipwrecked mariner and after a few days, vomited him up again upon dry land, when they wished to tell how the big empire of Babylonia conquered the little kingdom of Judah and after half a century, had been obliged to release her hold upon her captives. This was, of course, quite understandable to the people of twenty-five hundred years ago, but it is not so clear to those of us who know Babylon merely as a deserted heap of stones and rubbish.

All the same, the last twenty books of the Old Testament make up in quantity for what they lack in accuracy, and it is possible to reconstruct the fifth, the fourth and the third centuries B. C. with a fair amount of accuracy.

With the help of this somewhat unreliable material, we

shall now try to tell you what you ought to know if you are to understand the great spiritual drama which was to follow so soon afterwards.

Exile, in the case of the Judæan people, did not mean slavery.

From a purely worldly point of view, the change from Palestine to Mesopotamia was an improvement for the great majority of the Jews. The Israelites, a century and a half before, had been taken to four or five widely separated villages and towns and had been lost among their Babylonian neighbours. But the Judæan exiles of the year 586 were allowed to remain together and to settle in the same spot which became an honest-to-goodness Jewish colony.

They were in reality a band of involuntary pilgrims, travelling from the overcrowded slums of Jerusalem to the open spaces of Chebar. They left the sterile fields and valleys of the old land of the Canaanites to find a new home among the highly irrigated pastures and gardens of central Babylonia.

Nor did they suffer undue violence at the hands of a foreign taskmaster, as they had done in Egypt a thousand years before.

They were allowed to retain their own leaders and their own priests.

Their religious customs and ceremonies were not disturbed.

They were permitted to correspond with those of their friends who had remained in Palestine.

They were encouraged to practice the old arts with which they had been familiar in Jerusalem.

They were free men and were given the right to have servants and slaves of their own. No profession or trade was closed to them and soon a large number of Jewish names began to appear among the lists of rich merchants in the Babylonian capital.

Eventually, even the highest offices in the state were opened to Jewish ability and Babylonian kings more than once begged for the favour of Jewish women.

In short, the exiles had everything that can make men happy, except the liberty to go and come at will.

By going from Jerusalem to Tel-Harsha, they had shed many of the ills of the old country.

But now, alas, they suffered from a new ailment.

It was called homesickness.

This affliction, ever since the beginning of time, has had a strange influence upon the human soul. It throws a glowing light of happy reminiscences across the old country. It kills with sudden abruptness all recollection of past injuries and former suffering. Inevitably it turns "the old times" into "the good old times" and bestows upon the years spent amidst the old surroundings the dignified name of "the golden age."

When a man is a victim of homesickness, he refuses to see anything good in his new home. His new neighbours are inferior to the old ones (with whom, to tell the truth, he was for ever in open warfare). The new city (although ten times as large and twenty times as brilliant as his former village) is a mean and miserable hamlet. The new climate is only fit for savages and barbarians.

In short, everything "old" suddenly becomes "good" while everything "new" is just "bad" and "wicked" and "objectionable."

A century afterwards, when the exiles were given permission to return to Jerusalem, very few availed themselves of this opportunity. But as long as they were in Babylon, the land of Palestine was their lost Paradise and this attitude is reflected in everything they said or wrote.

Generally speaking, the lives of the Jews during this half-century of exile were dull and uneventful. The exiles went about their daily affairs and they waited.

In the beginning, they waited with the eager hope of those who expect that something "sudden" is going to happen. The words of doom of the great Jeremiah, who had predicted this terrible disaster, were still ringing in their ears.

But Jeremiah was dead and his place had never been quite filled.

In the earlier chapters, we have said a few words about the nature of the Jewish prophets. Since time immemorial, they have been the moral leaders of their people. Upon several occasions they had been the concrete expression of the national conscience.

But times were changing. The Jews no longer depended for their religious instruction upon the spoken word. They now had an alphabet of their own, and their language had acquired a formal grammar.

This alphabet, in the beginning, was rather crude. It had no vowels. It left a great deal to the imagination.

The same can be said of the rules governing the construction of written sentences. No clear distinction was made between the perfect and the imperfect tenses. One and the same verb could indicate that something had already happened or that it was about to happen. We have to guess at the real meaning from the contents of the sentence.

Such a form of expression lent itself very well to poetry. Hence the beauty of so many of the psalms. It was much less successful when the writer had to deal with concrete ideas or tried to give an account of the events of the past.

It does not quite show us where prophecy ceases and history begins.

But it was the best the Jews could do until they learned

the current Aramaic alphabet of their neighbours, and with all its crudities and imperfections, it served an excellent purpose.

It gave those prophets who had new ideas a chance to reach all their fellow Judæans, whether they lived in Egypt, in Babylonia, or on the islands of the Ægean Sea. It allowed them to bring order into the old and vague forms of worship. It made possible that great system of codified religious and civil law which we find in the Old Testament and in the Talmud. And it turned the prophet into something which he had never quite been before. He began to explain the written words of their ancestors to the children of the new generation. From a man of action, he became a contemplative sage who lived and died, surrounded with books. Now and then we shall still hear of prophets who walked among their fellow men and who spoke the language of the market-place. But as the number of schools where prophets were trained increased, the influence of their graduates diminished in proportion.

Jehovah ceased to be the Jehovah of the wind-swept plains and hills.

He became a set of rules and regulations. He no longer spoke to men amidst the crash of thunder in the desert. His voice from now on was heard in the solitude of the library. And the prophet became the rabbi—became the priest—who explained and expounded and interpreted and elucidated and gradually buried the spirit of the Divine Will underneath that philological rubbish-pile of learned annotations and criticisms which grew to enormous extent as the ages went by.

This new development, however (like all similar changes) did not come suddenly, and the period of exile produced several men who compare favourably with those among their predecessors who had been the acknowledged spiritual leaders of their race.

Two prophets stand out from the others.

One of these was Ezekiel.

Of the other (most unfortunately) we do not know the name. He was "the evangelist among the prophets." He spoke a new language, the like of which had never been heard either in Israel or in Judah. His works you will find hidden in the latter half of the twenty-third book of the Old Testament which is called Isaiah.

This book contains sixty-six chapters. The first thirty-nine may have been the work of the Prophet Isaiah, who lived during the reigns of Jotham, Ahaz and Hezekiah, and who predicted the fate of the two Jewish nations long before the days of Sennacherib and Nebuchadnezzar.

But the last twenty-six chapters are most evidently the work of a man who lived several centuries later and who used different language and a different style.

That these two dissimilar parts have been put together without a word of explanation need not surprise us. The compilers of the Old Testament (as we have repeatedly stated before) were not particular in such matters. They took whatever they liked wherever they found it and pasted their scrolls together without a vestige of what we modern people call "editing."

In this way, the identity of the man who wrote the second part of the book was lost in that of the prophet of the first half. It does not matter very much. As the "Unknown Author," the poet has gained more fame than many of his contemporaries whose genealogies have been incorporated in some very dull pages of the Old Testatment.

What makes his work so valuable is his new and unique

vision of the power and character of Jehovah. Jehovah, to him, is no longer the tribal god of a small Semitic nation. His name is written across the high heavens of all lands.

He is the ruler of all men.

Even the mighty King of Babylonia and the no less powerful King of Persia (to whom the Jews looked secretly for their ultimate deliverance)—they are both the unwitting servants of the One God whose will is law unto all men.

This God, however, is not a cruel God who hates those who know him not. On the contrary, he offers his love and his compassion even to those who live in darkness and who have never heard His Name.

He does not keep himself hidden from man behind the forbidding clouds of his own perfection. He is visible to all who have eyes to see. His words are clear to those who have ears to hear. He is the loving Father of all men, the Shepherd trying to lead an unwilling flock to the safe harbour of peace and righteousness.

Such language was far in advance of the times.

The average exile regarded it with profound misgivings.

This talk of a God who loved all living things did not appeal to a small community which depended for its existence upon its daily hate quite as much as upon its daily bread and which prayed incessantly for the days of vengeance when Jehovah should destroy the detestable Babylonian captors.

And eagerly they turned to other men who had been carefully grounded in the strict doctrines of an older day and who believed that Jehovah had chosen the descendants of Abraham and Jacob (and them only) to be the instruments of his divine will, and who never ceased to predict the day when all other nations should lie prostrate before the victorious hosts of the New Jerusalem.

Among the popular prophets of the exile, Ezekiel stands forth with granite strength.

He was born in the old country.

His father was a priest and the boy grew up in the highly religious atmosphere of Jerusalem, where he undoubtedly listened to the sermons of Jeremiah.

Later, he too became a prophet.

He seems to have been a young man of some importance in his community, for he was among the first to be driven away from the capital as soon as the Babylonians conquered Judah and several years before the beginning of the great exile.

News of the actual fall of Jerusalem reached him in the village of Tel-Abib (on the southern bank of the Euphrates), where he made his home.

He continued to live there until the day of his death.

The literary quality of his work is far beneath that of the Unknown Author of Isaiah. His style is rigid. The man himself lacks those human qualities which make such an appeal to us in many of the older leaders. He is far from modest.

He often gets into a veritable trance of artificial excitement. Upon such occasions he sees strange visions and hears mysterious voices.

But withal he was a man with a good deal of practical sense.

Like Jeremiah, he never ceased to argue against those misguided fanatics who believed that Jerusalem was bound to be impregnable because the town happened to be the capital of God's Chosen People.

He warned them. He told them that faith without deeds had never saved a nation.

But when the city had been taken and many people of little faith became at once despondent about the future of their race, Ezekiel stood forth as the triumphant advocate of a better future.

He never ceased to predict the happy day when the Temple should be restored and the altar of Jehovah drip once more with the blood of the offered bullocks.

This resurrected state, however (according to his views), could not survive unless the Jewish nation was willing to submit to certain practical reforms which Ezekiel then described in great detail.

Here, for a moment, he assumed the rôle of his Greek neighbour, Plato.

He gave us the description of an Ideal State, according to his own views of life. He wanted to strengthen and reënforce those parts of the Laws of Moses which in former times had given several heathenish forms of worship a chance to incorporate themselves within the holy rites of Jehovah.

In a general way, he advocated the reëstablishment of the Kingdom of David and of Solomon.

But in his new state, the Temple and not the royal palace must become the centre of all national life and activity.

The Temple, according to the Prophet, was the House of Jehovah, and the palace was merely the home of the sovereign

That difference ought to be severely impressed upon the people.

Furthermore, the average man should have a profound respect for the holiness of his God and should be made to understand that He was a Being far removed from ordinary human traffic.

The Temple, therefore, in Ezekiel's ideal state, was to be surrounded by two enormous walls and should stand in the middle of vast courtyards, so that the gaping multitude could at all times be kept at a respectable distance.

Everything connected with the Temple was to be holy ground.

No foreigner was ever to be allowed within the enclosure.

And the Jews, with the exception of the priests, were to be admitted only on rare occasions.

The priests were to form a closely knit union or guild.

Only descendants of Zadok should aspire to this dignity.

Their influence was to be greatly increased until they should be the actual rulers of the state, as it had already been planned by Moses.

In order to strengthen their hold upon the common people, the number of feast days was to be greatly increased and special attention was to be paid to the offerings of atonement for sin.

The idea of perpetual sin was to be held firmly before the nation.

Private offerings were to be discouraged.

Everything connected with worship in the Holy of Holies ought to be done in the name of the whole people.

The King, upon such occasions, was to act as the representative of the nation.

For the rest, he was to be merely an ornamental figurehead without any actual power.

In the olden days, David and Solomon had been given the privilege of appointing all priests.

This privilege was to be taken away from the sovereign.

The priestly class was to become a self-perpetuating body which was to treat the King as one of its servants and by no means as its master.

Finally, all the best land of the country, in the neighbourhood of Jerusalem, was to be given to the priests that they might be certain of a decent revenue, and there was to be no appeal from any law or decree they might wish to pass.

Here indeed was a strange programme.

But it sounded reasonable enough to the contemporaries of Ezekiel. And as soon as the Temple should have been rebuilt and the exiles allowed to return to their old home, they intended to establish such a rigid ecclesiastic state.

That day was to come sooner than most of the exiles expected.

Beyond the distant mountains of the east, a young barbarian chieftain was drilling his horsemen. He was to be the Messiah who delivered the Jewish captives from their foreign bondage.

His Persian subjects called him Kurus.

We know him by the name of Cyrus.

THE RETURN HOME

CHAPTER XV

MEANWHILE A SMALL TRIBE OF PERSIAN SHEPHERDS HAD GONE ON THE WARPATH AND HAD DESTROYED THE MIGHTY EMPIRES OF WESTERN ASIA. CYRUS, THE PERSIAN KING, ALLOWED THE JEWISH EXILES TO RETURN TO THEIR OWN COUNTRY. THE MAJORITY OF THE JEWS, HOWEVER, WERE PERFECTLY HAPPY IN THE COMFORTABLE BABYLONIAN CITIES AND REMAINED WHERE THEY WERE. BUT A SMALL MINORITY, WHICH TOOK ITS RELIGIOUS DUTIES SERIOUSLY, RETURNED TO THE RUINS OF JERUSALEM, REBUILT THE TEMPLE AND MADE IT THE ABSOLUTE AND ONLY CENTRE OF THE WORSHIP OF JEHOVAH FOR ALL THE JEWS IN EVERY PART OF THE WORLD

EARLY during the seventh century before the birth of Christ a small Semitic tribe, called the Kaldi (or Chaldeans), had left its desert home in Arabia and had moved northward.

After many adventures and several unsuccessful attempts to break into the domains of Assyria, the Kaldi had at last made common cause with the wild mountain-people who lived to the east of the Mesopotamian plain.

Together they had defeated the Assyrian armies and had taken and destroyed the city of Nineveh.

Upon the ruins of the old empire, Nabopolassar, the chieftain of the Chaldeans, had then founded a kingdom of his own which is now called New Babylonia by some historians and Chaldea by others.

His son, Nebuchadnezzar, had greatly strengthened the boundaries of his inheritance. And Babylon had become (what it had been three thousand years before) the centre of the old civilised world.

During his interminable war with his neighbours, Nebuchadnezzar had overrun and had conquered that remnant of the old Jewish state which was known as Judah, and he had transplanted several colonies of Judæans (or Jews) from the shores of the Mediterranean to the banks of the Euphrates.

His relations, however, with his Jewish subjects were pleasant enough, although somewhat indifferent.

Like all stern monarchs, Nebuchadnezzar took a great interest in fortune-telling. The man who could successfully explain a dream was certain to find favour in the eyes of the King.

Such a man, it seems, was the prophet Daniel.

According to the book which bears his name (but which was written four hundred years later) Daniel was a young Judæan prince who had been taken, together with three of his young cousins, to Babylon that he might there be educated at the Chaldean court.

The four boys were very faithful servants of Jehovah.

They obeyed his holy laws in all details.

For example, when they were given the regular palace food, they refused to eat it and insisted upon meat and vegetables which had been prepared according to those ancestral regulations which prescribed in detail how cows and sheep should be slaughtered and how vegetables should be cooked.

Fortunately, the Chaldeans were tolerant and easy-going and the little captives were given whatever they asked for.

They were diligent and eager boys.

They learned all that the Babylonian schools could teach them and promised to be useful subjects of their adopted country.

Now it happened during the last years of Nebuchadnezzar's reign that the old King had a dream.

He called his "wise men" together and bade them explain it to him on pain of death. The "wise men," quite reasonably, said: "Tell us the dream, Your Majesty, and we shall do our best to give you an explanation."

"I have forgotten my dream," he answered. "But I know positively that I dreamed something or other. It is your business to tell me both what I dreamed and what it means."

The magicians begged for mercy.

They asked their ruler to be reasonable.

"How can any man tell another that which the other does not know himself?" they shouted.

Eastern tyrants, however, are not interested in such details. Without further ado, Nebuchadnezzar condemned all his 'wise men" to the gallows.

He seems to have been in a bad humour on that particular day. He gave orders to kill not only these particular men who had failed in their duty, but to rid his court once for all of every magician and sorcerer.

An officer was despatched to the quarters of Daniel and his friends that they might share the fate of all their fellow-conjurors.

But Daniel, who in many respects was like Joseph, had

made friends with the military men at the Babylonian court. He asked the captain of the guard to give him a short respite.

Meanwhile, he would try to see what he could do.

He laid himself down to sleep and immediately Jehovah revealed to him the dream which Nebuchadnezzar had most inadvertently lost.

The next morning, the captain, whose name was Arioch, took Daniel before Nebuchadnezzar. The King was still greatly worried and was willing to give this young foreigner a chance.

Daniel first retold the dream, a strange story connected with the political events of four hundred years later.

Then he explained it.

As a result of his cleverness, he gained the everlasting gratitude of his royal master, who made him governor of the city of Babylon and who appointed Shadrach, Meshach and Abednego, his three companions, to be the rulers of three rich provinces.

All this was very pleasant but it did not last long. For, according to the unknown author of these chapters, Nebuchadnezzar, in his dotage, became addicted to a form of image-worship which was as foreign to the taste of the intelligent Chaldeans as to that of the Jews.

He ordered a large statue to be made. It was ninety feet high and nine feet wide and entirely covered with gold. It stood in the plain of Dura where it could be seen from far and wide. At a given signal (the blowing of many trumpets) all the people of the country were expected to prostrate themselves before this image and to worship it.

Shadrach, Meshach and Abednego, however, could not do this. They remembered the Second Commandment. They refused to obey the royal edict. All the people went down upon their faces, but Shadrach, Meshach and Abednego remained standing upright.

They knew the punishment which awaited them.

They were taken before Nebuchadnezzar, who ordered them to be thrown into a fiery furnace. To make sure that the victims should not escape their fate, the furnace was heated seven times hotter than usual.

Shadrach, Meshach and Abednego were bound, hand and foot, and were thrown into the flames.

But behold! when the doors were opened, the next morning, the three young men walked out as unconcernedly as if they were just returning from a cool swim.

After that, Nebuchadnezzar was convinced that Jehovah was the greatest of all gods. He forgot his idols and favoured his Jewish captors more than ever before.

Unfortunately, he was soon afterwards stricken with a strange nervous malady.

He imagined that he had become an animal. He went around on all fours and mooed, and died miserably in a field, where he had been eating grass, like an ordinary cow.

In all this, we are following the text of the book ascribed to the hand of Daniel. This volume, according to the painstaking investigations of modern scholars, was written sometime between the years 167 and 165 B. C. when the Jews were very lax in their religious duties. The author, taking the liberty of a novelist, laid his story during the reign of Nebuchadnezzar. He probably introduced the wholly imaginary episode of the fiery furnace to tell his contemporaries what faith can do for those who seriously believe that Jehovah is on their side and he made Nebuchadnezzar die a terrible death because such an unfortunate ending was sure to please his Jewish readers.

To do this was his good right as the teacher of certain religious morals. But we have too many Babylonian sources about the great Chaldean King to be in doubt about his ultimate fate. He died peacefully in the year 561 B. C. and six years later the dynasty of Nabopolassar came to an end and a general by the name of Nabonidus made himself master of the throne.

This Nabonidus seems to have had a son or a son-in-law by the name of Bel-shar-usur, who shared the throne with him.

In the book of Daniel he is called Belshazzar and according to the Jewish tradition, he was the last king of Babylon. But once more we are in the midst of very conflicting historical evidence. Darius, the Mede, who is mentioned in this same chapter of the Old Testament, was probably intended for Darius the Persian, who lived a hundred years later, and Belshazzar was not murdered until several months after the surrender of Babylon to the Persians.

But that some sort of feast was held just before the city was surprised by the enemy is borne out both by Herodotu and Xenophon, and it was at this very noisy celebration tha Daniel gained his greatest fame as a prophet of future events

Belshazzar, so the story goes, had invited more than thousand nobles to his party. They ate and they drank an the hall was full of the noise of very drunken people. Sud denly, on the wall opposite the King's couch, a hand appearec

Quietly it wrote four words upon the stones.

Then it disappeared.

The words, curiously enough, were written in Aramai No wonder that the King could not understand them. H sent for his magicians, but they too failed to decipher then Then some one remembered Daniel, just as ten centuri before, at the court of Pharaoh, some one had remembered Joseph.

Daniel came. He was well versed in the different arts of mystic writing. He read the words first down, then up, and then down again. This is what he saw:

M	U	P
E	L	H
N	E	A
E	K	R
M	E	S
E	T	I
N	E	N

And this is what he spelled out: MENE MENE TEKEL UPHARSIN.

Even then, this combination of letters did not make much sense.

A "mene" or "mina" was a Jewish coin or weight, about fifty times the value of a shekel.

A "tekel" was what we call a "shekel."

The "u" before the next word was merely a connecting particle, and "pharsin" (which became "Peres" in the translation) could mean "half-a-mina" or it could refer to the "Peres" or Persians.

Thus the words could have meant "Nebuchadnezzar was a mina. Nebuchadnezzar was a mina." (Repeated for the sake of strengthening the argument.) "Belshazzar, you are only a shekel. The Persians are half a mina."

Or, in plain English: "The big empire of the great Nebuchadnezzar, now dwindled to a small kingdom under your weak guidance, O King Belshazzar! will soon be divided into halves by the Persians."

All this, however, is a philological puzzle which we shall not try to solve.

Daniel appears to have regarded the substantives as the past participles of the verbs "to count," "to weigh," and "to number."

And he gave the following explanation of this very frightening riddle:

"Jehovah has weighed you in the balance, O King Belshazzar, and he has found you wanting."

As a reward for his prophecy and hoping to find favour in the eyes of the Jewish God, Belshazzar made Daniel his viceroy.

But this honour meant little. The Persians were at the gates of Babylon. The days of the empire were indeed numbered.

In the year 538, Cyrus entered the city through one of the water-gates.

DANIEL DECIPHERS THE MYSTERIOUS LETTER

He spared Nabonidus, the King. He killed Belshazzar when the latter, a short while later, tried to start a revolution against the conquering host.

And he turned the territory of Babylon into a Persian province just as the Babylonians (only half a century before) had turned the kingdom of Judah into a subordinate part of their own empire.

As for Darius the Mede, who is mentioned in the book of Daniel, we know nothing about him except his name. Cyrus on the other hand, is a famous hero of antiquity and he deserves some attention.

The Persian people over whom he ruled were of Aryan stock. That is to say, they were not Semitic like the Babylonians and the Assyrians and the Jews and the Phœnicians, but they belonged to the same general group of people from whom our ancestors are descended. Originally those tribes seem to have lived in the plains on the eastern shores of the Caspian Sea.

At an unknown date they appear to have left their old homestead to begin a great trek.

A few of them went westward and settled among the aborigines of Europe whom they soon killed or subjugated.

Others went southward and occupied the plateau of Iran and the plains of India. The Persians, together with the Medes, took hold of several mountain ranges which had been depopulated by the ferocious military expeditions of the Assyrians.

Here they organised themselves into something which at first resembled a cowboy republic. Out of these humble beginnings had grown that strange kingdom of Persia which was elevated to the rank of an empire by the conquests of Cyrus.

Cyrus himself was a very remarkable man. He only made war when he could not accomplish his purpose by means of intrigue and diplomacy. He did not march against Babylon until he had isolated that powerful city from all her former vassals and allies. This was slow work.

It took almost twenty years, and this period had been one of intense excitement for the exiles.

From the very beginning, they had suspected that "Kurus" might be the Messiah who at Jehovah's instigation was to deliver them from their Babylonian yoke. They had followed his adventures with breathless interest. First they had heard of him as making war upon the Cappadocians.

A little later, so travellers had told them, he was engaged in a struggle with Crœsus, King of the Lydians and a great personal friend of Solon, the law-giver of the Greeks.

Next, rumour had him in Asia Minor, where he was said to be building a fleet with which to invade the shores of Greece.

A whole chorus of prophets watched this man's campaigns with almost indecent zeal. Whenever there was a report of another Persian victory, all the people broke forth into songs of praise and hope.

The days of Babylon (of this they were convinced) were numbered. The wicked city had refused to listen to the words of Jehovah.

Jehovah was ready to punish her for her crime.

When at last the impossible happened and Babylon fell, the Jewish captives celebrated the event with frantic joy. Then they rushed forth to kiss the feet of their new masters and asked that they be allowed to return to the old country.

Cyrus made no objection.

He prided himself upon his tolerance.

All the subject races of the old Babylonian empire were at once given permission to return to their homes. Cyrus, however, went further.

He seems to have had an almost Roman indifference towards the private opinions of other people.

If the Jews or the Phœnicians or the Cilicians preferred their own gods to those of the Persians, that was their business.

They were welcome to build such temples as they thought best.

They could fill them with images or leave them bare, just as they preferred.

Provided they paid their taxes and obeyed the King's "satraps" or governors, they could shape their own political and religious lives as suited them best, and the King would see to it that no one dared to interfere.

Furthermore, the idea of a wholesale return of the Jewish exiles to the land of Canaan had a practical side which greatly appealed to this sagacious ruler. He hoped to make Persia a maritime nation.

The cities of Phœnicia already obeyed his will.

But between Phœnicia and Babylonia lay the deserted ruins of Palestine.

It was necessary to repopulate this desert.

A few vague attempts in this direction had already been made by the Babylonians. They had sent immigrants to the former kingdom of Israel. These had settled down among the half-starved remnants of the original population. Together with these, they had formed a new race, called the Samaritans, remnants of which may be found to-day in some of the Palestine villages of the north.

They had never been very prosperous. They were a strange mixture, composed of Hebrews and Babylonians and Assyrians and Hittites and Phœnicians, who were held in the most profound contempt by the pure Jews of the former Judæan kingdom. When Cyrus began to restore order in Palestine, he first of all tried to find the descendants of the captives from Israel. Not a trace could be found of these exiles or their children. They had been completely absorbed by their Babylonian neighbours and their fate is as much of a mystery to-day as it was in the year 538 B. C.

It was easy, on the other hand, to deal with the Judæans. They had maintained their racial integrity.

A royal edict of the year 537 urged them to return at once to Jerusalem. At the same time, it gave them permission to rebuild the temple. It restored to them all the golden and silver implements which Nebuchadnezzar had taken to Babylon, some forty years before, and it encouraged the Judæans to turn Jerusalem into a new national capital which should rival the extinct but not forgotten splendour of Solomon's old residence.

After half a century of prayer, the words of the prophet had come true.

The exile of Jehovah's children had come to an end.

The Jews were at liberty to leave their prison.

But now that the door stood open, behold! only a few of the captives availed themselves of the opportunity to go home.

The majority remained quietly in Babylon or moved to Ecbatana or to Nippur or to Susa or to one of the other great centres of the new Persian empire. A very small minority undertook the long and dangerous journey through the desert. They were pious men who took their religious duties very seriously.

And they now established upon the ruins of Jerusalem a new state which, devoid of all foreign influence, was to be devoted exclusively to the worship of Jehovah.

It would have been natural if Daniel had assumed the leadership over those who returned to Palestine.

But Daniel was too old to travel. The Persians treated him kindly and retained him in his office. For a short time he came under the suspicion of disloyalty, because he continued to pray to Jehovah when the king had issued a decree forbidding all petitions to either gods or men for the period of a month. As a result of this disobedience, he had been condemned to death and had been thrown before the lions.

But these ferocious animals had refused to eat so holy a prophet. In the morning, Daniel had walked out of the cage without a single scratch, and after that, he lived his life in peace.

When it became certain that he could not undertake the journey, the Persians looked for another candidate for the governorship of the reëstablished province of Judah.

Their choice fell upon a certain Zerubbabel, who was distantly related to the old Judæan kings. Zerubbabel went to Jerusalem and together with the high priest, Joshua, he began the work of reconstruction.

It was no easy task. The entire city had to be rebuilt. Most of the surrounding territory had been turned into farms and pastures by squatters from the Samaritans' country. They of course hated to be dispossessed and they did everything they could to make the life of the newcomers as difficult and as unpleasant as possible.

They hoped to make an honest penny working on the Temple but they were informed that no heathens need apply for a job on the holy shrine.

To revenge themselves, they sent mysterious messages to Cyrus, warning the Persian king of a rebellion which was to make Judah an independent kingdom as soon as the Temple should be finished.

Cyrus was a very busy man. He had no time to bother about such trifles as a Jewish revolt, but as a precautionary measure, he gave orders that the building of the Temple should be discontinued until the charge should have been investigated.

Soon afterwards Cyrus died and the matter was forgotten. Several years went by and the half-finished walls were beginning to be covered with weeds. Then the prophet Haggai appeared upon the scene. He denounced Zerubbabel for his indolence and timidity and told him to continue the work on the walls with or without royal permission.

Zerubbabel, who was sadly in need of a little encouragement, promised that he would do so. He told the people to go back to work.

But then he got into trouble with Tatnai, the governor of Samaria, who asked him by what right he was building this house of God which began to look more and more like a regular fortification. Zerubbabel answered that he had obtained the permission years ago from Cyrus. Tatnai sent this answer to headquarters. Meanwhile, Cambyses, the successor of Cyrus, had also died and had been followed by Darius. Darius ordered that a search be made of the archives. It was getting to be quite a complicated case. But fortunately, the original decree, signed by Cyrus, was discovered.

Tatnai thereupon withdrew his opposition and four years later the Temple was finished.

Slowly a few other exiles returned to their native country. The vast majority of the Jews, however, continued to live in the commercial centres of Egypt and Babylonia and Persia. Whenever circumstances allowed it, they celebrated their great religious festivals within the walls of their holy city. They acknowledged and honoured the old town as their spiritual home. But the little land-locked capital, with its narrow and dirty streets and its neglected workshops, did not offer sufficient opportunity for worldly success.

As soon as the last offering had been made and the last psalm had been chanted the visitors hastened back to the busy counting houses of Susa and Daphnæ. They were proud to be Jews and they loved Jerusalem, provided they did not have to live there all the year round.

In this way there developed that strange double loyalty which was to cause much trouble and suffering during the next four centuries. For although the Jews, in the dispersion, lived peacefully among the Persians and the Egyptians and the Greeks and the Romans, they never adopted the customs of these countries.

Everywhere they formed a state within a state.

They lived in a quarter of their own.

They went to a different temple.

They did not allow their children to associate with the boys and girls to whom Jehovah was just a funny name. They would rather kill their daughters than give them in marriage to a heathenish husband.

They ate different food which had been differently prepared.

They were careful to obey the laws of the land, but besides they obeyed certain very rigid and complicated laws of their own.

By preference they wore a garment which distinguished them from other people.

And they rigorously celebrated certain holidays which were a complete mystery to their fellow-citizens.

People are always suspicious of those of their neighbours whom they fail to understand. The aloofness of these Jewish colonies, the open scorn of all Jews for the gods of other races, together with their gift for racial team-work, often made them unpopular among their neighbours and frequently led to bitter feuds.

In one of these, early during the fifth century before the birth of Christ, the Jews in Persia perished and were for a moment in danger of complete annihilation.

The underlying causes for this sudden outbreak we do not know. But we find all the details of the plot in the book of Esther.

The book of Esther, the last of the so-called historical books of the Old Testament, like the book of Daniel, was written several centuries after the death of Xerxes and in this case there are no Persian inscriptions to help us out. We know a great deal about King Xerxes, who almost destroyed the new civilisation of the European mainland. He was both weak and worthless and the story of his behaviour towards his wife is entirely in keeping with his general character.

Xerxes, or Ahasuerus, as the Jews called him, had divorced his wife after a most disgraceful quarrel. The King had been drinking too much. So, for that matter, had the Queen. There had been hot words and Vashti, the wife, had been forced to leave the royal palace.

Xerxes had immediately searched the country for a new queen and he had selected Esther, a young Jewish girl who was an orphan and who lived with her cousin Mordecai, a man of considerable standing in the community and favourably known at the royal court.

Esther went to live in the royal harem and Mordecai often visited her there.

One day, in an anteroom, he overheard two men discussing a plot to kill the King. Mordecai warned Esther. Esther spoke to the King. The two men were arrested and executed, but Mordecai was forgotten and received no reward for having saved the King's life.

This did not worry him. He was well-to-do and did not need any money. Besides, as the Queen's former guardian, he received a great many honours and he was quite content. But his sudden rise in the world and the prominence which he now enjoyed brought him many enemies.

Just then an Arab by the name of Haman was one of Xerxes' most trusted ministers. Haman (who belonged to the tribe of the Amalekites, the age-old enemies of the Judæans) despised Mordecai and Mordecai returned this sentiment in a most cordial fashion.

Haman insisted that Mordecai bow to him first whenever they met. Mordecai refused. The matter was brought before the King. The King said that he did not want to be bothered. From that moment on, the two men hated each other with a deadly hatred. It seems a small matter about which to get excited, but thirty centuries ago, people did not know any better.

Haman was a dangerous enemy. He filled the heart of Xerxes with suspicion against all descendants of the former captives. He pointed to their rich houses and to their apparent success. As the King had never seen the slums where the greater part of his Jewish subjects lived, he believed all these stories. Without much trouble, Haman got his dissolute monarch to the point where he willingly signed a royal decree condemning all the Jews within his domains to death.

Haman was entrusted with the execution of this terrible law. Like all mean persons, he proceeded with slow and deliberate care, for he wanted to enjoy his revenge to the full. He threw lots to see what month would be best for the wholesale execution of the followers of Jehovah. In this way, the month of February was chosen. This gave Haman enough time to order the erection of a gallows on the top of a high hill, so that Mordecai, his enemy, "might be elevated above all men."

The plot, however, was so complicated that it could not remain a secret for very long. Esther, at Mordecai's urgent request, appeared unannounced in the presence of her royal husband and asked that her people be spared.

Xerxes was angry at first, but he remembered how Mordecai had once saved his life, and putting all evidence before him together, he began to understand how Haman had misled him out of personal spite. Messengers on horseback were sent at once to all parts of the country to warn the Jews against the coming attack. And Haman was impaled on the top of that same high hill where he had hoped to hang his enemy, Mordecai.

When the details of the plot became known, the Jews began to appreciate the danger from which they had escaped. They decided to perpetuate the memory of this important event.

Every year thereafter, between the 13th and the 15th of the month of Adar (a Babylonian month covering part of our February and March), there was to be a great celebration called the feast of the Lots or "Purim."

HAMAN'S PLOT TO MURDER
THE JEWS

Upon that occasion, the book of Esther was to be read aloud to every Jewish community and the name of Haman was to be publicly execrated. And the rich were to give liberally to the poor in memory of the good Queen who had saved her people from destruction.

The faithful Jews who had already returned to Jerusalem did not welcome this innovation and for a long time they opposed the annual celebration of Purim, which seemed a little bit too "foreign." But the feast (which probably was of Assyrian or Babylonian origin, and very old) rapidly gained in popularity in its new form and it has survived until our own time.

The story of Esther shows clearly how very important the foreign colonies were during the rule of the Persian kings.

They completely overshadowed the home country and all accounts seem to agree upon the desolate state of affairs in Jerusalem.

The Temple had been rebuilt after a fashion. But the walls of the city were still in ruins and commerce and trade were slow to revive. Zerubbabel had died and had been succeeded by a number of men who, hampered by a lack of funds and a lack of immigrants, had not been able to do anything to improve matters.

At last the Jews abroad decided that something must be done for the old homeland. A priest by the name of Ezra was given a sum of money to go to Judah and report upon conditions there. He asked for volunteers to accompany him. There was little enthusiasm. After a great deal of argument, Ezra persuaded some five hundred people to go back with him.

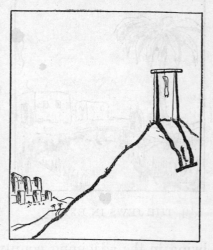

HAMAN HANGED ON HIS
OWN GALLOWS

After a journey of four months, this band of pilgrims came within sight of the ancient Temple.

But conditions in Jerusalem, as Ezra found them, were terrible. The colonists (for they were little else) had taken wives from among the neighbouring villages.

They had become very lax in the execution of their religious duties.

Judah was in a fair way to become another Samaria.

Ezra, ably assisted by Nehemiah (one of Artaxerxes' former body servants), came to the rescue and reorganised the decaying state. The walls of the city were at last rebuilt. The streets were cleared of all rubbish. The foreign wives were sent back to their parents. And outside the main gate of the Temple a wooden pulpit was built from which Ezra regularly read and explained certain parts of the holy laws that the people might forever be reminded of their duties.

THE JEWS IN EXILE

Even then the larger part of the old city remained an uninhabited wilderness.

As this meant constant danger (there were hardly men enough to defend the elaborate system of walls which had been laid out in the populous days of Solomon), some drastic steps were taken to complete the quota of necessary inhabitants.

One-tenth of all the Jews living in the adjoining country districts, selected by lot, were told that they must move into Jerusalem. A few came voluntarily and were given great honour as very unselfish patriots. The others were brought in by force.

Even then, Jerusalem remained a shadow of her former self. The old days of political and commercial importance were gone and they were gone for good.

The dream of Ezekiel could never come true.

But soon the city was to be the home of that great prophet whose ultimate appearance had been predicted by that "unknown author" whose courageous eyes had dared to look forward when all of his fellow-exiles placed their faith in the glories of the past.

THE MISCELLANEOUS BOOKS

CHAPTER XVI

THE MISCELLANEOUS BOOKS OF THE OLD TESTAMENT

HE Old Testament was a national Jewish scrap-book. It contained histories and legends and genealogies and love poems and psalms, classified and arranged and reclassified and rearranged without any regard for chronological order or literary perfection.

Suppose that there had been no American histories at all and that a patriotic citizen of the year 2923 should decide to compile such a volume. Very likely he would go through all the bound copies of our great magazines and newspapers (if any survived) gathering everything of an historical and literary nature that seemed to be of sufficient importance.

But unless he were very thoroughly prepared for his task, he would give us a compilation that would in many respects resemble the Old Testament.

There would be strange legends of some of the earliest Indians, dealing with their mysterious stories of creation.

There would be special Sunday stories, telling of the discoveries of Columbus and giving an account of the hardships of the first settlers along the banks of the Charles River and the Hudson.

These would be followed by a detailed description of the attempts to organise the thirteen little colonies (corresponding to the twelve tribes of the Jews) into a single nation, for which there would be a great deal of material.

The adventures of this new commonwealth would be described in detail with special reference to the Civil War, which almost turned the United States into another Judah and Israel.

Together with these historical narratives, there would be a miscellaneous collection of bits of poetry and of those songs that have become part of our great national inheritance.

And if our American patriot had had as little training for this sort of work as did the scribes of Jerusalem and of Babylon, we should find that those chapters dealing with the conquest of the west contained snatches of verse, gathered from the works of Longfellow, Whittier and Emerson; that an account of the Revolution had been added to the chapter dealing with the acquisition of Alaska; and that Roosevelt was mentioned as the author of almost every important measure of state.

Of course, this purely imaginary book would not be a very reliable historical guide. In our day and age, that would not matter very much. We could go to France and England and Spain and with the help of their libraries (taking it for granted that they had not been destroyed, as most of the libraries of Babylon have been) we could easily enough reconstruct our own past from these foreign sources.

In the case of the Old Testament, this is almost impossible. The Egyptians and Assyrians and Chaldeans and Persians paid very little attention to this strangely pious tribe, who held themselves aloof from the national life of their adopted fatherland.

In the main, therefore, we depend for our information exclusively upon the ancient Hebrew and Aramean texts. We have said this before, but we repeat it here for the last time, that you shall not miss this most important point.

Thus far we have, to the best of our ability, tried to reconstruct the era of legend and the period of written history. Now we must tell you something about those extra chapters of pure poetry which form the most attractive part of all Jewish literature.

The story of Ruth has already been mentioned. A counterpart (but of a very different nature) of this idyllic life of the old Judean villages is found in the book of Job.

It was an old, old popular story of a pious man who was sorely tried by circumstances, but who never lost his faith in the ultimate good of all things. He does not understand why all these terrible things should happen to him, why he should be stricken with a terrible malady, why he, a "wise man," should not be allowed to profit by his learning; why he, the kindest of fathers, should lose all his children.

He does not understand, yet he resigns himself quietly to his fate.

He does not argue.

He accepts.

But when he meets three of his old friends, then occurs that memorable conversation which has made the book of Job so dear to all lovers of imaginary literature.

Job steadfastly maintains that all his sufferings are for the benefit of his unworthy soul. He may not be able to follow the designs of Jehovah, but surely they are right, while he himself, in his ignorance, is wrong.

At last the days of his trial come to an end. Job is restored to the full possession of his former riches. He marries again and has seven stalwart sons and three beautiful daughters. And he lives to be a hundred-and-forty years old and dies, the most prosperous and important man in the country.

The book of Job is followed by the Psalms.

The Greek word "psalter" meant a stringed instrument, probably of Phœnician origin and at one time very popular in western Asia. It was used on festive occasions to accompany the people who chanted the holy songs, and it was played with a plectrum, like a modern mandolin.

It did not have a very wide range and was restricted to ten notes. But it served a good purpose.

It kept the congregation on the right pitch, like a modern organ.

As for the Psalms, they are as varied in subject as the poems of the last six centuries, which we find in "The Oxford Book of English Verse."

They range all the way from the sublime in goodness to the sublime in wickedness and revenge. They contain the oldest and the most beautiful descriptions of nature of which we have been able to find a written record. Whatever truly religious people have ever felt or dreamed or prayed for is contained in many of those sublime lines which speak of hope and consolation. The Psalms cover almost the entire period of Jewish national life. Some were written during the days of the kingdom. Others date back only to the great exile. As time went on, they became a regular part of all religious celebrations. As such, they have been adopted by our Christian Church. They have inspired most of the great poets of later ages. They have been translated into every known tongue. They have been set to music by the greatest of our western composers. Their sombre dignity reveals itself even when we are ignorant of the language in which they are read.

Whatever the future of many of the historical and prophetic books of the Old Testament, the Psalms will survive as long as man believes that beauty (in whatever form or guise) is something holy and venerable.

The same cannot be said of Proverbs.

This is a book without any vision or passion.

It contains just what the name implies, the wise sayings of several generations of shrewd old men and old women.

Every nation, since the beginning of time, has possessed such a collection of proverbs. Our own republic, based solidly upon the common-sense of our independent pioneers, has given the world a large number of such proverbs.

The wisdom of Confucius, the great teacher of the Chinese, is almost entirely composed of such mildly tolerant observations upon the foolishness of man and upon the patience of the gods. And just as to-day, we ascribe the kindly sayings of two entire generations to Abraham Lincoln, so the Jews of the Persian period, remembering Solomon as the greatest of their national heroes, proclaimed him the author of all this homely wisdom.

As a matter of fact, most of the Proverbs were written four hundred years after the death of that great monarch. This, of course, is of very small importance. The Proverbs would be just as good if they had been collected only yesterday. They show us what the man in the street thought and they teach us more about the ancient Jewish point of view than a dozen historical or prophetic works.

The next chapter, called Ecclesiastes, or "the Preacher," is a purely religious volume.

It is a tired but a very human book.

It delves deeply into the problems of life and faith.

It reflects the weary and rather personal wisdom of the famous Jewish physician who is said to be its author.

What is the use, so he asks, of those seventy years of toil and anxiety, which represent the average human life? The end of all things is the grave.

The good die.

The wicked die.

They all die.

What does it all mean? The righteous suffer persecution. The ungodly gather riches. Is there no reason in this human misery?

"Vanity of vanities, all is vanity." And so on for twelve whole chapters.

The Jews, like all Oriental people, were a moody race.

They dwelt upon the highest peaks of joy or miserably they descended into a deepest abyss of gloom.

Their literature was their music.

When they were sad and despondent, they listened to Ecclesiastes—which has the despondent beauty of an Etude by Chopin.

When they were happy, they read the jubilant Psalms which are reflected so well in the opening chords of Haydn's "Ode to Creation."

Man changes, but his soul remains the same. If we are wise, we too shall find much consolation in these books of poetry. What we suffer, others have suffered before us and still others will suffer in the years that are to come.

What has given new hope to those who died a thousand

years ago may some day give fresh courage to those who are not yet born.

Man changes, but his grief and his pleasure remain as they were in the days of Abraham and Jacob.

The last one of the miscellaneous works of the Old Testament is a very curious book. It is called the Song of Songs. This does not mean that it is really a collection of songs. The repetition of the word is used to indicate a superlative of literary perfection. It means, "This is the most beautiful song of all songs," just as we praise the happiest day of our lives as "the day of days."

The Song of Songs is in reality a very old love poem. Of course, King Solomon (as seems almost inevitable in view of his tremendous reputation) is said to be the author. At any rate, he is the traditional hero of this great lyric of love.

The heroine is a shepherdess.

The King has seen her and has taken her away from her home in the village of Shunem.

He has given her an honoured place in his harem.

He tries to gain her favour.

But she, the simple Shulamite, remains faithful to her shepherd lover. She has been installed in a lovely apartment in the heart of the royal palace. But she thinks only of the happy days when she and her own man wandered across the hills and tended their flocks.

She repeats old bits of their conversation. At night, she dreams of the strength and comfort of his arms. Finally (as in all such stories) the true lovers are united and all ends happily.

The Song of Songs is not a religious book, but it is the first evidence of something new and very fine which had at last come into the world.

In the beginning of time, woman had been a beast of burden.

She belonged to the man who captured her.

She worked his fields. She looked after his cattle. She bore his children. She cooked for him. She made him comfortable. And in return, she received the morsels which fell from his table.

But all this is beginning to change.

Woman is coming into her own.

She is recognised as the equal of man.

She is his companion.

She inspires his love and she receives it.

Upon this firm foundation of mutual respect and affec-tion, a new world was soon to be built.

THE COMING OF THE GREEKS

CHAPTER XVII

BUT WHILE THESE EVENTS OF WHICH WE HAVE JUST SPOKEN WERE TAKING PLACE, A GREAT CHANGE HAD COME OVER THE WORLD. THE GENIUS OF THE GREEKS HAD SET THE WORLD FREE FROM ITS ANCIENT IGNORANCE AND SUPERSTITION. THE FOUNDATION HAD BEEN LAID FOR OUR MODERN WORLD OF SCIENCE AND ART AND PHILOSOPHY AND STATECRAFT

AR to the east, where the purple sails of the Phœnician ships disappeared beyond the distant horizon, lay the rugged peninsula of Greece.

It was a small country, not quite as tiny as the modern state of Delaware, and not quite as large as South Carolina. But it was inhabited by a race of people who were to play a most remarkable rôle in the history of mankind.

The Greeks, like the Jews, were immigrants.

While Abraham was driving his flocks westward in search

of new pastures, the advance-guard of the Greek army was exploring the northern slopes of Mount Olympus.

The problem before the Greeks was not as difficult as that which Moses and Joshua encountered when they tried to get a foothold in the land of Canaan.

The Pelasgians, the original inhabitants of the Peloponnesian and Attican valleys, were weak and uncivilised and had not yet outgrown the habits of the late stone age. They were conquered and exterminated without great difficulty by an enemy armed with iron spears.

As soon as this had been done, the Greeks settled down behind the high walls of their little cities and laid the foundations for that civilisation which since then has become the common possession of all the nations of Europe and America.

In the beginning, the Greeks did not pay much attention to their neighbours across the sea. They conquered the Ægean Islands, but they did not try to get a foothold in Asia. The Phœnicians maintained their hold upon foreign commerce and the Greeks rarely ventured beyond Cape Males or the Straits of the Dardanelles.

There was the memorable exception when the Greek contemporaries of Jephthah and Samson started upon their famous expedition against Troy. But when the insult to Menelaus had been avenged, the Greeks returned to their own country and rarely ventured beyond the distant harbours of Pergamum and Halicarnassus. What lay hidden behind the blue mountain-ridges of Phrygia did not interest them. Babylon was only a name to the citizens of Athens. Nineveh was of small interest to the Puritan soldiers of Sparta. They spoke of these mysterious cities as our own grandfathers spoke of Timbuktu and Lassa.

The land of Canaan was unknown territory to them.

They had never heard of the Jews.

But in the fifth century before the birth of Christ, all this changed.

Europe did not come to Asia, but Asia tried to come to Europe.

And in this unholy endeavour, Asia almost succeeded.

We have heard the name of Cyrus before. To the Jews in their captivity, he came as the deliverer, who was to restore the glories of the old temple.

The Greeks had reason to regard him in a somewhat different light.

Cyrus himself was too busy consolidating his empire to march far beyond the plains of Mesopotamia. But eight years after his death, Darius, the son of Hystaspes, came to the throne and there was an end to the peace of Hellas.

The Persian army (after a long period of preparation) crossed the Hellespont and conquered Thrace. That happened in the year 492 B.C. The expedition met with disaster near Mount Athos, a defeat which the Greeks attributed to the timely interference of their great god Zeus.

Two years later, the Persians returned.

At Marathon, they were brought to a standstill.

Twice thereafter they repeated the experiment. But although they defeated and destroyed a Greek force near the Thermopylæ and plundered and burned Athens, they never gained a lasting foothold on the western continent.

It was the first clash between the old civilisation of Asia and the young civilisation of Europe, and Europe remained victorious.

As for the Greeks, the triumph of their arms was followed by a period of unparalleled mental and artistic development.

Within a single century they produced more scientists,

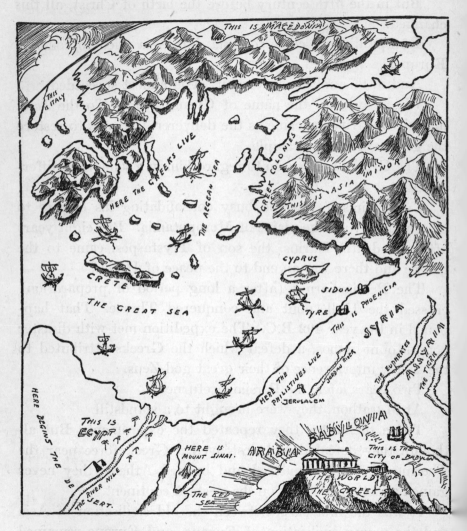

THE WORLD OF THE GREEKS

more sculptors, more mathematicians and physicians and philosophers and poets and dramatists and architects and orators and statesmen and law-givers than have graced the annals of any other country during the last twenty centuries.

Athens became the centre of the entire civilised world.

From far and wide, people travelled to Attica to study the graces of the body and the subtleties of the mind.

Among the crowds which gathered at the foot of the Acropolis there may have been a few Jews.

But we have reason to doubt this.

Jerusalem never heard of the Greek capital, and those things which filled the western mind with eager curiosity were a matter of deep contempt to the serious zealots of Palestine, to whom a knowledge of the will of Jehovah was the beginning and the end of all things.

JERUSALEM STOOD FOR-
GOTTEN

They did not know and they did not care what was happening in the land of the heathen.

They went to their temple.

They listened to the exhortations of their priests in the newly established synagogues. They minded their own business.

And they lived such inconspicuous lives that we know nothing of their history during this period.

Jerusalem had been forgotten. Which is exactly what the pious Jews had prayed for.

JUDAEA, A GREEK PROVINCE

CHAPTER XVIII

A CENTURY LATER A YOUNG MACEDONIAN CHIEFTAIN, TRAINED IN THE BEST GREEK SCHOOLS, DECIDED THAT HE MUST BRING THE BLESSINGS OF HIS ADOPTED CIVILISATION TO ALL MANKIND, AND CONQUERED ASIA. THE COUNTRY OF THE JEWS WAS OVERRUN BY THE ARMIES OF ALEXANDER AND WAS TURNED INTO A MACEDONIAN PROVINCE. AFTER HIS DEATH, ONE OF HIS GENERALS BY THE NAME OF PTOLEMY MADE HIMSELF KING OF EGYPT AND THE PROVINCE OF PALESTINE WAS ADDED TO HIS POSSESSIONS

URING their long residence in Persia, the Jews had made the acquaintance of a new religious system. The Persians were the disciples of a great religious teacher whose name was Zarathustra, or Zoroaster.

Zarathustra regarded all life as a constant struggle between Good and Evil. The lord of wisdom, called Ormuzd, was forever at war with Ahriman, the lord of ignorance and evil.

This was a new idea to most of the Jews.

Thus far they had recognised one single master of all things, who was called Jehovah. When things had gone wrong, when they had been defeated in battle or suffered from sickness, they had invariably attributed such disaster to the lack of devotion of their own people. The idea that sin was the result of the

ZARATHUSTRA

direct interference of a malevolent spirit had never occurred to them. Even the serpent in Paradise in their eyes had been less wicked than Adam and Eve, who wilfully had disobeyed the holy commands.

Under the influence of the doctrines of Zarathustra, the Jews now began to believe in the existence of a spirit who tried to undo all the good accomplished by Jehovah.

They called him Jehovah's adversary, or Satan.

They feared him and they hated him and in the year 331, they were sure that he had come to earth.

A young pagan prince by the name of Alexander destroyed the remnants of the Persian armies in the plains of Nineveh. Darius, the last of the Persian kings, lay murdered by the side of one of his own royal highways.

The mighty empire which had been such a good friend to the Jewish exiles was a thing of the past. Alexander and his Greeks were triumphant. It was a terrible time.

The end of the world seemed to have come.

Only the world never quite ends. There always is a "next chapter" and this now opened for the Jews under very strange aspects.

Alexander of Macedonia was really not a Greek. The true Greeks regarded him as a Macedonian, as a "foreigner." But he himself, convinced of his love for Greek life and civilisation, refused to share this point of view.

As a very young man he made himself the avowed champion of the Greek cause. Thereafter it was his ambition to carry the ideas of Solon and Pericles to the four corners of the world, that all men might be benefited by their noble appeal to human intelligence.

Alexander began his career in 336.

Thirteen years later his dead body lay in the palace which once had been the home of Nebuchadnezzar, and which now was to have been the centre of a new world empire.

In the meantime, the Macedonians had conquered all the land from the river Nile to the river Indus, and they had carried the rudiments of Greek civilisation to all the nations of western Asia and Egypt.

When the armies of the great conqueror began to overrun the plains of Syria, the Jews were faced with a difficult problem.

How should they behave towards this new master? Only

a few years before (in 345) they had dared to revolt against certain atrocities inflicted upon them by Artaxerxes, one of the later Syrian kings.

For a short while, aided by the Egyptian king, Nectabenus, and an auxiliary corps of Greeks, they had been able to maintain themselves. This easy victory had emboldened the Phœnicians to follow their example and begin a revolution of their own. As a result, the city of Sidon had been burned to the ground.

Shortly afterwards, Jerusalem had shared a similar fate. Most of the houses had been destroyed.

The temple had been desecrated by the solemn offering of unclean animals. A large number of people had been exiled to Hyrcania, a province on the southern shore of the Caspian Sea, and the dream of Jewish independence had gone up in the smoke of their pillaged land.

It had been a bitter blow to Jewish pride. They had for years tried to be very careful in their observation of the holy laws. They had felt convinced that their exemplary conduct had gained them the absolute support of Jehovah and that Jerusalem had become an impregnable fortress, defended by his flaming sword.

And now, after Artaxerxes and his terrible mercenaries, this new and unknown menace!

Unfortunately (or fortunately) Alexander did not give them much time for meditation.

Hardly had the news of the destruction of Tyre and the conquest of Samaria reached them, when the Jews were called upon to send money and provisions to the Macedonian king.

With Gaza in the hands of the Greeks and the road towards the sea cut off, there was no hope for escape.

According to a very untrustworthy tradition, Alexander

himself visited Jerusalem and there dreamed his famous dream in which he was urged to be lenient to the people of Judah.

As a matter of fact, the city quietly submitted to the demands of the conqueror and sent him the gold and silver for which he had asked.

In return for this service, the Jews were left unmolested and enjoyed a period of comparative rest while all around them empires and kingdoms came tumbling down into the dust.

A few years later, the city of Alexandria was built at the mouth of the Nile to take the place of the now extinct Phœnician trading stations. The Jews, whose business ability was required by Alexander, were offered homes in the northeastern part of the town. Many of them eagerly availed themselves of this opportunity to leave Jerusalem and migrated to Egypt. And the holy city, deserted by most of its energetic citizens, slowly lost its last characteristics as a national capital.

It then became what it was to remain until to-day—the spiritual centre of the Jewish race, revered by all and visited by few.

The death of Alexander did not change this. The empire of the great Macedonian was divided among his generals.

One of these, by the name of Ptolemy Soter, got Egypt. In the year 320 B.C. he made war upon his former colleague who now ruled Syria, of which the land of Judah had become a province.

He attacked Jerusalem on the Sabbath and the Jews, remembering the fourth commandment, refused to fight and lost their city.

Ptolemy, however, treated the Jews very well. As a result, still more of them moved to Egypt and grass began to grow in the busy streets which once had heard the tread of Solomon's pikemen.

The story of the next hundred years is devoid of all interest. The descendants of Alexander's former lieutenants quarrelled with each other without interruption. Judah often changed hands.

JERUSALEM SURRENDERED ON ONE SABBATH DAY
WITHOUT A FIGHT

Finally, during the second century before the birth of Christ, it became part of the domains of the family of the Seleucids.

In the year 175, Antiochus Epiphanes, the eighth ruler of

the famous Seleucidian dynasty, made himself master of the greater part of western Asia. With this intelligent but intolerant monarch begins a new chapter in the development of a conscious national Jewish life.

When he came to the throne, Judah was rapidly being depopulated.

The ease and charm of Greek city life were beginning to make their influence felt upon the last remaining adherents of Jewish culture.

Very soon the entire Jewish nation would have been absorbed by that strange Hellenistic civilisation which was a perfect blend of all that was good and bad in Asia and Europe.

But Antiochus Epiphanes had not learned the wisdom of leaving well-enough alone. Within a single lifetime, he undid all the work of his predecessors and turned the lukewarm Jews once more into ardent patriots.

REVOLUTION AND INDEPENDENCE

CHAPTER XIX

TWO HUNDRED YEARS LATER, A JEWISH FAMILY BY THE NAME OF THE MACCABEES BEGAN A REVOLUTION AND TRIED TO SET THE COUNTRY FREE FROM FOREIGN INFLUENCE. BUT THE STATE WHICH THE MACCABEES TRIED TO FOUND NEVER FLOURISHED AND WHEN THE ROMANS CONQUERED WESTERN ASIA THEY MADE PALESTINE A SEMI-INDEPENDENT KINGDOM AND APPOINTED ONE OF THEIR POLITICAL HENCHMEN TO BE KING OF THE UNHAPPY LAND

N the old land of Canaan there was not room for two conflicting forms of worship.

A tribe of people who accepted Jehovah as the one absolute and undisputed master of their world could not tolerate the rivalry of an indefinite Zeus who was said (by the heathen, of course) to live on the top of a savage rock somewhere in the land of the Barbarians.

Antiochus Epiphanes failed to recognise this. As a result, he wasted most of his years and all of his energy upon the unsuccessful attempt to turn his obstinate Jewish subjects into unwilling Greeks.

He was (as we have said) the eighth ruler of the family of the Seleucids, and he ought to have known better.

But when he was quite young, he had been sent to Rome as a hostage. He had spent fifteen years of his life in the city which then was the centre of the entire world, both civilised and otherwise.

Rome had grown immensely rich and the old simple virtues of the nation (if they had ever existed, which we sincerely doubt) had made room for the more amusing but less ponderous entertainment provided by a large and important colony of Greeks.

The Greeks in those days played the rôle of the foreigner in modern New York. The typical American builds and buys and sells and plans and looks after the material needs of his continent.

But his orchestras are composed of Germans and Dutchmen and Frenchmen, and his theatres devote much of their time to plays written by Russians and Norwegians, and his restaurants employ French cooks and his pictures are painted for him by half a dozen European nations.

The American is too busy to attend to all those matters, and patiently (if sometimes somewhat contemptuously) he leaves them to people who can do those things better than he can do them himself, but who lack the necessary ambition for a life of political or physical creation.

It was not different in the Rome of the late Republic and the early Empire.

The Roman was first of all a soldier and a law-giver and a statesman and a tax-gatherer and a road-builder and a city planner.

He conquered and administered the entire known world from the dark and foggy coast of Wales to the endless plains of Dacia and the scorching sands of northern Africa.

That was his job.

He did it well and he liked it.

But he was too busy to bother about such details as schools and academies and theatres and churches and candy-stores.

And so Rome soon was swarming with the brilliant but none too reliable progeny of Pericles and Æschylus and Phidias.

They were very plausible orators, those handsome black-haired Greek teachers who talked vaguely of a thousand things of which the honest Roman had never heard, and which therefore had meant nothing in his life.

They could argue about the Gods and in the same breath they could tell a man how to dress. They could explain the mysteries of a new Oriental religion to the women and at the same time give them a few useful hints about the use of cosmetics. They were never at a loss for a jesting word, and altogether, they turned the dull and dour Roman community into something which began to resemble that famed market-place at the foot of the Acropolis.

Young Antiochus, fresh from distant Syria, fell an easy victim to the agreeable lure of the great and wonderful city (like a youngster from a bleak farm in northern Michigan thrown into the heart of New York), and during the fifteen years of his residence, he developed into such an ardent admirer of Greek philosophy and Greek art and Greek music and everything Greek, that Alcibiades himself could not have been more devout in his love for the superior virtues of Athens than this little Asiatic crown-prince.

Of course, as soon as the young man was called back to his

own kingdom, he was bitterly disappointed by what he found at home.

Jerusalem had never regained the old splendour of David and Solomon. Even in those early days, it would have ranked as a backward village when compared to such worldly-wise centres as Corinth and Athens and Rome and Carthage.

It had always been just a little off the beaten track of civilisation. It was regarded by the Babylonians and the Greeks and the Egyptians (if they ever thought of it at all) as a nice but decidedly provincial centre, inhabited by a narrow-minded and uncomfortable set of people who regarded themselves with undue seriousness and showed a very evident contempt for everything foreign.

The period of the great exile had not improved matters. Many of the Jews had preferred to remain in Babylon. Two centuries later, the greater part of the survivors had been lured away to Alexandria and Damascus, and as we have seen in the last chapter, only the most pious had remained and they turned the intellectual life of Jerusalem into a very exclusive theological debating society.

And now Antiochus, fresh from the delights of Rome, talking and thinking of athletic feasts and Dionysian processions, was obliged to spend his days among sombre and morose scholars who were staring themselves blind upon obscure paragraphs of an ancient law for which their ruler and his friends felt and expressed a most profound dislike.

Antiochus rashly decided to become the apostle of the superior Greek culture.

But he was like a man who endeavours to hasten the natural progress of a glacier.

He accomplished very little and caused a great disaster.

At first he tried to make use of the usual dissensions among his Jewish subjects to further his own ends.

There was one small party in the country which was not entirely unfriendly towards the Greek mode of living.

Encouraged by these, Antiochus held athletic games in Jerusalem and sent some money to certain sacrificial festivals which were being held in honour of the Greek gods. This greatly offended his religious subjects, but they had just been caught in a scandal of their own and until that should have been straightened out, nothing could be done.

It happened that two rival candidates were both trying to become High Priest.

One of them, by the name of Menelaus, had offered the King several hundred thousand dollars if he were appointed. It seemed a great deal of money to his neighbours, and truth to tell, it was much more than the poor man could ever hope to pay.

To get hold of the initial instalment, he was obliged to steal the Temple funds. When this was discovered, there was a great outcry against Menelaus, and suddenly every one was in favour of Jason, his opponent, who was not a whit better.

A quarrel followed, which the King of Egypt used as an opportunity to raid the city of Jerusalem, and plunder the Temple (in which by this time very little of any value had been left).

Antiochus appealed to his friends in Rome for help.

But one difficulty leading to another, he decided to visit the capital himself and plead his own cause before the senate.

The great Republic, however, had no interest in the private quarrels of its allies. Provided the tribes of western Asia did not upset the peace of the Empire or interfere with the safety of the great international roads, they could do whatever they wanted. A war in the Orient would probably have interfered with Asiatic commerce. Antiochus and Egypt therefore were both warned to behave, but nothing was done beyond this.

The turbulent young man, once the Egyptians were gone, was free to devote all his time and all his attention to the noble task of eradicating what he was pleased to call his subjects' superstitions.

ONCE MORE JERUSALEM WAS TAKEN

He certainly worked with a will.

He gave curt orders that the old Jewish ceremonial must come to an end. The Sabbath was no longer to be observed and sacrifices to Jehovah must be discontinued as belonging to an old and happily forgotten period of barbarism.

Those books of the Law which could be gathered by his henchmen were burned and the possession of such a book by a private citizen was identical with a self-imposed sentence of death.

The people of Jerusalem, living in an imaginary world of rules and regulations and prophetic visions, were rudely awakened to these brutal and unwelcome facts. They closed the gates of the city and tried to resist the royal commands. But the Syrian general attacked the temple on the Sabbath day. Again the Jews refused to fight and Jerusalem was at the mercy of Antiochus.

Those inhabitants who could be profitably sold as slaves were spared. The others were killed. No mercy was shown to the Temple.

In the month of December of the year 168 before the birth of Christ, a new altar was erected upon the site of the altar of burnt-offering which had been pulled down.

When it was ready, it was dedicated to the worship of Zeus, with a liberal offering of dead pigs.

As the pig was the most offensive animal to the Jew (the touch, yes, the sight of which made him feel uncomfortable and unclean), the insult was without parallel in the history of the world.

The Jews submitted because they had to. A strong garrison, comfortably housed in a newly built fortress, watched over the survivors with relentless eagerness. And woe to the man or the woman who tried to substitute the flesh of an ox for that of a pig which now had to be placed upon the desecrated shrines of their unfortunate city.

Of course, this silly tyranny brought its own punishment, as Antiochus was to experience ere long.

Some six miles away from Jerusalem, well towards the north in the little border village of Modin, lived an old priest called Mattathias together with his five stalwart sons.

In the course of the new dispensation, the messengers of Antiochus came to Modin and demanded that the inhabitants should worship Zeus according to the latest regulation. The people came together in the market-place. They did not quite know what to do. Antiochus was near and Jehovah was far away.

Soon a poor, frightened peasant was found willing to perform the prescribed ritual.

This was too much for Mattathias. He took his sword and he cut down the poor rustic and with a second blow he killed the official who had dared to suggest such a terrible act of sacrilege to the faithful children of Jehovah.

Thereafter, of course, there was only one thing which Mattathias and his sons could do.

They fled.

They crossed the mountains and escaped into the valley of the river Jordan.

THE HOME OF MATTATHIAS

All through the land the people heard the good news. The power of the King had been openly challenged.

Jehovah had found his champion.

And those who still believed in the future of their own race escaped in the dark of night and hastened to the Jordan to join the rebels.

Antiochus at first hoped to quell this riot by resorting to his former strategy.

Once more his troops were told to attack the Jews on the Sabbath day.

But Mattathias was a practical man. He preferred to live by the letter of the law rather than die by it.

He ordered his men to fight and the Syrian army was repulsed.

Mattathias was too old for the hardships of campaigning. He died, but his sons, John, Simon, Judas, Eleazar and Jonathan, succeeded him as leaders of the Jewish patriots and the war continued.

Of these sons, Judas, the third, gained the greatest fame. He was for ever in the thick of the fighting and the people called him Judas Maccabee, or Judas the Hammer, on account of his bold courage. He wisely avoided an open encounter with the well drilled troops of his enemies and inaugurated that strategy of guerilla warfare which twenty centuries later was used so successfully by General Washington.

He never allowed the Syrians a moment of rest.

He attacked their flanks and their rear and surprised them by sudden assaults in the middle of the night. When, however, the Syrians made halt and drew up their regiments in battle formation, Judas and his followers would vanish into the mountains. But as soon as their exasperated opponents had grown tired of waiting and had relaxed their guard, they returned, and killed them off by small detachments.

After several years of this sort of skirmishing, Judas had so skilfully strengthened his position that he could risk an expedition against Jerusalem.

He took the city and the Temple was restored in all its former glory and holiness.

Unfortunately, just when at the height of his fame, Judas was killed in a skirmish and the Jews once more were without leader.

John and Eleazar Maccabee were both dead.

John had been captured in ambush a few years before and had been executed, while Eleazar had accidentally been crushed by a war-elephant.

Jonathan, the youngest, was elected commander-in-chief, but he held his office for only a few weeks. Then he was murdered by a Syrian officer and the leadership fell to Simon, the only surviving son of old Mattathias.

Meanwhile on the other side, Antiochus had died.

His son had succeeded him; but immediately afterwards, Demetrius Soter, a nephew of Antiochus, had returned from Rome, had murdered his cousin, and in the year 162 had proclaimed himself King of the greater part of western Asia.

This was a stroke of luck for the Jews.

Demetrius was beset by so many difficulties at home, that he could not afford the extra burden of a Jewish revolution.

He made peace with Simon Maccabee, who thereafter ruled over Judah as "High Priest and Governor," a somewhat vague dignity which we can best compare to the position held eighteen centuries later by Oliver Cromwell, when he was made "Lord High Protector of England."

The outside world, impressed by the ability of the Maccabees, virtually recognised the new Jewish state as an independent kingdom and accepted the "High Priest and Governor" as the legitimate ruler of a new country.

Then the High Priest set to work to put order into his state. He concluded treaties with his neighbours.

Coins were struck with his picture.

The army recognised him as their chief.

When he and two of his sons were murdered in the year 13? B.C., the Maccabee family was so firmly established that th throne automatically descended to John, called Hyrcanus, wh ruled for almost thirty years and was the recognised sovereig of a small but well organized kingdom in which Jehovah wa worshipped according to the most rigid exactions of the ancier laws and in which no foreigner was tolerated, except for a short visit, connected with important business.

But alas! as soon as a period of comparative peace had been inaugurated, the Jews once more became a victim of those old religious discussions and controversies which in bygone days had done so much harm to their land.

Theoretically, the country was still a theocracy. The High Priest was recognised as the highest official of the state and as Mattathias Maccabee had belonged to a family of hereditary priests, everything was according to the strict interpretation of the law.

But the world was moving rapidly.

The idea of a theocracy had died out long since in all other parts of Asia and Europe and Africa.

It was practically impossible to maintain it in this little land-locked community, surrounded on all sides by people who had willingly adopted the modern Greek and Roman ideas upon the subject of statecraft.

Under pressure from abroad, the Jews were now beginning to be divided into three distinct and separate parties, each one of which believed in a different set of principles of government and worship.

These three groups were to play a very important rôle in the history of the next two centuries. It is therefore necessary to discuss them in some detail.

Most important of all were the Pharisees.

We do not know much about their origin.

The party seems to have been founded during the difficult years preceding the Maccabean revolt. For as soon as Mattathias had raised his brave sword in token of revolt, he found himself backed up by a group of men who were known as the "Hasideans," or "the pious."

When the struggle for independence had been crowned with success, and when the first religious enthusiasm was beginning to wane, the Hasideans, under the new name of the "Pharisees," came to the front and maintained themselves until the end of the independent kingdom.

Even the fury of Titus, the Emperor, could not subdue their ardour and many of them have survived until this very day, although they are no longer restricted to the old Jewish faith.

The Pharisees were exactly what the Hebrew name implied. They were the "separated people." They were different from the rest of the people on account of their fanatical allegiance to the letter of the law.

They knew the ancient books of Moses by heart. Every word, almost every letter, suggested something to them.

They lived in a world of strange ordinances and even more incomprehensible taboos. There were a few things which they must do and a thousand things which they must omit doing.

They and only they were the true followers of almighty Jehovah. While the rest of humanity was condemned to eternal perdition, the Pharisees, by their painstaking obedience to every comma and every exclamation mark in the law, were sure to enter the kingdom of Heaven.

Generation after generation, they spent the valuable hours of the day and of the night, poring over the ancient scrolls, explaining, annotating, expounding, interpreting and elucidating obscure and totally irrelevant details of some half forgotten sentence in a dark chapter of Exodus.

They made a virtue of great public humility.

But in their heart of hearts, they were inordinately proud of those qualities which distinguished them (in their own eyes) from all other men and women, for whom, to speak the truth, they felt only the deepest contempt.

At first the Pharisees were undoubtedly inspired by very high motives and an exalted and unselfish patriotism, based upon an invincible faith in the power of their God.

But as time went by, they developed more and more into a meddlesome sect which would tolerate no dissension from the old-fashioned prejudices and superstitions.

Deliberately they turned their backs upon the future and fastened their eyes firmly upon the bygone glory of the Mosaic era.

They hated everything that was foreign.

They detested all innovations and decried all reformers as enemies of the state.

And when the greatest of all prophets spoke to them of a kindly and loving God and preached the common brotherhood of all men, the Pharisees hurled themselves against their enemy with such violence that they upset and wrecked the very nation which they had helped to found only a short time before.

Next to the Pharisees in power, but not quite so numerous, were the Sadducees.

The Sadducees (who probably derived their name from a priest called Zadok) were much more tolerant than the Pharisees. Their tolerance, however, was not based upon conviction but upon indifference.

They belonged to the small class of well-educated Jews. They had travelled. They had seen other lands and other people, and while they were faithful in their worship of Jehovah, they acknowledged that much might be said for the noble doctrines of life and death which were preached by an increasing number of Greek philosophers.

They were not much interested in the world of the Pharisees, which was being increasingly populated with devils and angels and other queer imaginary creatures, brought to Palestine by travellers from the east.

They accepted life as they found it and tried to live an honourable existence without placing too much faith in the promise of a future reward.

Indeed, when the Pharisees tried to argue with them on this point, they were apt to ask for some corroborating testimony in one of the ancient books, and none was forthcoming, as none was given in those venerable scrolls.

In short, the Sadducees, much more than the Pharisees, were in daily contact with the age in which they happened to live.

Consciously or unconsciously they had absorbed the wisdom of their great Greek neighbours.

They recognised the importance of one God, be he called Jehovah or Zeus.

But they did not feel that so great a power could be interested in the petty details of human existence. Hence, all the purely legalistic considerations of the Pharisees appeared to them to be a sheer waste of time and energy.

They held it to be more important to live bravely and nobly than to flee from life and concentrate upon the salvation of one's own soul behind the safely sheltering walls of a scholastic study.

They looked forward, rather than backward, and expressed scant regrets at the illusory virtues of the past ages.

Gradually they lost all interest in purely religious matters and in a very practical fashion devoted themselves to politics.

Years afterwards, when the Pharisees insisted upon the death of Jesus on account of his religious heresies, the Sadducees made common cause with them and denounced the

Nazarene prophet because he seemed to be a menace to the established law and order.

They were not interested in the doctrines of Jesus.

But they feared the political consequences of his ideas and therefore were in favour of his execution.

They arrived at their conclusions in a different way from the Pharisees.

But their tolerance was as sterile and as narrow-minded as the avowed intolerance of their opponents and they bore an equal share in the final drama of Golgotha which will be told in one of the last chapters of this book.

There remains one other party which we must mention for the sake of historical accuracy. It plays, however, no great rôle in our story.

Many of the Jews lived in endless fear of what we might call unconscious sin.

Their laws were so complicated that no one could ever hope to obey every jot and tittle of the ancient books.

But such disobedience (however involuntary) was a terrible sin in the eyes of Jehovah, who himself was the incarnation of the law, and would be punished almost as severely as a breach of one of the Ten Commandments.

To escape this difficulty, the Essenes, or Holy Men, deliberately abstained from what we might call all "acts of living."

They did nothing at all.

They fled into the wilderness, far away from all strife, and held themselves aloof from their fellow men.

For the sake of greater protection, however, they often lived in small colonies.

They did not believe in private property. What belonged to one, belonged to all. With the exception of his clothes and his bed and the bowl in which he carried his food from the common kitchen, no Essene had anything that he could call his own.

Part of each day the members of those pious settlements were expected to give to the tilling of the few poor corn fields that provided them with food.

THE ESSENES LIVED IN THE WILDERNESS

The rest of the time they could spend perusing the holy scriptures and torturing their unworthy souls with the study of dark and dismal points in the books of long-forgotten prophets.

It was not a very attractive programme to most people and the number of the Essenes remained small compared to that of the Pharisees and Sadducees.

They were never seen in the streets of the cities.

They did not engage in business, and they avoided all contact with political life.

They were happy because they knew that they were saving their own souls, but they did remarkably little for their neighbours and exercised no direct influence upon the life of their nation.

Indirectly, however, they played a great rôle.

For when their austere asceticism was combined with the practical eagerness of the Pharisees (as it was in the case of John the Baptist) they could influence large numbers of people and had to be reckoned with very seriously as a power in the state.

From this short explanation, the reader will understand that it was no easy task to rule this country where the balance of power was held by several conflicting groups of religious fanatics.

The Maccabees did their best, under very trying circumstances.

During the first hundred years, they succeeded fairly well.

But with John Hyrcanus, the last of the great leaders of this dynasty came to the throne.

His unworthy son, Aristobulus, the "Friend of the Greeks," was entirely incompetent, and with him the period of decline began.

It greatly angered him that his Jewish subjects would not let him assume the title of King, although he really held all the powers usually associated with that name.

To the Pharisees, however, with their love for detail and their respect for tradition, such small distinctions were matters of the gravest importance.

The Jews had accepted the rule of the Judges because the Judges had always most carefully abstained from claiming the royal title.

Now a man who was not even a descendant of David insisted that he be given a title which was only very occasionally used for Jehovah himself.

The Pharisees were in a fury, and Aristobulus, looking around for some support, foolishly enough made common cause with their enemies.

To make the situation still more complicated, this incident was followed by one of those family quarrels which were so common in those early days.

The mother and the brothers of the new "King" took the side of his enemies.

It came to open warfare.

The mother was killed.

A little later, through the mistake of an over-zealous officer, Antigonus, the favourite brother of Aristobulus, was stabbed to death.

Trying to make his subjects forget these unpleasant incidents by some excitement of a different nature, Aristobulus next began a campaign against his powerful northern neighbours.

He got hold of the greater part of the old Kingdom of Israel, which had been extinct these last four centuries. He did not revive the name Israel, but called the conquered land Galilee, after one of the districts in the northern hills.

What future plans Aristobulus had, we do not know, for he was taken sick and died after a reign of only one year.

He was succeeded by his brother, Alexander Jannæus, the third son of John Hyrcanus.

This young man had been in exile ever since he had been old enough to attract the attention of his father, who thoroughly detested him. He ruled for almost thirty years and when he died, the entire kingdom had been wasted away.

Like Aristobulus, the young prince made the fatal mistake of taking sides in the quarrels between the two religious parties.

And following the example of his ancestors, he tried to extend his territories at the expense of his neighbours.

Although he was as unsuccessful abroad as he was at home, he never learned from experience.

His wife, Alexandra, was no better. She became a tool of the Pharisees and the actual government of the country was in the hands of a small kitchen cabinet of clever leaders who ruled Judah and Galilee for the benefit of their own friends.

That they might the better maintain their hold upon the country, the Pharisees encouraged Alexandra to appoint Hyrcanus, her elder son and one of their most tractable pupils, High Priest.

This was not at all to the liking of Aristobulus, the younger boy, who had been called after his uncle and who had inherited many of the less desirable qualities of that defunct and unregretted relative.

When the Pharisees, carried away by their own success, began a reign of terror and tried to execute the Sadducean leaders, Aristobulus proclaimed himself the defender of the Sadducean cause.

The Sanhedrin, or Council, continued to be dominated by the Pharisees, but Aristobulus and the Sadducees got hold of several very important country towns and soon they were strong enough to threaten the safety of Jerusalem.

At this moment Alexandra died.

Her sons were left with a depleted treasury and a country split wide open by civil strife.

There was nothing new in the situation.

This turbulent little corner of the world had forever been in a turmoil of some sort.

But times and circumstances, as we have said before, had changed.

A thousand or five hundred years before, no one had cared what those Semitic tribes were doing, provided they stayed within their own boundaries.

But the greater part of western Asia was now in the hands of the Romans, who had inherited the empire of Alexander.

They were mainly interested in a steady and uninterrupted flow of taxes.

As most revenue in that part of Asia was derived from trade, they insisted upon that outward semblance of peace and orderliness without which no credit (and therefore no commerce) was possible.

A certain king of Pontus, in Asia Minor, by the name of Mithridates, had just tried to interfere with the Roman policy. After a long and disastrous war, he had been forced to commit suicide and his empire had been added to the Republic.

Oblivious of the fate of this rich and powerful tyrant, Hyrcanus and Aristobulus continued to quarrel and caused such a disturbance that Rome heard about it.

The general commanding the troops in the east was ordered to proceed to Jerusalem and report upon conditions. When he reached the city, Aristobulus and his friends were inside the temple and Hyrcanus with his followers was outside, laying a formal siege to the sacred building, which was really a very strong fortress.

As soon as the Romans appeared upon the scene, both princes asked for their support.

The Roman general, with that cold understanding of complicated issues so characteristic of his race, decided that it would be much easier to defeat Hyrcanus, whose troops were out in the open, than Aristobulus, who was hiding behind the high walls of a steep rock.

He drove away Hyrcanus, and by this simple process, Aristobulus became ruler of the land of Judah and of Galilee.

But not for long.

No one less than famous Pompey was coming east and Hyrcanus hastened to meet him that he might plead his cause in person.

Aristobulus no sooner heard of this than he too drove post-haste to the Roman camp to tell his side of the story and recommend himself as the most suitable (because the most obedient) candidate for whatever government the Romans intended to establish in his part of the world.

But ere Pompey fully realised what all these arguments meant, there was a blast of trumpets.

A third delegation had arrived.

The Pharisees had come to explain to Pompey that the Jewish people were as heartily tired of one prince as of the other and wished to return to the old form of a pure theocracy on a strictly Pharisaical basis.

Pompey, not caring what happened as long as caravans could safely pass from Damascus to Alexandria, listened boredly to all three, and then refused to commit himself.

He said that he would give a definite answer as soon as he returned from an expedition against certain Arab tribes who were beginning to make trouble in those districts which formerly had belonged to the Assyrian Empire.

Meanwhile, all three parties must keep the peace and wait.

Even then, the Jews did not fully understand the hopelessness of their position. For the moment Aristobulus was back in his capital, he behaved as if he were really the king of all Judah and could rule his domains as if there were not a single Roman soldier in all the world.

This lasted just as long as Pompey remained in the east.

But immediately after his victory over the Arabs, he returned westward and asked why his wishes had been disregarded in this flagrant manner.

Aristobulus, badly advised, then took another fatal step.

He tried to play the role of his great-great-grandfather.

He retired to the Temple, cut down the bridge which connected the fortress with the rest of the city and openly hoisted the flag of revolt.

It was a most unequal fight. Hyrcanus, the elder brother, went over to the enemy and the siege of the Temple began, according to the best and the most efficient methods of that day.

It lasted three months.

Inside the holy edifice, the starving garrison suffered great privations.

Their despair, however, gave them added courage.

Betrayed by Hyrcanus, they felt themselves to be the defenders of the holy cause of Jehovah and that of Jewish independence.

Deserters told Pompey of this outburst of religious fanaticism.

Remembering what the Syrians had done a few generations before, he ordered a general attack to be made on the Sabbath day.

It was the month of June of the year 63 before the birth of Christ.

The Roman legions stormed the Jewish citadel and captured the Temple together with all its defenders.

According to tradition, more than twelve thousand soldiers were killed on that day.

The captive officers were decapitated, while Aristobulus and his wife and children were taken to Rome that they might march in the triumphal procession of the Roman general

Afterwards, however, they were allowed to settle peacefully in one of the suburbs of Rome, where they laid the foundations for that Jewish colony which was to play such an important part in the imperial history of western Europe in the days of Paul and Peter.

Once the fighting was over, the Romans, with that wise moderation which characterised them until the end of their history, refrained from plundering the Temple and allowed its continued use as a place of worship. But Pompey got scant gratitude for this act of generosity.

Out of sheer curiosity and totally ignorant of the prejudices of his former enemies, Pompey and his staff in the course of a tour of inspection happened to wander into the Holy of Holies.

It proved to be a small stone room, entirely bare and empty.

As soon as the Romans had convinced themselves that this sacred chamber contained nothing of interest, they left it.

But to the Jews, this visit, however short, on the part of unclean foreigners, meant a sacrilege which must bring forth a terrible revenge on the part of Jehovah.

They never forgave Pompey.

Whatever he tried to do for his newly acquired subjects was as naught compared to this one unconscious insult to their religious pride.

Pompey, of course, never knew what he had done.

From his point of view, he had been most unusually lenient.

He had allowed Hyrcanus to return to Jerusalem and he had even appointed him High Priest to pacify the Pharisees. As a final act of grace, he had given him the rank of Ethnarch. This was a rather hazy title sometimes bestowed upon former independent sovereigns. It carried little power but flattered the national pride of the conquered race. The Romans were very generous with this titular distinction, provided the candidate followed their instructions and behaved with the necessary discretion.

If Hyrcanus had been a capable man, even then something might have been saved out of the ruin of his country.

But the Ethnarch was wholly incompetent and soon lost what little prestige he still enjoyed.

Some thirty years before, when Alexander Jannæus, the father of Hyrcanus and Aristobulus, was king, he had appointed a certain Antipater to be governor of the district of Edom or Idumæa, situated south of Jerusalem.

The original Antipater loved to fish in that troubled water which according to the old proverb is apt to provide a clever and unscrupulous sportsman with a liberal catch.

He pretended to be a faithful friend of Hyrcanus and often whispered discreet words of advice into his ear.

But such bits of gratuitous council were inevitably followed by further complications and by additional difficulties in the land of Judah.

So intelligently did Antipater play his game that he soon found himself basking right royally in the pleasant sun of Roman favour.

When civil war broke out in Rome and when the armies of Pompey were pitched against those of his rival, Cæsar, Antipater waited to see who should be the victor.

As soon as Pompey had been defeated on the field of Pharsalia in the year 48 before the birth of Christ, the Idumæan ruler made common cause with Cæsar.

In return for this loyal support, Cæsar bestowed upon Antipater the dignity of a Roman citizen and tacitly allowed him to become the power behind the tottering throne of the country which was now called Judæa.

The new "citizen" made good use of his favoured position. He strengthened his hold upon the people.

His Jewish subjects were given a greater degree of liberty than they had enjoyed for a long time.

They were exempted from service in the Roman armies and were allowed to rebuild the walls of Jerusalem.

They were no longer forced to pay the small tribute which Pompey had exacted from them.

And they regained almost complete judicial and religious independence.

But Antipater fared no better at the hands of the Pharisees than Pompey had done. They accused him of being a foreigner and an upstart and a usurper who had no right to the throne of David.

They talked of making Antigonus, the son of Aristobulus and the grandson of Alexander Jannæus, their king. Once more they behaved as if they, and not the Romans, were the masters of western Asia.

In this instance it did not matter very much, for Antipater was easily their superior both in his shrewdness and in his complete lack of scruples.

He had certain ambitious plans for his own dynasty and felt that the hour had come to dispose of the house of Maccabee.

He moved slowly, but never lost sight of his ultimate purpose.

Just when everything was ready, he was unfortunately poisoned by a friend of Hyrcanus.

But his son Herod continued the work along the lines laid down by his father and with equal success.

Antigonus was foolishly encouraged to begin a revolution against the Roman government.

This ill-timed uprising ended in the disaster which Herod had anticipated.

Antigonus with a few soldiers fled to the Temple and after a long siege which greatly embittered the Romans he was forced to surrender.

Antigonus begged that his life be spared.

The Romans, however, refused to show mercy upon this occasion.

Hardly a year had gone by without some sort of disturbance in their Judæan province.

They had granted the Jews all sorts of privileges, and the Jews in return had repaid them with a succession of very costly rebellions.

This time they were resolved to make an example which should be remembered until the end of time.

Antigonus was treated like an ordinary criminal.

He was publicly whipped and thereupon decapitated.

The Maccabee dynasty came to an end and Herod received the throne.

He married Mariamne, the granddaughter of Hyrcanus, and thereby established a vague relationship with the legitimate rulers of Judæa.

In this way, Herod, by the grace of the Roman legions, became king of part of the Jews.

It was the thirty-seventh year before the beginning of our era, and much was wrong with the world.

THE BIRTH OF JESUS

CHAPTER XX

NOW IT HAPPENED DURING THE REIGN OF ONE OF THOSE KINGS, BY THE NAME OF HEROD, THAT MARY, THE WIFE OF JOSEPH THE CARPENTER FROM NAZARETH, GAVE BIRTH TO A SON WHO WAS CALLED JOSHUA BY HIS OWN PEOPLE AND JESUS BY HIS GREEK NEIGHBOURS

N the year 117, Tacitus, the Roman historian, tried to account for the persecutions of a new sect which had just taken place throughout the Empire.

He was no friend of Nero.

All the same, he did his best to find some excuse for this particular outrage.

"The Emperor," so he wrote, "has inflicted cruel tortures upon certain men and women who are hated for their crimes and who are called 'Christians' by the mob. The particular Christ from whom they have taken their name was put to death under the Emperor Tiberius by a certain Pontius Pilate, who happened to be procurator of Judæa, a distant province in Asia. Although repressed for a while, his terrible and detestable superstition has broken out again, not only in Judæa, the ground of the evil, but also in Rome, to which city, unfortunately, all the infamies and irregularities of the world tend to gravitate."

Tacitus mentioned the whole matter in that detached way in which an English journalist of the year 1776 might have referred to certain insignificant revolutionary outbreaks which had occurred in a distant colony of the Empire but which were not supposed to be of a very serious nature.

The Roman did not know exactly who those "Christians" of whom he wrote so contemptuously were or who that Christ was from whom "they had taken their name."

He did not know and he did not care.

There always was trouble of some sort in a state as big and as complicated as the Roman Empire and the Jews who were to be found in most of the larger cities were always quarrelling among each other and invariably exasperated the magistrate to whom they carried their disputes by their faithful tenacity to certain incomprehensible laws.

The Christ in question had probably been a preacher in some obscure little synagogue in Galilee or Judæa.

Of course there was more than a probability that Nero had been a bit too severe.

On the other hand, it was better not to be too lenient in such matters. And there the question rested, as far as Tacitus was concerned.

He never mentioned the offending sect again.

His interest was entirely academic and such as we ourselves might take in the trouble between the Canadian Mounted Police and those strange Russian sects which inhabit the western portion of that vast empire of forests and grain fields.

The information which other writers of that period throw upon the same subject leaves us little wiser.

Josephus, a Jew, who in the year 80 of our era published a detailed history of his country, mentions Pontius Pilate and John the Baptist, but we do not find the name of Jesus in the original version of his work.

Justus of Tiberias, who wrote at the same time as Josephus, had apparently never heard of Jesus, although he was thoroughly familiar with the Jewish history of the first two centuries.

There is complete silence on the part of all contemporary historians and we depend for our knowledge entirely upon the first four books of the New Testament, which are called the four "gospels," an old English word which meant "good tidings."

JOSEPHUS

Like the book of Daniel and the Psalms of David, and many other chapters of the Old Testament, the Gospels bear fictitious names.

They are called after the apostles Matthew, Mark, Luke and John, but it seems very unlikely that the original disciples had anything to do with those famous literary compositions.

The subject is still shrouded in deep mystery. For many centuries it has been a favourite subject for scholastic dispute, but as no form of altercation seems more futile and unprofitable than that connected with theological subjects, we shall refrain from giving a definite opinion, but shall in a few words try to explain why this topic has given rise to so much discussion.

Of course, to the people of the modern world, who from childhood on are obliged to wade through a veritable mire of printed wood-pulp (newspapers, books, time-tables, menus, telephone directories, passports, telegrams, letters, income tax blanks, and what not), it seems incredible that we should not possess a single written scrap of contemporary evidence for the life and the death of Jesus.

But historically speaking, there is nothing very unusual or startling in this.

The famous songs of Homer were not written down until centuries after the disappearance of those travelling bards who used to wander from village to village and recite the glories of Hector and Achilles to admiring groups of young Greeks.

In those early days, when people depended for their information upon the spoken word, they developed very accurate memories. Stories were transmitted from father to son just as carefully as they are now handed over to posterity by means of the printed word.

Furthermore, we must not forget that Jesus, once he had refused to assume the rôle of a Jewish national leader (a fond hope of many of his own people), was obliged to associate almost exclusively with very poor and simple fisherfolk and inn-keepers, none of whom were expert editors, and most of whom were undoubtedly ignorant of the art of writing.

And finally, once he had been crucified, it seemed a sheer waste of time to give an account of his life or his teaching.

The disciples of Jesus firmly believed that the end of the world was near at hand. While preparing for the final judgment, they did not care to compose books which soon would be destroyed by the fire from Heaven.

As the years went by, however, and it became more and more certain that the world was going to continue upon its tranquil voyage through space for many centuries to come, efforts were made to gather the memoirs of those who had known Jesus personally and who had heard him speak and who had been the companions of his last years.

Many of these were undoubtedly still alive and they told all they knew. Gradually torn bits of the prophet's famous sermons which they remembered were put together until they made a book.

Next the parables were retold and gathered into another volume.

Old men and old women in Nazareth were interviewed.

In Jerusalem, several people who had gone out to Golgotha to witness the execution gave an account of the last hours and the agony of Jesus.

Soon there was quite a literature upon the subject.

It increased as the demand for such books grew more popular. Within a very short time, the material assumed unwieldy proportions.

If you want a modern example, take the case of Abraham Lincoln. There is a steady outpouring of volumes, big and little, devoted to the life and death of the greatest of our American prophets. It is impossible for the average person to read all these books. Even if he knew where to find them all, he would hardly be able to choose what was really essential.

Therefore, every now and then, some scholar who has devoted his life to this subject sifts all the evidence and gives the public a short and concise "Life of Lincoln" which throws light upon the important issues but leaves out what would not really interest those who are not professional historians.

That is exactly what the authors of the four gospels did with the life of Jesus. Each one, according to his own tastes and ability, retold the story of the suffering and the triumph of his Master in his own words.

No one can state with certainty who Matthew was or when

he lived. But from the way in which he gives us his good tidings, we know him as a simple fellow who loved the homely stories which Jesus used to tell to the peasants of Galilee and who therefore by preference dwelt upon the subject of parables and sermons.

Far different was John. He must have been a learned if somewhat dull professor, thoroughly familiar with the most modern doctrines then being taught in the academies of Alexandria, and giving to his "Life of Jesus" a dignified theological turn which is entirely lacking in the other three gospels.

Luke, after whom the third gospel is called, was a doctor, according to tradition.

He well may have been a schoolmaster.

He stated with great solemnity that he had read all the other lives of Christ which were then in circulation, but that he did not think any of them quite satisfactory. He therefore had decided to write a book of his own.

He expected to tell his readers all that was already known, and to add a few details which had never been published before. True to his promise he bestowed much time and attention upon details which had escaped Matthew and John, and by his pains-taking research, rendered us all a great service.

As for Mark, he was (and still is) a subject for the special attention of all Biblical scholars.

Against the hazy background of the last days of Jesus, we get frequent glimpses of a bright and intelligent young man who played a definite although very minor rôle in the tragedy of Golgotha.

Sometimes we see him running errands for Jesus.

On the night of the last supper he comes rushing into the garden of Gethsemane to warn the Prophet that the soldiers of the Council are coming to arrest him.

We hear of him again as the secretary and the travelling companion of Paul and of Peter.

But we never know quite who he was or what he actually did or in what relation he stood to Jesus himself.

The gospel which bears his name makes the matter more complicated. It seems to be just the sort of work which just that sort of young man might have done exceedingly well. It shows a personal familiarity with many events. It omits a great deal which is given in the other gospels, but when it stops to describe a certain event with some detail, the story becomes at once a living document and is full of picturesque little anecdotes.

This intimate and personal touch has often been used as absolute proof that in this instance at least we have to do with the work of a man who had first-hand knowledge of his subject.

But alas! the gospel of Mark, like all the others, has certain literary characteristics which place it definitely in the second century and make it the work of one of the grandchildren of the original Mark and Matthew and John.

The complete absence of all contemporary evidence has always been a strong argument in the hands of those who claim that all our efforts to re-create the life of Jesus upon an historical basis must be futile and must remain so until further evidence (which may lie buried almost anywhere) shall have given us the connecting link between the first half of the first and the latter half of the second century.

Personally, however, we cannot share this opinion.

While it is undoubtedly true that the actual authors of the Gospels, as we have them to-day, had not personally known Jesus, it is equally evident to any one who has seriously studied those documents that they derive their common information from a number of texts which were current in the year 200 but which have been lost since then.

Such gaps are quite common in early European and American and Asiatic history. Even the famous book of nature is apt to indulge in an occasional jump of a couple of million years, during which period we are allowed to use our imagination as best pleases our fancy, or our scientific convictions.

In the present case, however, we are not obliged to deal with vague prehistoric figures, but with a personality of such extraordinary charm and such definite strength, that it has outlived everything else that existed twenty centuries ago.

Besides, the direct documentary evidence which is so desirable in the historical laboratory seems utterly superfluous when we speak or write of Jesus. The very literature written around the figure of the prophet of Nazareth will bear us out.

The number of books which deal with him and his work written during the last two thousand years cannot be counted. They represent every language, every dialect and every conceivable point of view.

With equal zeal they either prove or they disprove his existence.

They affirm or question the authority and the reliability of the evidence presented to us by the gospels.

They doubt or reverently uphold the absolute trustworthiness of the letters written by the apostles.

But that is not all.

Every single word of the New Testament has been most carefully submitted to the acid tests of philological and chronological and dogmatic criticism.

Wars have been fought and countries have been devastated and whole nations have been eradicated because two eminent expounders of the Scriptures happened to disagree upon som difficult point in the Apocalypse or the Acts which had nothing at all to do with the ideals of Jesus. Mighty churches have been built to commemorate certain facts which never took place and terrific assaults have been made upon certain events which are of undeniable truth.

Christ has been preached to us as the Son of God and he has been denounced (sometimes with incredible violence and persistency) as an impostor.

Patient archæologists have dug deep into the folklore of a thousand tribes to explain the mystery of the Man who became a God.

The sublime, the ridiculous and the obscene have been dragged into the discussion with a wealth of texts and sources and clauses and paragraphs which seemed absolutely irrefutable.

And it has made no difference.

Perhaps the early disciples knew best.

They did not write, they did not argue, and they did not reason overmuch.

They gratefully accepted what was given to them and they left the rest to faith.

Out of this loving inheritance, we must try to reconstruct our story.

*　　　*　　　*　　　*　　　*

Herod was King, and a bad King he was.

His throne stood based upon murder and deceit.

He knew no principles, but he had an ambition.

The memory of great Alexander was still alive in western Asia.

What a little Macedonian prince had done, three hundred years before, a more powerful Jewish king might do to-day.

And so Herod played a game of cold and brutal calculation

and worked for the greater glory of the house of Antipater and cared for neither man nor God, with the sole exception of that Roman governor by whose grace he was allowed to hold his nefarious throne.

A thousand years before, such despotism might have gone unchallenged.

But much had changed in this world, as Herod was to experience before the hour of his miserable death.

HEROD

The Romans had definitely established order in the lands around the Mediterranean Sea. At the same time, the Greeks had charted the unknown vastness of the soul and in their scientific pursuits had endeavoured to reach a logical conclusion about the nature of Good and Evil.

Their language (greatly simplified for the convenience of those who lived abroad) had become the tongue of civilised society in every country.

Even the Jews, with their violent prejudice against everything foreign, fell victim to the spell of the handy Greek alphabet.

Although the authors of the four gospels were without exception of Jewish parentage, they wrote their books in Greek and not in that Aramaic vernacular which in turn had taken the place of the old Hebrew ever since the return from the Babylonian exile.

To counteract the influence of Rome as the acknowledged centre of the universe, the Greeks of the Hellenistic era had concentrated their forces in a rival city, called Alexandria after the inevitable Macedonian hero. It was situated at the mouth of the river Nile and not far removed from that famous centre of Egyptian civilisation which had been dead for many centuries before Jesus was born.

The Greeks, brilliant, unsteady, but of insatiable curiosity, had carefully examined and clarified all human knowledge.

Furthermore, they had passed through every possible experience of success and failure.

They could remember their golden age when, single-handed, their little cities had defeated the hordes of the mighty Persian kings and had saved Europe from foreign invasion.

They could recall (how could they help it?) other days when, through their own selfishness

NAZARETH

and greed, their country had fallen an easy prey to the better organised power of Rome.

But once deprived of their political independence, the Greeks had gained even greater fame as the teachers of those same Romans who had conquered them only a few years before.

And having tasted of all the joys of living, their wise men had come to the conclusion (with which we are already familiar from the author of that book called "Ecclesiastes") that all is Vanity and that no life can ever be complete without that spiritual contentment which is not based upon a cellar full of gold or an attic replete with the riches of the Indies.

The Greeks, who based all their conclusions upon strict

scientific reasoning, did not take much stock in vague predictions about the future.

They called their intellectual leaders philosophers or "friends of wisdom" rather than prophets, as was the common use among the Jews.

There was, however, one great point of similarity between

JOSEPH

such men as Socrates in Athens and the Unknown Prophet in Babylon.

They both strove to do whatever was right according to the inner conviction of their own souls without regard to the prejudices and the gossip of their fellow-townsmen.

And they earnestly tried to teach their own ideas about righteousness to their neighbours, that the world in which they found themselves might become a more humane and reasonable place of abode.

Some of them, like the Cynics, were as severe in their principles as those Essenes who dwelled in the mountains of Judæa.

Others, called the Epicureans and the Stoics, were more worldly. They taught their doctrines in the palace of the Emperor and were often used as private tutors to the wealthy young men of Rome.

But all of them shared one common conviction. They knew that happiness was entirely a matter of an inner conviction and not of outward circumstances.

Under the influence of these new doctrines, the old Greek and Roman gods were rapidly losing their hold on the masses

First of all, the upper classes deserted the ancient temples.

Men like Cæsar or Pompey still went through all the forms prescribed by the worship of Jupiter, but they regarded the story about a Mighty Thunderer, enthroned high above the clouds of Mount Olympus, as a fairy tale which might impress little children and the uneducated masses of the suburbs on the

ZACHARIAS

other side of the Tiber. But that such fables should be taken seriously by men who had been trained to use their brains, that seemed simply preposterous.

Of course, no society has ever been entirely composed of intelligent and high-thinking people. From the beginning of its history, Rome had been full of war-profiteers. As the capital of the world for more than three centuries, it had attracted that strange international society which inevitably drifts towards such cities as New York or London or Paris, where social success is comparatively easy and where no embarrassing questions are asked about one's antecedents.

The conquest of so much new land in Europe and western Asia had turned many a poor Roman into a rich country squire.

His sons and daughters, living on the revenue of the parental estates, had joined the ranks of that smart society which regarded religion as a question of the latest fashion. They found little to attract them in the simple and unostentatious doctrines of the Epicureans and the Stoics (not to speak of such unwashed monomaniacs as Diogenes, who insisted upon

living in an old barrel for the sake of greater convenience).
They demanded something a little more picturesque and perhaps not quite so serious. Something that should appeal to
the imagination without interfering to any considerable extent
with the agreeable demands of daily life.

Their wish was fulfilled. Impostors and visionaries and
swindlers and medicasters from all over the world, from Egypt

MARY

and from Asia Minor and from
Mesopotamia, hastened to Rome
and in return for a certain pe-
cuniary remuneration preached
short-cuts to happiness and salvation which would have earned
them millions in our own en-
lightened days.

They called their spiritual
quackeries by the dignified name
of "mysteries."

They knew that most men
(and most women) dearly love to be the owners of some secret
which they are not obliged to share with their neighbours.

A Stoic would bluntly state that his rules of life could
make all the people of this world, both rich and poor, white,
yellow or black, happy and contented and virtuous.

The shrewd possessors of the invisible knowledge upon
which the wonderful Oriental mysteries were based never made
that mistake.

They were very exclusive.

They appealed only to small groups and sold their wares
dearly.

They did not preach under the high dome of Heaven, which
was free to all. They withdrew to a badly lighted little room,

filled with the smell of incense and with strange pictures. There they performed that wonderful hocus-pocus which never fails to impress the half-educated.

Undoubtedly a few of those new missionaries were honest. They believed in their own visions and actually thought that they heard those voices which spoke to them in the dark and which brought them messages from the other world. But the great majority was composed of clever adventurers who fooled their public because that public insisted upon being fooled and paid well for the privilege.

ON THE WAY TO BETH-LEHEM

For quite a long time they were very successful. The competition in mysteries was almost as eager as that among the palmists and horoscope professors of our modern cities. Then there was a sudden slump. The public was growing tired of this novelty, and its indifference was the result of certain outward changes which were taking place in the Empire.

Usually the happiness of a people is in inverse ratio to their riches. When they grow rich and prosperous beyond a certain definite point, they begin to lose interest in those simple pleasures without which life becomes a vast span of boredom which stretches from the cradle to the grave.

The Empire was perhaps the best example of this historical axiom. To a rapidly increasing number of Romans, existence became a burden. They had eaten too much and drunk too much and enjoyed too many pleasures to get the slightest satisfaction out of normal human experiences. They asked for a solution of their problems and they received no answer.

The old Gods failed them.

The dispensers of the new Truth failed them.

The learned doctors connected with the worship of Isis and Mithras and Bacchus failed them.

Nothing was left but despair.

And then Jesus was born.

* * * * * * *

It was the fourth year before the beginning of our era.

THE NATIVITY

On the sloping hillside of a quiet valley in Galilee stood the village of Nazareth.

There lived Joseph the carpenter and his wife Mary.

They were not rich, and they were not poor.

They were just like all their neighbours.

They worked hard and they told their children that the world expected something of them as both their parents were descended from King David, who, as they all knew, was a great-great-grandson of the gentle Ruth, whose story was well known to all Jewish boys and girls.

Joseph was a simple man who had never been outside of his own country, but Mary had once spent quite a long time in that big city called Jerusalem.

This had happened while she was still engaged to Joseph.

Mary had a cousin, by the name of Elisabeth, who had been married to a certain Zacharias, a priest connected with the service of the Temple.

Both Zacharias and Elisabeth were old folk and they were quite sad because they never had had any children.

But behold one day Mary heard from Elisabeth. There was to be a baby in the family, and could Mary come and take care of her kinswoman? for there was a lot of work to be done and Elisabeth needed a little attention.

THE SHEPHERDS

Mary went to Juttah, the suburb of Jerusalem in which her people lived, and stayed there until her little cousin John lay safely tucked away in his cradle.

Then she returned to Nazareth where she was to marry Joseph.

But ere long she had been called upon to undertake another journey.

In distant Jerusalem, wicked Herod was still King.

But his days were numbered and his power was waning.

In still more distant Rome, Cæsar Augustus had taken hold of the reins of government and had turned the Republic into an Empire.

Empires cost money and subjects must pay.

Therefore almighty Cæsar had decreed that all his beloved children from east and west and north and south should duly enroll their names upon certain official registers that henceforth the tax-gatherers might know who had paid their just shares of all dues and who had failed to do their duty.

It is true, both Judæa and Galilee were still nominally part of an independent kingdom. But when it came to a question of revenue, the Romans were apt to stretch a point or two, and far and wide the order went forth that the people must present themselves at a given date at the particular spot which happened to be the original home of their family or tribe.

Joseph, as a descendant of David, therefore had trav-elled to Bethlehem and his wife, faithful Mary, had gone with him.

THE ADORATION

It had been no easy journey. The road had been long and tiring.

And when at last Joseph and Mary had reached Bethlehem, all the rooms in the city had already been occupied by those who had arrived earlier.

It had been a very cold night.

Kind people had taken pity upon the poor young wife. They had made her a bed in the corner of an old stable.

And there Jesus had been born, while outside in the fields, the shepherds were guarding their flocks against thieves and wolves, and were wondering when the long-promised Messiah should set their unhappy land free from those foreign masters who mocked at the power of Jehovah and laughed at all that was sacred to the heart of the Jews.

All this had occurred long ago.

It was rarely mentioned, for it had been followed by that hasty and terrible flight into the wilderness, which had been caused by the cruelty of Herod the King.

One evening, Mary had been nursing her baby in front of the old stable which served her and Joseph as a home.

Suddenly there had been a great noise in the street.

A caravan of Persian travellers was passing by.

With their camels and their servants and their rich clothes and their golden rings and the bright colours of their turbans, they were a sight which brought all the village to its wondering doorsteps.

The young mother and her child had attracted the attention of these strange men. They had halted their camels and they had played with the little boy and then, when they left, they had given his pretty mother some presents from among their bales of silk and their boxes of spices.

All this had been innocent enough, but Judæa was a very small country, and news travelled fast.

HEROD'S GLOOMY PALACE

In Jerusalem, in his gloomy palace, Herod was sitting in dark dread of the future. He was old and he was sick and he was very miserable.

The memory of his murdered wife was forever with him. The shadows were falling fast.

Suspicion was the companion of his last days, and fear for ever followed him with silent tread.

When his officers began to talk about the visit of the Persian merchants to Bethlehem, Herod became panic-stricken. Like all men of that age, the King of Judæa firmly believed that the dark-skinned Magi could perform such miracles as had not been seen since the wondrous days of Elijah and Elisha.

They could not be just ordinary merchants. They must have some special mission. Were they to avenge the evil deeds of the usurper who now sat on the throne, which centuries before had belonged to David, a native of that selfsame village of Bethlehem where the Magi had created such a stir?

King Herod had asked for details. He had heard of many other strange occurrences in connection with the mysterious child.

A short time after his birth, the boy, being the oldest son, had been taken to the Temple, and there, when the offering had been completed, an old man by the name of Simeon, and a very

old prophetess called Anna, had spoken strange words about the coming of the day of deliverance, and Simeon had asked Jehovah to let him die in peace now that he had seen the Messiah who should lead his people back from the path of wickedness and depravity.

Whether all this was true or not did not interest Herod. It had been said and it was being

SIMEON AND ANNA

believed by great numbers of people. That was enough. Herod had given orders that all boys born in Bethlehem within the last three years should be killed.

In this way he had hoped to rid himself of any possible rival for his throne. But the plan had not been entirely successful.

Several of the parents, warned by the officers or by their friends in Jerusalem, had been able to escape. Mary and Joseph had gone southward and tradition (which loved to connect the early story of Jesus with that of Abraham and Joseph) long maintained that they had gone as far as Egypt.

As soon as the massacre had come to an end by the welcome death of Herod, they had returned to Nazareth.

Joseph once more had opened his carpenter shop and Mary found her hands busy tending the ever increasing nursery.

For she became the mother of four other boys who were called James and Joseph and Simon and Judas, and of several girls, who lived to see the triumph and the death of that strange older brother who

MURDER IN BETHLEHEM

was to include all mankind in the tender affection which he had learned at the knees of his mother.

JOHN THE BAPTIST

CHAPTER XXI

THE PROPHETIC SPIRIT HAD NOT YET DIED OUT AMONG THE JEWS, FOR DURING THE DAYS OF JESUS' YOUTH, A MAN BY THE NAME OF JOHN (OR JOHN THE BAPTIST, AS WE CAME TO KNOW HIM) WAS WARNING THE PEOPLE IN A THUNDEROUS VOICE TO REPENT OF THEIR CRIMES AND OF THEIR SINS. THE JEWS HAD NO IDEA OF CHANGING THEIR WAYS. WHEN JOHN CONTINUED TO BOTHER THE PEOPLE OF JUDÆA WITH HIS SERMONS AND EXHORTATIONS, HEROD THE KING ORDERED HIM TO BE KILLED

EROD was dead and Augustus was dead, and Jesus had grown to manhood and was living peacefully in Nazareth.

Much had happened since the days of his childhood.

The division of the many possessions of Herod, who had been married ten times, had caused very considerable difficulty.

Originally, the number of his children had been very large, but murder and execution had brought down the number of possible candidates to just four.

The Romans, however, had refused to listen to the rival claims of the ambitious heirs.

They had divided the domains of Herod into three unequal parts and had given these to such candidates as best suited the momentary political need of the Empire.

The largest share, almost one-half, including Judæa, had gone to Archelaus, the oldest son. Galilee and most of the northern territory had been given to Herod Antipas, who was a brother of Archelaus by the same Samaritan mother. What remained, a very negligible strip of land, had gone to a certain Philip who does not seem to have been a relative of Herod at all, but who happened to enjoy the particular favour of the Romans. On account of his name, which was very common in those days, he has caused the historians a great deal of trouble.

And to make matters worse, there was another Philip, usually called Philip Herod after his father, who was married to a certain Herodias, the daughter of the first Herod's half-brother Aristobulus. Herodias in turn became the mother of a girl called Salome, and this same Salome eventually seems to have married that Philip who ruled the country towards the north of the Sea of Galilee.

A few years afterwards, all these Philips and Herods were to play leading rôles in a most atrocious family scandal which indirectly caused the untimely death of John the Baptist. That is the only reason why they are mentioned here at all.

To make this long and complicated chapter as short as possible, the spoils of old Herod had been divided, the ever patient subjects had welcomed their new masters, and Tiberius, the Emperor, had given instructions to his procurator in Judæa to keep a discreet but watchful eye upon all further developments within this turbulent bailiwick.

The name of that procurator has come down to us.

He was called Pontius Pilatus (or Pilate, as we say) and he was the personal representative of the Emperor in one of those provinces which paid their taxes directly to His Majesty and not to the Senate.

It is difficult to describe the position of Pilate in terms which mean anything to modern people.

But a condition similar to that in Judæa still prevails in several parts of the British and the Dutch colonies. Many districts in the Indies continue to be ruled by so-called independent sultans and chieftains, who go through the formality of commanding their body-guards and promulgating laws, although they are deprived of all actual power and are completely at the mercy of their foreign masters.

For reasons of policy it has seemed expedient not to annex such territories and they have been left an outward semblance of self-government. But a "governor" or a "resident" or a "consul-general" is maintained in the capital of the national sovereign. He superintends the acts of the King and those of his ministers. As long as the latter follow his tactful suggestions, they are allowed to continue to hold office. But Heaven help them if they forget that they are subordinate officers of an invisible but ever watchful power. His Excellency the Governor, in unmistakable terms, gives expression to his respectful discontent. And if he has reason to feel that his first warning has fallen upon deaf ears, there is a sudden stir in the dock-yards of the home country, and soon afterwards a lonely, dark-skinned exile is rowed to the silent shore of a distant island.

Pontius Pilate was the unfortunate official whose duty it was to exercise such hidden but ever evident authority among the Jews. His territory was quite large, and only once each year (and sometimes less) did he find occasion to leave Cæsarea on the coast and come to Jerusalem. He timed his visits in such a way that he should be present at the great Jewish festival. He could then meet all the district leaders without wasting his time travelling from one village to another. He could hear their complaints and could offer his suggestions and in case of trouble (which was always possible among the highly excitable masses of the old capital) he could personally superintend those measures which had to be taken to re-establish order.

The procurator had no palace of his own in the capital. Whenever he came to town, he occupied one wing of the royal palace. The owner of that ancient edifice probably did not like this arrangement, but the austere and abrupt Roman official was no more interested in the private views of a Jewish

THE ROMAN GUARD

king than the Governor General of India is disturbed by the personal preferences of an humble Mohammedan prince who thus far has escaped direct annexation at the hands of the British.

Besides, Herod knew exactly how he could get rid of his unwelcome guest in the shortest possible time.

Provided that all the taxes had been duly paid up and that the roads had been kept free from robbers and that the personal differences of the religious leaders in the great council had not led to civil war, the procurator was more than willing to leave the capital almost as soon as he had entered it.

Like many other Roman institutions, this dual form of government was by no means ideal. But it worked, and that was all the conquerors wanted. They cheerfully left the theory of government to those Greek publicists who were interested in that sort of thing, and themselves stuck to the prosaic facts of daily life. As they were usually successful along these practical lines, the world accepted their rough-and-ready methods as the most practical solution that had as yet been offered by any race of men.

And now, behold! just when everything was going smoothly, the peace of Judæa was rudely upset by the sudden and most inconvenient appearance of a wild man from the desert.

To the people who lived west of the river Jordan, the Essenes, who despised all worldly possessions and loved to acquire holiness in the lonely desert, were an old story. They were harmless folk, who kept to their own little settlement and who rarely ventured forth into the villages and never into the towns, where bad people were buying and selling things and growing rich without a thought of that hereafter which so greatly worried the pious hermits. But the new prophet, although he dressed and lived like an Essene, did not in the least share their proverbial shyness. He went up and down the valley of the Jordan, indulging in that sort of religious exhortation which the modern world associates with the revival meetings which were so popular a few years ago.

When people refused to agree with him, he denounced them in terms that could not possibly be mistaken.

Soon there were clashes between him and the Sadducees. This was deplorable, for a breach of the common peace meant official reports from Palestine to Rome and commissions of inquiry from Rome to Palestine and perhaps a change of government which would make the King of Judæa an exile, passing his embittered days in a Roman city or in a far hamlet on the shores of the Black Sea.

Before the procurator in distant Cæsarea therefore could hear of the trouble, the strong arm of the law was invoked against the religious firebrand, who dared to upset the peace and quiet of the land.

And behold! the man proved to be the son of Zacharias and Elisabeth, the little boy who was born while Mary was visiting the old couple some thirty years before.

John (who was just twelve months older than Jesus) had been a very serious child. At an early age he left his home and had gone into the desert to contemplate holiness on the lonely shores of the Dead Sea.

Far away from the turmoil of the farm and the factory, he thought deeply upon the wicked-

JOHN THE BAPTIST IN THE DESERT

ness of that world, of which, truth to tell, he knew nothing.

He himself was without desires and without needs.

An old shirt made of camel's hair was his only possession.

He ate the simplest food and only just enough to keep him alive.

He read no books but those written by his ancestors, and knew nothing of what had been said or thought or done by the more civilised people of the Near-West.

He served Jehovah with an absolute and unswerving loyalty and soon began to compare himself to Elijah and to Jeremiah and to the other great leaders of his race. He himself was good and he wanted all the world to share his virtues. And when he saw the harm done by old Herod and his terrible sons, and noticed the lukewarm allegiance of his fellow men to the laws of their fathers, he felt it his duty to go forth and tell the people of Judæa of certain things which they ought to know and which, unfortunately, they seemed to have forgotten long ago.

His uncouth appearance and the violence of his language caused large crowds to gather wherever he made his appearance.

THE DEAD SEA

Dirty and unkempt, a long wild beard flowing in the wind, his arms waving excitedly as he spoke of the coming day of Judgment, John was a man to inspire fear and doubt in the heart of the most hardened sinner.

Soon the crowds began to whisper to each other that this man was none other than the long-expected Messiah.

But he would not hear of that.

He was not the Messiah. Jehovah had merely sent him to prepare for the day when the real Messiah should come.

But the people, who dearly love a mystery, would not believe this simple statement. If this man were not the Messiah, he was at least the prophet Elijah, come back to this earth to perform some more of his miracles.

But that too John denied.

He stuck closely to the rôle which he had selected for himself. He was but a humble messenger from Heaven, commanded to bring tidings of despair and of hope.

JOHN THE BAPTIST

In the meantime, and while waiting for the day when all people should be forced to undergo the final baptism of fire (to cleanse them of their sins) he was willing to baptise those who showed signs of repentance with the water of the river as a token of their renewed faith in the power of Jehovah.

The Judæans were greatly impressed. John's fame rapidly spread from village to village and from far and wide the Jews came to see and hear and received baptism at the hands of their strange new Prophet.

At last the news of John's successful career reached Galilee.

There in his home at Nazareth, Jesus had been living the peaceful existence of a carpenter's apprentice.

At the age of twelve his parents had taken him to Jerusalem, to keep the feast of the Passover. The visit to the Temple had made a deep impression upon the boy. As soon as the necessary ceremonies had been finished, Mary and Joseph had returned northward. Jesus was not with them but they thought that he had joined another group of Nazarenes and would probably turn up in the evening.

But when night came, their son was still missing and no one had seen him. Joseph and Mary feared an accident and went back to Jerusalem as rapidly as they could.

After a day of searching, they found Jesus in the Temple, where he was engaged in a deep religious discussion with a crowd of rabbis.

When Jesus saw how greatly he had frightened his poor

mother, he had promised that he would never run away again.

But now he was grown up and he was very much interested in the questions of the day and when he heard of John (who by now was generally spoken of as John the Baptist) he left Nazareth and went on foot to the Dead Sea and joined the crowds which were forever at the heels

JESUS IN THE WILDERNESS

of the grim prophet, clamouring loudly to be immersed beneath the muddy waters of the river Jordan.

The sight of his cousin moved Jesus strangely.

Here at last was a man who had the courage of his convictions.

John's manners and his method of attack were not exactly to his taste.

But Jesus had grown up amidst the pleasant meadows of the north and John was the product of the barren farms of the south, and these early associations had put their stamp upon the characters of the two cousins.

Jesus felt that John could teach him much. He too asked to be baptised and then, after a short while, he decided to go into the wilderness that he too might find his soul in solitude.

When he came back, the career of John was rapidly coming to an end and thereafter the two men met only on rare occasions.

It was not the fault of Jesus, but a result of certain circumstances over which he had no control.

As long as the Baptist had merely spoken of the approaching Kingdom of Heaven, the authorities had not bothered him. But when he began to criticise the more tangible Kingdom of Judæa, it was a very different matter.

Unfortunately, John had excellent reason to find fault with the private life of his sovereign. Herod, the Tetrarch, was a chip off the old block.

When he and his half-brother Philip had been called to Rome on some political business, he had fallen desperately in love with his brother's wife, Herodias.

Herodias, who cared not at all for her own husband, was quite willing to marry Herod provided he (Herod) first divorce his own wife, who happened to be an Arab woman from the famous city of Petra.

THE UNDERGROUND DUNGEON

In Rome, in those days, all things could be arranged, provided one was very rich, and the divorce had been procured.

Herod had taken Herodias as his queen and Salome, the daughter of Herodias, had gone to live with her stepfather.

The people of Galilee and Judæa had been greatly shocked at this callous arrangement. But they wisely kept their own counsel and did not express their opinions too loudly where the soldiers of the King were near at hand and could overhear them.

John, however, conscious of his high duty as a minister of Jehovah's will, found it impossible to remain silent before so wicked a deed.

He denounced Herod and Herodias wherever and whenever he could.

In time, his fulminations might have incensed the people to such an extent that riots would have taken place, and this, of course, the authorities were obliged to prevent at all cost.

JOHN WAS TAKEN OUT OF HIS DUNGEON

Orders were given for the arrest of John.

Even then the prophet refused to keep quiet. From the bottom of his dark dungeon he continued to thunder away against the royal couple who in his eyes were no better than common adulterers.

The Tetrarch was in a difficult position. He had a wholesome dread of the mysterious power of this unknown man.

But he feared his wife's sharp tongue more.

One day he was going to have John executed. The next day he relented and offered clemency if John would only promise to keep quiet.

At last Herodias grew tired and decided to make an end of all further hesitation. She knew of her husband's great admiration for his stepdaughter Salome. The girl was a very graceful dancer and Herod loved to watch her.

She told her daughter that she must not dance at court,

unless the King promised to give her whatever she should ask for.

Herod rashly said "Yes," and then Salome, following the urging of her mother, demanded the head of John the Baptist.

The stepfather, repenting of his folly, offered her his whole kingdom if she would release him of his oath. But mother and daughter remained steadfast and John was condemned to be killed.

The executioner clambered down into the pit where the prophet lay chained. A minute later the head of John was handed to the frightened Salome.

Such was the death of John, who had dared to speak of serious things to a world which only cared to be amused.

THE CHILDHOOD OF JESUS

CHAPTER XXII

AS FOR JESUS, HE GREW UP AMONG THE SIMPLE PEAS-
ANTS AND ARTISANS OF A LITTLE VILLAGE CALLED
NAZARETH. HE WAS TAUGHT THE TRADE OF A CAR-
PENTER, BUT THIS LIFE DID NOT SATISFY HIM. HE
LOOKED UPON THE WORLD AND FOUND IT FULL OF
CRUELTY AND INJUSTICE. HE LEFT HIS FATHER
AND HIS MOTHER AND HIS BROTHERS AND HIS SIS-
TERS, AND WENT FORTH TO TELL OF THOSE THINGS
WHICH IN HIS HEART HE HELD TO BE TRUE

JESUS spent only a short while in the wilderness.

During that time he rarely ate or slept.

And well might he need all his hours to plan the future.

He was almost thirty years old, un-married, free to come and go and live according to the very simple standards of his day.

But the words of John had set him thinking. All the im-pressions and experiences of his quiet and uneventful exist-ence in Nazareth seemed to lead up to that moment near the river Jordan when he had suddenly asked himself the question, "What does life really mean?"

He knew little of the great political events which had just turned the old Roman Republic into an Empire based upon the strength and the loyalty of a few regiments of highly paid mercenaries.

Of the Greek language and of everything that had been written in that tongue, he was profoundly ignorant.

He spoke Aramaic and probably had a reading knowledge of the ancient Hebrew tongue in which the holy books had been written, many centuries ago.

But Greek thought and Greek science meant as little to him as Roman jurisprudence and Roman statecraft.

He was withal a child of his own people and his own age— a humble Jewish carpenter, steeped in the knowledge of the old Mosaic laws and the traditions of the Judges and the Prophets, of whom he had heard in the synagogues and in the Temple.

He was very faithful in his religious duties.

Whenever it was necessary, he went to Jerusalem, that he might give burnt offering in the Temple, as it was required by ancient usage.

He accepted his little Galilean world as he found it and did not question what Joseph and Mary had taught him.

And yet he was not without certain doubts.

He was not like other people.

He felt within himself a certain spiritual quality which set him apart from other men. The good neighbours of Nazareth hardly noticed this. They knew him too intimately. To them he always was the carpenter's son.

But once he left his native village, it was different.

He was pointed out.

There was something in his eye, in his gesture, which attracted the attention of the casual passer-by. And when he reached the river Jordan where the crowd lived in momentary expectation of a great miracle, he heard how the followers of the Baptist whispered behind his back and asked each other the oft-repeated question: "Is that the man who is to be our Messiah?"

But the Messiah, to those who flocked together to hear the sermons of John, was a great warrior and a stern judge— a sort of imperial avenger who was to establish a great Jewish kingdom and make all the nations of the world subject to the laws of Jehovah's chosen people.

And nothing was further removed from the simple mind of Jesus than this worldly idea of another Samson, astride a big black horse, waving a sword and leading his victorious armies against those who did not happen to share the religious prejudices of the Pharisees or the political convictions of the Sadducees.

It was a question of four letters.

That which separated Jesus from the merciless Roman, the sophisticated Greek and the dogmatic Jew, was his understanding of the word "love."

His heart was filled with love of his fellow-men. Not merely towards his own friends in Nazareth, his neighbours in Galilee, but towards the people of that vaster world which lay hidden beyond the last curve of the road to Damascus.

He pitied them.

Their strife seemed so senseless, their ambitions so futile, their desire for gold and glory such a waste of valuable time and energy.

It was true that many of the Greek philosophers had come to an identical conclusion. They too had discovered that true happiness was a matter of the soul and did not depend upon a pocket filled wth drachmas or the noisy approval of the crowd in the stadium.

But they had never carried their ideas beyond that small and exclusive circle of well-born gentlemen who alone in those days were allowed the luxury of an immortal soul.

They had resigned themselves to the existence of slaves and of the poor people and of those millions for ever doomed to dwell in misery, as being part of an established and inevitable order of things—as something unfortunate which just could not be helped.

They would as soon have explained the principles of their Epicurean or Stoic philosophy to the dogs of the fields and to the cats of their backyards as to the labourers who worked in their farms and to the cook who prepared their dinner.

In some ways they were far in advance of those early Jewish leaders who had steadfastly refused to acknowledge the rights of any man who did not belong to their own tribe.

But to Jesus (who knew nothing about them) they had not gone far enough.

He included all that lived and breathed within the compassion of his great heart. And although he had vague forebodings of the fate which awaited him if he were to teach his doctrine of patience and kindness and humility to a country dominated by the uncompromising Pharisees, he could not well refuse to follow the voice which bade him give his life for the cause of a better world.

It was the crisis of his career.

He could do one of three things.

In the first place, there was the prospect of a quiet old age in Nazareth, doing odd jobs about the town and discussing profound questions of law and ceremony with the rustics who in the evening gathered around the watering trough and listened to the village rabbi.

This did not appeal to Jesus. It would mean slow spiritual starvation.

If, on the other hand, he cared to lead a life of adventure, he now had his opportunity.

He could make use of the enthusiasm which his mere appearance had created among the followers of the Baptist. If

JESUS LEAVES HOME

he would allow these simple people to believe what they were only too eager to believe, he could easily get himself recognised as the long-expected Messiah and could become the head of a nationalistic movement which, after the example of the Maccabees, might (and then again, might not) bring independence and unity to the sorely divided Jewish nation.

But the temptation to do this (and who during his lifetime does not have a momentary dream of such a future?) was immediately discarded as utterly unworthy of the ambition of a serious man.

There remained therefore but one other course.

He must go forth, must leave father and mother, run the risk of exile, hatred and death, to tell all those who cared to listen of the things which were uppermost in his own mind.

He was thirty years old when he started upon his great work.

In less than three years, his enemies had killed him.

THE DISCIPLES

CHAPTER XXIII

FROM VILLAGE TO VILLAGE HE WANDERED. HE TALKED
TO ALL SORTS AND CONDITIONS OF PEOPLE. MEN,
WOMEN AND CHILDREN CAME TO LISTEN EAGERLY
TO THE NEW WORDS OF GOOD-WILL AND CHARITY
AND LOVE. THEY CALLED JESUS THEIR MASTER
AND FOLLOWED HIM WHEREVER HE WENT AS HIS
FAITHFUL DISCIPLES

N the days of Jesus it was comparatively easy for an intelligent man with
a new idea to get a hearing.

He did not need a lecture room and
he was not obliged to spend his valuable
time waiting until some one had made
him a professor or had ordained him as
a minister.

The problem of board and lodging was as easily settled in
Judæa as it was almost anywhere in Egypt or in western Asia.

The climate was mild. One suit of clothes would last almost a lifetime. Food was plentiful in a land where most
people ate only just as much as was necessary to exist and
where they could pluck their daily bread from the trees.

In the time of the Judges and the Kings, when the priestly class had ruled supreme, wandering orators who preached strange heresies were not tolerated. But now the Roman policeman stood guard on the highroads and watched the traffic in the busy cities.

The Romans, indifferent in matters of a spiritual nature, allowed all men to seek salvation after their own fashion, provided they kept away from subjects too closely connected with politics. As long as one did not advocate open rebellion or sedition, there was practically no limit to the freedom of speech. The Roman magistrate existed to see that this rule was enforced and woe to the Pharisee who would have dared to disturb such a meeting.

No wonder that the new prophet was soon followed by a large number of curious villagers and ere he had been gone a month, he had gained a reputation as a speaker and a prophet which reached far beyond the narrow confines of Galilee.

It was then the turn of John to be curious. He was still at liberty although he was closely watched by members of the National Council. He left his beloved Judæa and travelled northward to meet Jesus.

It was the last interview between the two men.

It seems extremely doubtful whether John ever understood what was in the mind of his cousin. The two prophets looked upon this world from entirely different angles. John urged the people to repent of their sins in fear of a wrathful and avenging Jehovah.

In this he was only following what he had learned from the Old Testament, which had been hacked out of the granite rock of Mount Sinai.

Jesus, on the other hand (not yet with any great decisiveness), conceived of life in terms which like the flowers of his native land had been smiled upon by the pleasant sun of a warm climate.

John the Baptist preached "Nay!"

Jesus, just as eagerly, answered "Yea!"

John shared the belief of his fellow Jews, who had created the coming Messiah after the image of their relentless Jehovah.

BETHLEHEM

Jesus had a vision of something nobler and endowed the common Father of all things with everlasting forbearance and a love that surpassed human understanding.

Between those two views, no compromise was possible.

For a moment, John seems to have had a glimpse of what Jesus might come to mean. He told his disciples that they must not expect too much of him, that he was only the forerunner of another teacher, greater than himself. And when two of those pupils (acting upon this suggestion) left him to follow Jesus, he was not angry.

He had given the best there was in him.

Somehow or other, he felt that he had failed.

His death, however terrible, came to him as a welcome relief.

As for Jesus, almost immediately after the encounter with John, he went back to Galilee for a short visit to Nazareth.

Joseph no longer lived, but Mary cleverly kept her small household together and the children could always return to the old home whenever they needed a vacation.

It is not easy to be the mother of genius. Mary never quite

understood this strange son who came and went and who wandered all over the land and whose name was mentioned with the awe of admiration or the hatred of vengeance whenever three Jews met together by the roadside.

But she was by far too wise to stand in the way of one who seemed to know so well what he was doing.

And if she sometimes failed to appreciate the Prophet, she never ceased to love her son.

This time, when her boy came back from his first trip into foreign lands, she had good news for him.

There was to be a wedding in the family and they had all been invited.

Jesus said that he would be glad to go, but he was no longer alone. There were his new friends who had followed him to Nazareth. He made it plain that he regarded them as his brothers and as such he took

CANA

them along when he went to Cana.

This was the beginning of that close and intimate friendship which lasted until the day of the crucifixion.

Several hundred years later, when a touch of the miraculous was added to every event in the life of Jesus for the benefit of the simple-minded barbarians who had to be gained for his straightforward message of a loving God, the story of a pleasant family gathering, where everybody had been happy and where Mary for the last time had enjoyed the sight of her son in the midst of his friends and relatives, was not considered sufficiently convincing. It had been adorned with a mysterious tale which the painters of the Middle Ages used repeatedly as a popular subject for their pictures.

According to this new account, the sudden arrival of so many extra guests had caused a shortage of wine.

The waiters had been in great distress. There was nothing but water, and no Jew or Greek or Roman would have dreamed of offering water to the strangers within his gate.

The servants had rushed to Mary, who was a careful house-wife and who might perhaps know what to do.

Mary in turn had spoken to her son and asked for his advice.

Jesus, lost in deep thought, had been somewhat irritated by this interruption on account of a matter of mere food and drink. But he was a very human person and appreciated the importance

THE WEDDING AT CANA

of details. He had understood the embarrassment of his host whose careful arrangements had been upset by the unexpected appearance of half a dozen uninvited guests.

To save his relatives from their predicament, he had quietly changed the water into wine and the dinner had been finished to the satisfaction of all.

As the ages went by, similar bits of magic were continually added to the original stories. That was quite natural.

People have always loved to connect superhuman power with those whose memory they worship.

The Greek gods and heroes had all performed a score of miracles. The old Jewish Prophets had made iron float upon the waters and had walked across deep rivers and occasionally had even been able to interfere with the regular order of the planetary system.

In China, in Persia, in India, and in Egypt, wherever we turn, we meet with strange records of supernatural feats which have been common among the earliest inhabitants of those far-away lands.

This proves that the need for an imaginary world wherein the impossible becomes the self-evident is very general and not restricted to a particular country or race.

But to many of us, the influence which Jesus exercised upon the world was so astonishingly profound and inexplicable that we are willing to accept him without the doubtful embellishments of conjuration and exorcism.

In this we may be entirely wrong.

But as the reader can find full descriptions of all the miracles in a thousand other books, we shall content ourselves with a sober relation of those events which occurred when Jesus left his family for the last time and began to teach that gospel of mutual forbearance and love which led to his death on the cross.

THE NEW TEACHER

CHAPTER XXIV

SOON IT BECAME KNOWN ALL OVER THE LAND THAT HERE WAS A PROPHET WHO TAUGHT THE STRANGE DOCTRINE THAT ALL THE PEOPLE OF THIS EARTH (AND NOT ONLY THE JEWS) WERE THE CHILDREN OF ONE LOVING GOD, AND THEREFORE BROTHERS AND SISTERS TO EACH OTHER AND TO ALL MANKIND

ROM Cana, Jesus, accompanied by his friends, walked to Capernaum, a little village built only a short while before on the northern shore of the Sea of Galilee.

There lived the families of Peter and Andrew, two fishermen who had left their work that they might follow Jesus when he began his great voyage of discovery for the soul of God and the soul of Man.

They remained in Capernaum for a few weeks and then decided to go to Jerusalem.

This was done for two reasons.

In the first place, the feast of Passover was near at hand,

367

when it was the duty of all good Jews to pass the holy season near the Temple.

And in the second place, it would give Jesus a chance to find out what the people of the capital thought of him.

The Galileans, although openly despised by the true Jeru-

CAPERNAUM

salemites (because they were not supposed to be as careful in their devotions as those who worshipped in the Temple—a survival of the ancient rivalry between Judah and Israel), were really a kindly people, willing to listen to new ideas.

Perhaps they were not always over-enthusiastic, but they could be counted upon to be polite. Jerusalem, on the other hand, dominated by the Pharisees, was the mighty fortress of the old faith, where intolerance had been elevated to a national virtue, and where no mercy was shown to the dissenter.

Jesus safely reached the town, but before he had an opportunity to explain his ideas, something happened which obliged him to leave in greater haste than he had come.

In the beginning of time, people had slaughtered their captive fellow-men whenever they wished to gain the favour of their gods.

Later on, with the coming of a primitive form of civilisation, oxen and sheep had been substituted for human beings.

When Jesus was born, the Jews still sacrificed animals to Jehovah.

ANDREW AND PETER

Rich people killed a cow and burned the meat and fat upon the altar in the Temple, with the exception of the edible parts which went to the kitchens of the priests.

Poor people, who could not afford to spend so much money, bought a lamb, or if they were very, very poor, a couple of pigeons, and cut their throats in the strange belief that such an act of useless slaughter would be pleasant to that selfsame God who with such infinite care had created the pretty beasts only a short time before.

Now that most of the Jews lived abroad (for they had never been willing to give up the comforts of Alexandria and Damascus for the crooked and dark streets of Jerusalem, and more than half a million of them were to be found in Egypt alone) it became necessary to keep a large supply of live stock on hand for the benefit of those who came from afar and could not drive their own beasts before them all the way from the Nile to the brook of Kedron.

Years ago, when the Temple was built, the doomed oxen and sheep had been offered for sale in the street, just outside the entrance gate of the Temple. Later, for greater convenience of the customers, the cattle-dealers had taken their herds inside the Temple courts. They had been followed by the money-changers, who, seated behind their wooden banks, offered to change Babylonian gold into Jewish shekels and Corinthian silver into Judæan minas.

THE MONEY-CHANGER

These good tradesmen meant no disrespect. They hardly realised what they were doing. It was just a very bad custom which had developed so gradually that no one had noticed it.

To Jesus, fresh from the quiet valleys of Galilee, his mind upon problems far removed from trade and barter, the presence of the bellowing oxen and the barking money-changers seemed a blasphemy and an outrage. God's house had become a noisy market-place—surely such a thing was unpardonable!

He took a whip (there were any number of them lying around) and he drove that whole mob out of the Temple and he sent the poor beasts scurrying after their masters and the house of Jehovah stood cleansed of its shame.

The mob, eagerly hoping for something to happen, came

JESUS DRIVES AWAY THE MONEY-CHANGERS

rushing to this scene of violence as fast as the uneven cobblestones would let them.

There were many who thought that Jesus was right. It was scandalous that the Temple should be used as a cow-shed.

Others, however, were very angry. No doubt it was perhaps not entirely desirable that there should be quite so much noise so near the Holy of Holies, but then again, it was hardly the part for an unknown young man from the provinces—Galilee, was it? or Nazareth, or some such place—to create a disturbance and upset all the tables, covered with money, and make the poor bankers go down upon all fours to find their lost pennies.

Still others did not know what to make of it. Among these was a member of the Supreme Council, a staunch old Pharisee by the name of Nicodemus.

NICODEMUS

He could not well afford to be seen in public with one who had just behaved with such unseemly lack of dignity in a very holy place, but he wanted to know what sort of man it was who had dared to do such a rash thing.

He sent for Jesus and bade him come to his house as soon as it should be dark.

Jesus accepted the invitation and he and Nicodemus had their talk. The Pharisee was convinced that Jesus had been entirely sincere if somewhat over-eager in his efforts. What he heard of his activities in Galilee strengthened him in his conviction, and in his liking for the young Nazarene he advised him to leave the city as soon as possible.

The palace of the King had sensitive ears for anything that sounded like a breach of the common peace and the cattle-dealers and money-changers would undoubtedly set the people against so energetic a prophet, who preferred action to mere talk.

And so Jesus left and together with his friends he travelled back to Galilee by way of the land of Samaria.

That poor country, as we have told you before, enjoyed (or rather failed to enjoy) a very unfortunate and quite undeserved reputation as a hotbed of godlessness.

Centuries before it had been a part of the old kingdom of Israel. After the fall of that country, the inhabitants had been driven away to Assyria and their deserted farms had been handed over to settlers from Mesopotamia and from Asia Minor. Together with the few remaining Jews, these immigrants had formed a new race which was known as the Samaritans.

THE PHARISEE AND THE SAMARITAN

In the eyes of the true Jews, a man who dwelled within this land was something too despicable for words. Those terrible expressions which we so unthinkingly and insultingly bestow upon the strangers within our gate—"wop" and "kike" and "hunky"—are no more offensive than "Samaritan" when used by a hardened Pharisee to describe a citizen from Shechem or Shiloh.

As a result, whenever a Jew was obliged to travel to Damascus or to Cæsarea Philippi, he passed through Samaria as fast as his donkey could carry him and associated no more with the natives than was absolutely necessary.

The friends of Jesus, good conservative followers of the strict Mosaic laws, fully shared the common prejudice against the "dirty Samaritans."

They had to learn their lesson.

Not only did Jesus tarry by the way, but he actually spoke in a very friendly fashion to several Samaritans, and once he even sat down by the side of a well to explain his ideas to a woman who belonged to the despised race.

CÆSAREA

But when the disciples came near and listened to the conversation, they discovered that the words of their teacher were better understood by this "Samaritan" than they had been by those excellent Judæans who prided themselves so arrogantly upon their piety and their zeal for the law.

This was the first time that they were taught the principle of a common brotherhood. It was also the beginning of Jesus' career as the prophet of a new faith.

The methods which he used were quite unusual.

Sometimes he told his disciples stories.

But he rarely preached to them. A word and a hint were enough to give meaning to his hidden thoughts.

For in this, as in all other matters, Jesus was a born teacher. And because he was a great teacher, he understood the heart of man and he was able to help many who lacked the strength to help themselves.

Ever since the beginning of time there have been people who were able to exercise great influence upon those who are stricken with certain forms of illness. They could not heal broken bones and they were not able to stop an epidemic by a nod of the head. But as all the world now knows, imagination has a great deal to do with sickness. If we think that we have a pain, we actually feel that pain. If some one can only convince us that we were wrong in our amateur diagnosis, the pain will disappear immediately.

This gift has often been bestowed upon simple and kindly people who can gain the confidence of their patients and who can cure them although they are utterly ignorant of the principles of medicine.

Jesus, who inspired confidence and faith by the absolute honesty of his person and the lovable simplicity of his character, was undoubtedly able to help those who came to him in the agony of imagined distress.

When it became known that the young Nazarene (prophet, Messiah, or whatever else the

JESUS AND THE SAMARITAN WOMAN

people in their blind devotion believed him to be) could give people a temporary relief from their ailments, men and women and children came from far and near to ask that they be restored to health.

Tradition, in its eagerness to make a good story better, insisted upon depicting the second journey through Galilee as the triumphant progress of a wonder-doctor.

First, on the way back to Capernaum, it was the child of a rich man which had been given up by the local physician and which was brought back to life.

Next it was the mother-in-law of Peter who was ailing with a severe fever and who, in the twinkling of an eye, was sufficiently recovered to cook a meal for her guests and serve it to them at her own hospitable table.

Then there followed a steady stream of patients; people who thought that they were lame and had to be carried to

THE LAME, THE HALT AND THE BLIND

Jesus on stretchers; people who for years had suffered from strange and indescribable maladies; nervous patients of every form and description who needed but one reassuring word to be set upon the road to recovery.

Whatever the truth of several of those stories (dead people rarely come back to life) they certainly created great excitement and curiosity in Galilee and were soon repeated in Jerusalem.

But the Pharisees could not entirely approve. They were undoubtedly grateful for what Jesus had done for their suffering fellow-men, but they thought that he had gone much too far when he refused to make a difference between members of his own race and foreigners and had cured the servant of a Roman officer and the daughter of a Greek mother, and had relieved the pain of an old woman who insisted upon being sick on the Sabbath day, and when he had allowed lepers to touch the hem of his garment, in their desperate hope that this would ease their misery.

Besides, his willingness to accept a tax-gatherer, employed by the Romans and stationed at Capernaum, as one of his pupils, was a terrible thing. It seemed little short of treason to the cause of the much-suffering fatherland and several good people told Jesus so.

But although he appreciated their motive, he was not convinced that he had done any wrong.

To him, all men and all women, tax-gatherers, politicians, saints and sinners, were alike.

He recognised and accepted their common humanity.

And that there might be no doubt about his stand upon this matter, he took all his disciples and together with them he went to dine at the house of one of the offending officials as f it were an honour to sit at the humble table of a Roman enchman.

When the Pharisees heard of this they did not say anything openly.

But they told each other what they would do when Jesus again should venture to come within their jurisdiction. And when Jesus came back to Jerusalem for the last Passover of his life, he was met by the silent enmity of a determined group f men who understood that their little world would come to n end just as soon as the ideals of this strange prophet should ave been turned into realised facts.

THE OLD ENEMIES

CHAPTER XXV

OF COURSE THOSE WHO PROFITED FROM THE EXISTING ORDER OF THINGS (AND THERE WERE MANY) DID NOT LIKE TO HEAR SUCH DOCTRINES PUBLICLY PROCLAIMED. THEY DECLARED THAT THE NEW PROPHET WAS A DANGEROUS ENEMY TO ALL ESTABLISHED LAW AND ORDER. SOON THESE ENEMIES OF JESUS MADE COMMON CAUSE. THEY SET TO WORK TO BRING ABOUT HIS DESTRUCTION

PON his next visit, before he had even reached the Temple, Jesus was in open conflict with the powers that ruled Jerusalem.

It happened that when he came near the pool of Bethsaida, just outside of the Sheep Gate, he heard a man crying out to him for help. The poor fellow had been lame for more than thirty years. He had been told (like every one else) of the miraculous cures in Galilee. He too hoped that he could be cured.

Jesus looked at him. Then he told him that there was

ncthing the matter with his legs and ordered him to pick up his mattress and go home.

The delighted patient did as he had been told but he forgot that it was the Sabbath day and that it was against the law of the Pharisees to carry so much as an extra pin in one's clothes.

In his joy at being able to walk, he hastened away to the Temple that he might give thanks to Jehovah for his recovery.

But of course several of the Pharisees were told of what had just happened and as they could not allow such a breach of the holy commands to go unpunished they

THE POOL OF BETHESDA

topped the poor cripple (who was now possessed of two perfectly good legs) and they told him that it was against all law nd precedent to be seen with a mattress on one's back on the Sabbath day and that he ought to be punished for this breach f decorum.

But the excited man, as was quite natural, had his mind n other things.

"He who cured me told me to take my mattress and go ome," he answered, "and I am doing what he told me."

Thereupon, without further ado, he went his way, and the

Pharisees were left alone with their rage. One thing they understood very clearly. Unless this sort of thing were stopped, right then and there, no one could foretell what would happen next.

At their instigation, the Sanhedrin was called together to decide what to do. Like all magistrates who are not just certain of their position, the members of the council decided to investigate. Jesus was ordered to appear before them and give an account of himself. He came willingly enough and listened patiently to the many accusations of his enemies. Then he made it clear that law or no law, he did not intend to stop doing good just because it happened to be a particular day of the week.

THE SANHEDRIN MEETS

This answer meant open defiance of the established authorities.

But the Great Council, well knowing in what veneration this man from Nazareth was held by many people, thought it better to let him go this time and wait for another occasion when they could accuse him of something more definite.

By now they were beginning to understand that it would not be quite so easy to destroy Jesus as they had expected. Apparently it was impossible to rouse him to anger. He never showed any feeling towards those who hated him. He quietly walked out of every trap, and when he was driven into a corner, he told a simple little story which brought all those who listened over to his side.

The Sanhedrin plainly was puzzled. Of course, they could lay the matter before the King. But their King (whose title was very uncertain) would refuse to act without consulting the procurator. And what was the use of trying to explain anything to a Roman?

Upon more than one occasion, Pilate had already shown his total lack of sympathy for those who came to him with their religious grievances.

In this instance, he would do what he had repeatedly done before. He would promise that the matter would have his close attention. Then after many months, he would come to the official conclusion that Jesus had committed no crime against the Roman law. Next he would throw the case out of court and everything would be as it had been before, except that the position of Jesus would have been greatly strengthened by his acquittal.

Herod, therefore, offered the only hope for redress and vengeance, if he were approached in the right way and were told to keep the matter quiet. It was true that for several years the King had been at odds with the Council, but this was no time to remember personal feuds.

The Sanhedrin buried the hatchet (which they had been carefully whetting to destroy Herod) and meekly went to the royal palace and poured forth a long list of grievances against the person of one Jesus, a self-styled prophet who was preaching seditious doctrines which would upset the old theocratic state (or what remained of it) and who was quite as dangerous a person to the safety of the nation as that John whom some people had called the Baptist, who now fortunately was unable to cause any more trouble.

Herod, as suspicious as his father, listened with willing ears.

But when the time came to arrest Jesus, he could not be found. For the second time he had left the town, and followed by an ever increasing number of pupils, he was slowly wending his way back to Galilee where he felt more at home than he did in Judæa.

From a worldly point of view, his career was already reaching its climax. The belief that Jesus was really the Messiah had taken hold of the masses. They would have marched against Jerusalem, or for that matter, against the entire Roman army, had Jesus been willing to lead them.

But that, alas for them, was still furthest away from his dreams.

He had no personal ambition.

He did not work for riches or crave the glory and the doubtful pleasure of being acclaimed a national hero.

He wanted the people to look beyond the immediate desires of this earth and to seek the companionship of that spirit who was to unite them in love and in charity and pity for their fellow-men.

He had no patience with those who saw in him simply another (if better) representative of that old royal power which was now associated with the name of Herod.

Instead of confessing himself the Messiah, he stated repeatedly and clearly and as publicly as possible that his life his own happiness and comfort meant nothing to him but that his ideals about the kinship of all men and the love of a kindly God meant everything.

Instead of harking back to those commandments which had been revealed to a few people amidst the thunder of Moun Sinai- he told the masses who listened to him on the smiling hillsides of Galilee that the God of whom he spoke was a spirit of love which knew neither race nor creed. Instead of giving practical advice about saving money and acquiring wealth, he cautioned his friends against those useless treasures which lie

THE SERMON ON THE MOUNT

ccumulated in the attic of the miser (where they are an easy rey to cunning thieves) and asked them to make their own ouls an imperishable storage-house of good deeds and noble houghts.

Finally he summed up his entire philosophy of life in one

single discourse, the famous Sermon on the Mount, whose most exalted passage I here repeat:

"Blessed are the poor in spirit: for theirs is the kingdom of heaven. Blessed are they that mourn: for they shall be comforted. Blessed are the meek: for they shall inherit the earth. Blessed are they which do hunger and thirst after righteousness: for they shall be filled. Blessed are the merciful: for they shall obtain mercy. Blessed are the pure in heart: for they shall see God. Blessed are the peacemakers: for they shall be called the children of God. Blessed are they which are persecuted for righteousness' sake: for theirs is the kingdom of heaven. Blessed are ye, when men shall revile you, and persecute you, and shall say all manner of evil against you falsely, for my sake. Rejoice, and be exceeding glad: for great is your reward in heaven: for so persecuted they the prophets which were before you. Ye are the salt of the earth: but if the salt have lost his savour, wherewith shall it be salted? It is thenceforth good for nothing but to be cast out, and to be trodden under foot of men. Ye are the light of the world. A city that is set on an hill cannot be hid. Neither do men light a candle, and put it under a bushel, but on a candlestick: and it giveth light unto all that are in the house. Let your light so shine before men, that they may see your good works, and glorify your Father which is in heaven."

And as a daily and practical guide on the difficult path of life he gave them that short prayer which is this very day repeated by a hundred million people when they say:

"Our Father who art in heaven, Hallowed be thy name. Thy kingdom come. Thy will be done on earth, as it is in heaven. Give us this day our daily bread. And forgive us our trespasses as we forgive those who trespass against us. And lead us not into temptation, but deliver us from evil. For thine is the kingdom, and the power, and the glory, for ever. Amen."

Then, having laid down the general outline of a new philosophy both of life and of death entirely at variance with the old and narrow faith of the Pharisees, he asked those twelve men who were now his steady and faithful companions to follow him that he might show all the world how completely he had broken with those old Jewish prejudices which had made his race the enemy of all other men.

He left Galilee and visited the territory which since time immemorial had been known as Phœnicia.

Next he once more traversed the country of his birth, rowed across the river Jordan and deliberately passed into the land of the Ten Cities, which the Greeks (who formed a majority of the population) called the Dekapolis.

There the cures of a few demented people which he performed among the heathen caused as much grateful wonder as similar cures had done in his native land.

And it was then and immediately afterwards that Jesus began to illustrate his teaching with those very simple stories which appealed so greatly to the imagination of the people who flocked together to hear him and which have become part of the language of every European country.

It would be foolish, however, for me to try to retell them in my own way.

I am not, as I have so often said before, writing a new version of the Bible.

I am merely giving you the general outline of a book which (especially in its early parts) is often somewhat too complicated for the readers of our own hurrying days.

The gospels, however, are simple and direct and very short. Even the busiest of men can find leisure to read them.

Fortunately they have been translated into English by a group of scholars who were masters of the language. Several attempts have been made since the seventeenth century to re-valuate the ancient Greek ideas into modern words. All of these are rather disappointing, and none of them has been able to replace the version made by order of King James. It stands supreme to-day as it did three centuries ago.

If my little book can give you the desire to read the original, to study those wise parables, to comprehend the immense vision of this greatest of all teachers, I shall not have written in vain.

And that is really all I am trying to do.

THE DEATH OF JESUS

CHAPTER XXVI

THE ROMAN GOVERNOR BEFORE WHOM THE CASE OF JESUS WAS LAID DID NOT CARE WHAT HAPPENED AS LONG AS AN OUTWARD SEMBLANCE OF PEACE AND TRANQUILLITY WAS MAINTAINED WITHIN HIS PROVINCE. HE ALLOWED JESUS TO BE CONDEMNED TO DEATH.

 HE end of course was inevitable, as Jesus knew very well and as he had intimated to his disciples and his relatives more than once when he was still in Galilee and among his friends.

Jerusalem for many centuries had been the centre of a religious monopoly which not only brought great personal profits to most of the inhabitants but depended for its continued success upon the strictest observance of the ancient laws, as they had been laid down in the days of Moses.

Ever since the great exile, the vast majority of the Jewish people had insisted upon living abroad. They were much happier in the cities of Egypt and Greece and of the Italian peninsula and of Spain and of northern Africa, where trade was brisk and money flowed freely, than in Judæa, where the barren and exhausted soil could only be coaxed into a faint activity by endless hours of toil.

When the Persians had allowed the Jews to return to their home-land it had been impossible to bring a sufficient number of inhabitants back to the city without the use of soldiers. Since then, conditions had not improved.

THE DESERTED FARM

The Jews, wherever found, continued to regard Jerusalem with deep respect as the religious centre of their nation, but their fatherland was there where they happened to have found a comfortable home and nothing short of absolute force would bring them back to the land of their birth.

As a result, those people who dwelt within the gates of the old national capital were almost without exception connected with the Temple, just as to-day the inhabitants of many of our smaller college towns depend directly or indirectly upon the University for their daily bread and butter and would either starve or be obliged to move if the University were obliged to close its doors.

The economic and spiritual aristocracy of this group consisted of a small number of professional priests.

Next came their assistants who had to look after the complicated ritual of the burnt offerings and the minor sacrifices They were really highly trained and skilful butchers, personally interested in the number and the quality of the animals which were brought to them and which provided them with the greater part of their daily food.

Then there were the common servants who kept the Temple clean and washed the courts in the evening after the crowd had dispersed.

Then there were the money-changers, the bankers as we

THE MERCHANTS OF JERUSALEM

would call them to-day, who trafficked in the strange metals that were brought to them from every part of the world.

Then there were the hotel-keepers and the inn-keepers and the boarding-house-keepers, who offered board and lodging to the hundreds of thousands of pilgrims who annually travelled to Jerusalem that they might keep the law and worship at the appointed time at the ancestral altar.

Then there were all the usual shopkeepers and tailors and shoemakers and wine merchants and candlestick makers who are to be found in any city which has become a tourist centre. For that is what Jerusalem really was.

A religious tourist centre to which the people flocked, not for the purpose of amusement, but to perform certain rites which (so they firmly believed) could not possibly be performed in another place or by another set of men than those who since time immemorial had exercised the office of Priest.

JESUS ENTERS JERUSALEM

You must get firm hold of these facts if you are to understand the scorching looks of hatred which were thrown at Jesus when he once more dared to enter the city.

There he came, this carpenter, from a forlorn village in Galilee—this humble teacher whose great love embraced even sinners and publicans.

Twice before he had been told to leave.

He was not wanted in Jerusalem.

Had he returned to cause more trouble? or would he content himself with a few speeches?

It is true, these little talks which he sometimes delivered to his companions sounded very harmless. But they were really most dangerous. The man was for ever hinting at things. No in those vague terms which were so popular with the learned scribes who loved to hide the meaning of everything they said underneath a copious verbiage of Hebrew sentences which created an impression of profound erudition.

No, he used words which all the people could understand. Jesus said: "Thou shalt love the Lord thy God with all thy heart, and with all thy soul, and with all thy mind. This is the first and great commandment. And the second is like unto it: Thou shalt love thy neighbour as thyself."

And then, there were those parables about shepherds and all sorts of every-day things which went straight to the heart of the matter.

Some people had tried to answer the unmistakable allusions to false leaders and to unworthy gods.

But Jesus had confused them with a new array of stories and the crowd had laughed its approval. Even the children had come to listen and because they had liked this man they had clambered upon his knees. Jesus said: "Suffer little children to come unto me: and forbid them not; for of such is the kingdom of God."

In short, the Nazarene was for ever doing and saying those things which a decent and self-respecting rabbi would never have done or said, and he went his way so pleasantly and so quietly that the police were powerless to interfere.

And then the doctrines which this man seemed to hold!

Had he not stated. upon more than one occasion, that the Kingdom of God was everywhere and stretched far and wide beyond the borders of Judæa where dwelt the chosen few of Jehovah's predilection?

Had he not openly broken the Sabbath under the pretext of curing a sick woman?

Didn't they say in Galilee that he had dined in the homes of foreigners and Roman officials and people who would never be tolerated within the outer portals of the Temple?

What was to become of Jerusalem and of the Temple and of the priests and of the inn-keepers and of the butchers and of everybody else, if the people of the city were to take such words seriously and actually began to believe that the spirit of God could be worshipped just as well in Damascus or Alexandria as on Mount Moriah?

JESUS EATS WITH A FOREIGNER

The town would be ruined and the priests and the inn-keepers and the butchers and everybody else would be ruined along with it.

And, ghastly to contemplate, the whole complicated fabric of Mosaic law would come tumbling down before this terrible new slogan of "Love your neighbour."

For that, in truth, was the gist of everything Jesus taught during the last months of his life.

He wanted, he implored people to love their neighbours and to stop quarrelling among themselves. He was crushed by the cruelty and the unreasoning injustice of everything he saw around him. By nature he was cheerful and full of fun. Life was a joy to him and not a burden. He loved his mother, his family, his friends. He took part in all the simple pleasures of his village. He was not a hermit and did not encourage those who tried to save their own souls by running away from life. But the world seemed so needlessly full of waste, of pain, of violence and disorder.

In the simplicity of his great heart, Jesus offered a cure of his own for these ills. He called it love. And that one word was the sum total of his teaching.

He did not greatly interest himself in the existing order of things.

He did not argue against the Empire.

He never spoke in favour of it.

The Pharisees slyly tried to catch him in an expression of sedition when they asked him what he thought of the Emperor. But Jesus knew that all form of government is merely a compromise and he refused to commit himself. He advised his hearers to obey the law of the land and to think more of their own faults than of the virtues or the defects of their rulers.

He did not tell his pupils to keep away from the service in the Temple, but encouraged them to be faithful in the performance of their religious duties.

He had a sincere admiration for the wisdom of the Old Testament, and continually referred to it in his own conversation.

In short, he refrained from saying or preaching or advocating anything that could be construed as an open challenge of the established laws.

But from the point of view of the Pharisees, he was much more dangerous than the fiercest of all rebels.

He made the people think for themselves.

*   *   *   *   *   *   *

As for the last days of Jesus, they have so often been told that we can be short about them. No part of the life of the great Prophet has received so much attention from Christian chroniclers as the few days immediately preceding his death.

It was really part of the eternal struggle between those who keep their backs turned firmly upon the future and one man who courageously dared to look forward.

The last entrance of Jesus into Jerusalem was in the nature of a triumph.

This did not mean that the people really had begun to understand the new ideas which he so patiently tried to explain to them. But for ever in search of a hero whom they could worship (for however short a time) they had now begun to idolise the Nazarene prophet who had appealed to their imagination by his lovable personality and the calm courage which he displayed in the presence of the almighty Councillors.

THE FANATIC

They were willing to believe anything that was told about Jesus, provided it had a touch of the extraordinary.

Mere cures were not enough to satisfy their primitive need of excitement.

The patient was very sick when Jesus happened to come to his village?

Nay!

The patient had been on the verge of death!

Until at last the poor patient had actually been dead and buried and had been taken out of the grave to be restored to life by the man of miracles.

This last story, the famous case of Lazarus, had made an enormous impression upon the credulous peasants of Judæa. Repeated from farm to farm, it had soon acquired a wealth of lurid detail which made it a very popular subject for mediæ-val legends and pictures.

When finally the cause of all this commotion was said to be in Jerusalem, every one wanted to see him, and when Jesus entered the city gate on his little donkey, the crowd lustily shouted hooray and threw flowers and generally made a great noise, as it will do whenever it finds an excuse for a celebration.

Unfortunately such public approval is like a bonfire on a rocky hill. It makes a great blaze, but it does not last very long.

Jesus knew this and he did not flatter himself that all these hosannas and hallelujahs meant anything.

He had heard them before. Other people have heard them since.

And if they have been wise, they have not taken them seriously. The wisdom of which remark the following pages will show clearly.

The first thing which Jesus did after his arrival was to look for lodgings. He did not stop in the city itself but in the suburb of Bethany which was situated upon the Mount of Olives. There in former years he had often stayed with Laza-rus and his faithful sisters, Mary and Martha.

It was only a short walk to Jerusalem and as soon as he had eaten something and rested from the fatigue of the day before, he went back to the Temple and for the second time took a whip and drove the cattle dealers and the money-changers out of the holy enclosure.

The next morning, very early, he had his answer.

The Sanhedrin had taken up his challenge.

And when Jesus appeared at the door of the Temple, he was stopped by armed guards and was asked upon whose authority he had committed the sacrilegious act of the afternoon before.

At once a mob was formed. People took sides.

Some said: "This man is right."

Others shouted: "He ought to be lynched."

And they argued and gesticulated and would have come to blows, when Jesus turned around and looked at them. Then they became very quiet and Jesus told them a few more stories.

Nothing else could have given such offence to the Pharisees.

Again Jesus was taking the initiative and was talking right over the heads of the priests to the multitude, and as always happened when he made a personal appeal, Jesus gained the immediate good will of his audience.

He was the victor in this opening battle with the authorities. The soldiers were obliged to let him go, and followed by his friends he quietly walked back to his lodgings and that day he was not molested any further.

But all this meant very little.

When the Pharisees set out to destroy a man they did not rest until their victim had been killed. And Jesus, who knew this, was in a very serious mood as night approached.

There was something else which gave him reason for anxiety.

Thus far his pupils had been very faithful to him, and the twelve who were always with him had really loved each other like so many brothers and had borne with each other's shortcomings with exemplary kindness.

But with one of them, all was not well.

Judas he was called and he was the son of a man who lived in the village of Cariot or Kerioth. He therefore was a Judæan, whereas the other eleven were Galileans. This may have had something to do with his attitude towards Jesus.

He felt all the time that he was being slighted—that the Galileans were trying to get the better of him—that he was a victim of his national antecedents.

None of this was true, but given a mean man with a petty mind, the most harmless remark may be turned into an unpardonable insult.

And Judas, who seemed to have joined Jesus on the impulse of a very momentary enthusiasm, was a greedy scoundrel with all the vengeful hatreds of a person aware of his own inferior qualities.

He had a great gift for figures and the other disciples had therefore asked him to be their treasurer and book-keeper and see that their slender funds were equally divided among all twelve.

Even in that quality, Judas had not given complete satisfaction and had gained the distrust of his fellow disciples. He was forever grumbling at the expense of some of the presents which were forced upon Jesus. More than once he had publicly given signs of his irritation when money was squandered upon what he was pleased to call "useless luxury."

Jesus had spoken to him about this and had tried to show him how foolish and ill-mannered it was to show resentment at a gift which had been offered with the kindest of intentions.

But Judas could not be convinced.

He did not say anything.

Neither did he leave Jesus. He continued to call himself one of "the twelve" and listened with assumed eagerness whenever Jesus explained one of his favourite ideas. But in his mind he was working on an idea of his own. His vanity had been hurt by the reprimand, and he decided to commit the lowest of all crimes. He was going to "get even."

Here in Jerusalem, where he was among his own people, the opportunity for revenge would offer itself easily.

When all the other disciples were asleep, Judas escaped from the house, and soon the Great Council, sitting late to discuss the steps which were to be taken, heard that there was a

man outside who offered to give them some very important information.

They told the guards to bring him in and they crowded around him to listen to his story.

Judas went straight to the heart of the problem.

The Council wanted to get hold of the person of Jesus?

They most certainly did.

But they were afraid of causing a disturbance in view

THE REWARD

of the Nazarene's well-known popularity with the crowd?

That again was true.

And if they arrested him in public, and there was any trouble, then the Roman soldiers would be called out and that would be fatal to the prestige of the Pharisees and would be used by the Sadducees for political purposes?

Quite correct.

Therefore, whatever was to be done must be done quietly and under the guard of darkness and with the least possible noise?

Judas had understood the situation very well indeed.

But suppose that some one who was thoroughly familiar with the movements of Jesus should offer to tell them how he

could be captured so that no one would hear of it until he was
safely in prison?

That would fit in excellently with the plans of the Council.

How much were they willing to pay for this very valuable
information?

There was a momentary consultation.

JUDAS

A certain sum was mentioned.

Judas was satisfied.

The bargain was struck.

Jesus had been sold to his enemies.

The price was thirty pieces of silver.

*   *   *   *   *   *   *

Jesus spent his last few hours of liberty quietly in the suburb of Bethany.

It was the day of Passover. The Jews observed this feast
by eating roast lamb and unleavened bread.

Jesus asked his disciples to go to town and reserve a room

in one of the smaller inns and order a dinner, that they might all be together.

When evening came, Judas, looking bland and innocent, left the house together with the others.

They went down the Mount of Olives and entered the city and found that everything was ready.

They took their seats around one long table and began to eat.

But it was not a cheerful meal. They felt the dread of those coming events which already were casting their terrible shadow over the small group of faithful friends.

Jesus spoke very little.

The others sat in gloomy silence.

At last, Peter could stand it no longer and he blurted out what was in everybody's mind.

"Master," he said, "we want to know. Do you have reason to suspect one of us?"

Softly Jesus answered: "Yes. One among you who is now sitting at this table will bring disaster upon us all."

Then all the disciples got up and crowded around him. They protested their innocence.

At that moment Judas slipped quietly out of the room.

They now all knew what was to come.

They could no longer stand it in that little room.

They needed fresh air, and they left the inn and walked out of the gate and went back to the Mount of Olives and opened the wicket to a garden which a friend had told them to use whenever they wished to be alone.

It was called Gethsemane, after an old oil-press which stood in a corner.

It was a warm night.

They were all very tired.

After a while Jesus walked away from the little group. But three of the disciples who were closest to him, followed at a distance.

He turned around and bade them wait and watch while he prayed.

The time had come for a final decision. Escape was still possible, but escape would mean a silent confession of guilt and defeat for his ideas.

He was alone among the silent trees and fought his last great battle.

He was a man in the fulness of his years.

Life still held a great promise.

Death, once his enemies captured him, would come in a most terrible form.

He made his choice.

He stayed.

He went back to his friends.

THE GARDEN OF GETH-
SEMANE

And behold! they were fast asleep.

A moment later, the whole garden was in an uproar.

Led by Judas, the guards of the Sanhedrin rushed upon the prophet.

Judas was at their head.

He threw his arms around his master and kissed him.

That was the sign for which the soldiers had waited.

At that moment, Peter realised what was happening.

He grabbed the sword from the hand of one of the assailants and fiercely he hacked at him. He hit him on the side of the head and the blood spurted from a ghastly wound.

Jesus put his hand upon Peter's arm.
There must be no violence.
The soldier was only doing his duty.

GETHSEMANE

One blow would only lead to another, and ideas were not fought with daggers and spears.

Jesus was handcuffed and through the dark streets of Jerusalem he was taken to the house of Annas, who together with Caiaphas, his son-in-law, was acting as High Priest.

They shouted with joy.

Their enemy was at their mercy.

The questioning began at once.

Why had Jesus been teaching those pernicious doctrines?

What did he mean by his attacks upon the old ceremonies?

Who had given him the right to speak the way he did?

Jesus answered quietly that it was useless to reply. The

priests knew the answer to their own questions. He had never hidden anything from any one. Why waste time upon further talk?

One of the guards, who had never heard a prisoner speak in

CAIAPHAS AND ANNAS

that fashion to a member of the Sanhedrin, hit Jesus a terrible blow. Then the others took him and bound him even tighter than before and they dragged him to the house of Caiaphas, where he was to spend the night.

It was too late to call the Great Council together.

But as soon as the excited Pharisees and the much-disturbed

Sadducees heard of the arrest, they left their beds, and through the dark rushed to the room where Jesus sat, peacefully waiting for what was to happen next.

Suddenly there was a rumour near the door. The guards had got hold of one of the disciples. One of the maids, so they explained, had just told them that this fisherman was a great friend of Jesus and had often been seen with him when they came to town.

Poor Peter was struck by panic.

The lights and the noise and the curses filled his heart with terror.

Tremblingly he denied that he had ever known Jesus.

Angrily the disappointed guards kicked him out of the room.

Jesus once more was alone with his enemies.

In this rough and tumble fashion the night was spent, but the next morning, as early as possible, the Great Council convened, and without examining the evidence or listening to any witnesses, they condemned the Nazarene to death.

According to tradition, it was Friday, April the seventh.

The main purpose had been accomplished. The Pharisees had rid their city of a great menace.

But their work remained as yet only half done.

There came insistent messengers from Roman headquarters.

Pilate wished to know what this commotion meant.

He was told.

No doubt all this was very interesting, but might he remind the Jews that neither their King nor their Council had the right to execute a man without a hearing before the Roman governor of the district?

Much against their will, the Sanhedrin let go of their

victim and Jesus was conducted to the royal palace, where Pilate was staying, to be questioned.

The pious Pharisees remained outside. It was the time of Passover, when no Jew should touch anything belonging to the heathen.

Pilate was greatly annoyed. Ever since he had been in Judæa, there had been trouble. Some one was for ever bothering him with questions which he did not understand and which seemed utterly absurd and futile.

He gave orders that Jesus be taken into his private rooms.

There he talked with him.

A few minutes' conversation convinced him that here was no cause for a death-warrant.

The charges were absurd.

PETER DENIES JESUS

Jesus ought to be set free.

Pilate sent for the spokesman of the Council and informed him bluntly that he had not been able to find Jesus guilty of anything known to Roman law.

That was a terrible blow to the Pharisees.

It looked as if their victim might escape.

They pleaded with the governor. They told him that Jesus had been stirring up trouble all the way from Judæa to Galilee.

That gave Pilate an idea.

"Is this man a Galilean or a Judæan subject?" he asked.

"Galilean," he was told.

"Then take him before Herod Antipas, who is King of Galilee, and let him decide," Pilate answered, glad to have found an excuse for washing his hands of this affair.

But His Majesty was as little inclined to take the responsibility as was the Roman official. He had come to Jerusalem to celebrate the Passover and not to judge people who were to be executed. He had heard a great deal about Jesus and he had always imagined him to be some sort of magician.

PONTIUS PILATE

He asked Jesus to show him the secret arts of sorcery, and Jesus, of course, refused to give an answer to so absurd a request. At that point, the interview was interrupted.

There was no reason why the faithful should keep away from one of their own compatriots, and the crowd now freely pushed into the court-room.

"He says that he is a King," they shouted. "He has told us himself that he is above the law." And all the foolish accusations which by now were shouted through the streets of Jerusalem were repeated with renewed violence.

Herod understood that he would have a riot on his hands unless he acted quickly. Better sacrifice an unpopular subject than run the risk of losing a throne.

"Take this man," he ordered. "Dress him up like the King he pretends to be, and then send him back to Pilate."

Somewhere a dirty old cloak was found and it was thrown across the shoulders of Jesus. The guards took him in their midst and back the whole mob went to see Pilate.

A man of courage might have saved Jesus. But Pilate was merely well-intentioned. He had talked the case over with his wife, who had urged him to use clemency. But there was only

JESUS IS TAKEN TO PRISON

a small garrison in Jerusalem, and the members of the Council grew more and more threatening. For by this time, the Sadducees had made common cause with the Pharisees. They were

GOLGOTHA

politicians, and their interest in religion was only secondary. They feared the practical consequences if Jesus were allowed to go free and decided therefore that he must die for the good of the state. Darkly they hinted to Pilate of certain secret reports which were ready to be sent to Cæsar, explaining in detail just what had happened and how his governor had openly taken the side of an enemy of the Empire.

That would mean dismissal without the benefit of pension. Pilate weakened.

Then he yielded.

The High Priest and his friends could have their victim and do unto him whatever they wanted.

The Council met to debate upon the exact method of execution.

As a rule, criminals were killed by stoning. But the case of Jesus was exceptional. There must be something humiliating in the form of his death. Runaway slaves were nailed upon a cross and were then left hanging until they died of hunger and thirst. It was decided that Jesus should be crucified.

Four Roman soldiers and a captain were told to do the work.

They took Jesus and made him stand up.

Once more the dirty purple robe was pulled across his shoulders. A crown, hastily woven of thorns, was pressed upon his head. A cross, made out of two heavy beams, was laid across his back.

There was a wait until two thieves, condemned to die at the same time, had been brought from their cells.

Late in the afternoon, the dreadful procession began its way to the hill where the gallows stood. It was called Golgotha, from the "gulgalta" or skulls which lay around.

Jesus, weak from lack of food and dizzy with the blows and the flogging which he had received, was hardly able to walk.

The road was lined with people.

They watched him as he dragged himself and his cross up the steep path of the low hill.

The tumult had died down.

The anger of the mob had spent itself.

An innocent man was being killed.

There were cries for mercy.

THE ROAD TO GOLGOTHA

But it was too late.

The ghastly drama had to be enacted unto the bitter end.

Jesus was nailed to the cross.

Over his head the Roman soldiers fastened a slip of paper, carrying the words "Jesus of Nazareth, King of the Jews."

They wrote it down in Roman and in Greek and in Hebrew, that all might read it and understand. It was meant as an insult to the Pharisees and Sadducees, who were responsible for this terrible miscarriage of justice.

When the last nail had been driven in, the soldiers sat down to gamble. In a wide circle, the people stood and looked. Some of them were merely curious. Others were former pupils. They had ventured back into the town to be with their Master at the last moment. There were a few women.

THE DEATH OF JESUS

It was growing dark rapidly.

On the cross, Jesus was softly murmuring words which few could understand. A kindly Roman soldier had soaked a sponge in vinegar and thrust it to Jesus on the end of a pike. Such a potion would deaden the pain of his lacerated hands and feet, but Jesus refused it.

By a last and supreme effort, he held to his consciousness. And he uttered a prayer.

He asked that his enemies be forgiven for what they had done unto him.

Then he whispered, "It is finished."

And he died.

That same evening, a certain Joseph from the village of Arimathea came to Pilate and asked to be allowed to take the body of Jesus from the cross and bury it. He was a rich man, but for many years he had listened to the words of this strange new prophet and he now easily persuaded the Roman governor to grant him his request.

However, when news thereof reached the ears of the Pharisees, they too hastened to the palace of the Viceroy. For they feared that the disciples might remove the body of their victim and then spread the rumor that he had been able to do what he had foretold a short while before when he had publicly proclaimed that after three days he would come back to life.

To prevent this they intended to seal up the grave and place a guard over it. Pilate, weak and vacillating until the very end, bade them do whatever they liked, provided they cause no further strife.

But when on the third day after the tragedy, two pious women went forth into the wilderness to weep upon the grave of their beloved teacher, behold! the soldiers lay prostrate, the stones had been rolled away and the tomb was empty.

And that night the trembling disciples could tell each other the glorious tidings—"Verily, our Master was the Son of God, for he has risen from the dead."

THE STRENGTH OF AN IDEA

CHAPTER XXVII

BUT THE NEW WORDS OF LOVE AND HOPE WHICH HAD BEEN WHISPERED INTO THE EARS OF AN UNHAPPY HUMANITY COULD NOT BE SUPPRESSED BY THE ACTS OF ROMAN GOVERNORS AND ENVIOUS JEWISH PRIESTS. NAY, NOT EVEN THE EMPEROR HIMSELF COULD PREVENT THE DISCIPLES OF JESUS FROM CARRYING THE MESSAGE OF THEIR MASTER TO ALL THOSE WHO CARED TO LISTEN

HE teaching of Jesus was the noblest expression of a human soul seeking happiness in the exercise of love and justice.

And this accounts for the survival and the final triumph of an idea which so many people during so many centuries have tried to destroy.

The world in which Jesus lived was very badly balanced. Those who sat in the seats of the mighty had too much and those who lived in slavery had too little.

But the latter outnumbered the former a thousand to one.

413

It was among the very poor that the words of Jesus were first heard; that his lessons of kindliness, his assurance that the Mighty Spirit which dominates this universe was a spirit of love, were first discussed and accepted.

Those simple folk had never been touched by the plausible philosophies of the Sceptics and the Epicureans.

They could not read and they did not know how to write.

They had ears, however, with which to hear.

To their masters they were little better than the cows grazing in the fields.

They lived and died and were forgotten and no one mourned their loss.

Then suddenly the door of their bondage was opened wide and they were given a glimpse of the truth that all men are children of One Heavenly Father.

As was to be expected, the first people to accept the new faith were those Jews who lived in the same neighbourhood and who had been able to hear him and feel the charm of his words and see the fearless light in his eyes.

A few centuries later, the Middle Ages, in their naïve acceptance of all written tradition, conceived a fierce hatred for the Jews, because certain Jews had been directly responsible for the death of him whom they called God's son.

This attitude was utterly indefensible as we have since come to understand.

Jesus was a Jew. His mother was a Jewess. His friends and his disciples were Jews.

He himself rarely left the Jewish community in which he had grown up. He was quite willing to associate with foreigners, with Greeks and Samaritans and Phœnicians and Syrians and Romans, but he lived and died for his own people and lay buried in Jewish ground.

He was the last and the greatest of the Jewish prophets and a direct descendant of those intrepid spiritual leaders who had stepped forward at every national crisis.

No, those Pharisees and Sadducees who killed Jesus were Jews only in the most narrow and bigoted sense of the word.

They were the selfish defenders of an intolerant creed which had outlived its usefulness by many hundred years.

They were the self-appointed administrators of an outrageous monopoly of outward holiness.

They committed a terrible crime, but they committed it as members of a political and a religious party, and not as Jews, and if they were without rivals in their hatred for the new prophet, others of their race were equally staunch in the love which they bore their murdered Master.

And it was among those faithful pupils living in the land of Galilee and of Judæa that the first Christian community, the first combination of people who believed that Jesus was the Christos, or Anointed, was founded.

It is not quite correct to speak in this connection of a Christian community, for that name was not used until several years later in the city of Antioch in Asia Minor. But the community of disciples existed and prospered and the members met regularly, almost under the shadow of the cross, in that same city of Jerusalem which had sent Jesus to his terrible death.

Soon, however, there were dissensions and little groups were formed by those who shared the same ideas and could not quite agree with their neighbours. Some, like Stephen, who was familiar with the current Greek philosophies, understood that there must be a definite break between the old and the new and that there was not room in their church for the stern Jehovah of Moses and the loving God whom Jesus had preached.

But when they said this, the others arose in their wrath and killed them, for they seemed to be in favour of letting down all barriers against foreigners, and that was still a horrible thing in the eyes of those whose childhood had been spent within sight of the old Temple.

Presently, however, the breach widened. In less than a dozen years after the death of Jesus, his teachings had been put into a definite shape which forever separated the Christian from the Jew, as it separates him from the Buddhist or the Mohammedan.

From that moment on it was comparatively easy for the new doctrine to spread across western Asia.

The wisdom of the old Jewish law lay buried in the unknown tongue of the forgotten Hebrew language.

But everything connected with the "Christos" was being written down in Greek, and Alexander the Macedonian had made that tongue the international language of antiquity.

The stage was set.

The world of the west was ready for the message from the east.

There was need of a man who could carry Galilee to Rome.

He came.

And his name was Paul.

THE TRIUMPH OF AN IDEA

CHAPTER XXVIII

ONE THING, HOWEVER, WAS NECESSARY BEFORE CHRISTIANITY COULD BECOME A WORLD-RELIGION. THERE MUST BE A BREAK WITH JERUSALEM AND THE NARROW TRIBAL PREJUDICES OF THE OLDER FAITH. A BRILLIANT SPEAKER AND ORGANISER BY THE NAME OF PAUL SAVED CHRISTIANITY FROM THE FATE OF DEGENERATION INTO ANOTHER LITTLE JEWISH SECT. PAUL LEFT JUDÆA, CROSSED OVER INTO EUROPE AND MADE THE NEW CHURCH AN INTERNATIONAL INSTITUTION WHICH RECOGNISED NO DIFFERENCE BETWEEN JEW AND ROMAN AND GREEK

E know Paul well.

Historically speaking, we know him really much better than we do Jesus. The Acts of the Apostles, the fifth book of the New Testament, which follows immediately upon the Gospels, devotes sixteen chapters to the life and the works of Paul. And in the letters written by him when he was travelling among the heathen of the west, we find a very minute description of his doctrines.

He was the son of Jewish parents who lived in the city of Tarsus, in the district of Cilicia in the northwest corner of Asia Minor. Their son was given the name of Shaul or Saul.

He was well connected, had relatives in several parts of the empire, and when quite young he had been sent to Jerusalem

ST. STEPHEN

to go to school. Here his position was somewhat anomalous, for although a Jew, he happened to be a Roman citizen. This honour seems to have been conferred upon his father for certain services rendered to Rome. In those days it was a passport which allowed the owner a great many privileges.

After he had finished his education (the conventional education of all Jewish children) Saul was apprenticed to a tentmaker and afterwards he set up for himself in the same business.

Trained in the strict school of the Pharisees, young Saul was heart and soul with the Great Council when they ordered the execution of Jesus. Afterwards, he eagerly joined the group of young patriots who tried to eradicate the seditious doctrines which the hated Nazarene had spread throughout Galilee and Judæa.

He was present when Stephen was stoned to death and moved not a finger to save the poor man who was the first martyr to give his life for the new faith.

But as he was for ever at the head of a band of young rowdies, who in the name of the old law were committing new crimes, he came in almost daily contact with the followers of Jesus.

These earliest Christians, in great contrast to most of their contemporaries, were exemplary in their personal conduct.

They lived sober and abstemious lives, they told no lies, they gave liberally to the poor, they shared their possessions with their needy neighbours and went to the gallows with a prayer upon their lips for those who persecuted them.

At first, Saul was puzzled.

Then he began to understand that Jesus must have been something more than a revolutionary agitator to have inspired such devotion in people who had never even seen him.

DAMASCUS

He was a very intelligent pupil. Jesus had been a very intelligent teacher. Suddenly Saul understood Jesus, and surrendered himself to the will of his unknown Master.

His conversion took place on a lonely road.

He was on his way to Damascus. The authorities in Jerusalem had heard that a number of Jews in that city were beginning to show a leaning towards the Christian doctrines. The High Priest had given Saul letters to his colleague in Damascus asking that those heretics be surrendered and be brought to Jerusalem for trial and execution.

Saul had gone upon this gruesome errand as happy as a boy. But ere he reached the capital of Syria, he had a vision.

His blind eyes became seeing.

Jesus was right, and the High Priest was wrong.

It was the logical conclusion to which millions of people have come ever since.

Instead of presenting his credentials and asking that the dissenters be given into his custody, Saul went straightway to Ananias, who was the leader of the Damascan community and begged that he might be baptised.

ANTIOCH

From that moment on he was called Paul and under that name he gained his fame as the apostle to the heathen.

He gave up his profession and at the request of Barnabas (an early convert from the island of Cyprus) he went to the city of Antiochia, where the name Christians was for the first time publicly given to those who accepted Jesus and no longer worshipped in the old synagogue.

Paul stayed in Antioch only a short time and then commenced that life of a wandering missionary which carried him to all the corners of the Empire and gave him as his final reward a martyr's grave in an unknown Roman cemetery.

At first he worked chiefly among the coastal cities of Asia Minor and made many converts. The Greeks listened to him with evident pleasure. They could follow his line of reasoning. They were impressed by the tact he used to overcome their objections and willingly they joined the new faith.

THE APOSTLE

But the little groups of Jewish-Christians which were to be found in most Mediterranean ports hated Paul and did their best to make his work a failure.

Prejudices inherited from twenty generations of orthodox ancestors cannot be shed in a minute. To those good people it seemed that Paul was going much too far, that he was too friendly to the followers of Zeus and Mithras, that he should first of all be a Jew and that his Christian ideals should be of secondary importance and should conform as closely as possible to the old Mosaic laws.

When Paul tried to prove to them that the two had nothing in common, that one could not serve Jehovah and the God of Jesus at the same time, their dislike was turned into open hatred.

Several times they tried to kill the hated tent-maker, until Paul began to understand that Christianity, if it were to survive, must appeal to an entirely new public, and must break definitely and unequivocally with Judaism.

He still remained in Asia Minor, but finally in Troas (a

seaport not far from the ruins of the old city of Troy of which Homer had sung) he made up his mind to go to Europe.

He crossed the Hellespont and went straightway to Philippi, an important town in the heart of Macedonia.

TROAS

He was now in Alexander's old country and there, being familiar with the Greek language, he preached the words of Jesus to his first western audience.

Before he had spoken more than a couple of times, he was arrested and taken to prison.

But the people had liked him and he was quietly allowed to escape.

Nothing daunted by this unfortunate experience, he decided to attack the enemy in their own stronghold. He went to Athens. The Athenians listened politely enough. But they had heard so many new doctrines during the last four hundred years, that missionaries no longer interested them.

Paul's work was never interfered with, but no one stepped forward and asked to be baptised.

In Corinth, Paul secured a great success, as we know from the two letters which afterwards he wrote to the Corinthian congregation, and in which he explained some more of his ideas, which as time passed grew further and further away from those old formulas which were still so dear to the hearts of the Jewish-Christians.

Paul by this time had been several years in Europe.

The fundament for all future missionary work had been laid. He could return to his own world of Asia Minor.

First he visited Ephesus, on the western shore. In that city since time immemorial there had been a shrine to Diana. Diana (or Artemis, as the Greeks called her), the twin sister of Apollo, was something more than the goddess of the moon. The people believed that she could influence all living matter

THE TEMPLE OF DIANA

and in their imagination she was more powerful than her father Zeus, just as during the Middle Ages, Mary the mother of Jesus was thought worthy of greater homage than Jesus.

Paul, not knowing the conditions in the city, asked permission to speak in the local synagogue. This was granted, but withdrawn as soon as the Jews had heard a few of his sermons. He then hired the lecture hall of a former Greek philosopher and for two years he conducted what one might call the first theological seminary.

Ephesus, like Jerusalem, was a city with a religious monopoly. The services in the temple of Diana brought profit to many people.

There were visitors and there were offerings. There was a brisk trade in statues of Diana which pilgrims carried home, just as to-day we buy statues of the Madonna in Lourdes and images of Peter in Rome.

This business of course was threatened with ruin if Paul should be successful and should destroy the ancient belief in the supernatural powers of the wonder-working goddess. The goldsmiths and the silversmiths and the priests of the temple did exactly what their colleagues of Jerusalem had done a few years before. They tried to kill Paul in the same way as the Pharisees and the Sadducees had murdered Jesus.

Paul, warned of his danger, fled. But his work had been done.

The Christian community of Ephesus was too strong to be destroyed and although Paul never visited the city afterwards, Ephesus became the most important centre of the early Christian world and several of the earliest councils which gave the new doctrines their final shape were held in this town, as you may read in the chronicles of the second and third centuries of our era.

Paul was now growing older.

He had suffered many hardships and did not know whether he could live much longer.

Before his death he decided to visit once more the scene of his Master's death.

There were many who warned him.

The so-called Christian community of Jerusalem was in truth a branch of the Judaic faith. The very name of Paul was execrated by those who could not forgive the apostle his love for the heathen. His success in Greece counted for nothing in a town which was still dominated by the spirit of the Pharisees.

Paul refused to believe this, but as soon as he had set foot in the Temple, he was recognised and a quickly gathering crowd threatened to lynch him.

The Roman troops, however, came to his rescue and took him to the castle.

They did not know exactly what to do with him. At first they thought that he was a revolutionary agitator, come from Egypt to Judæa to stir up trouble. But when Paul proved that he was a Roman citizen, they hastily offered their apologies and removed the handcuffs which had been placed upon him as a matter of precaution.

Lysias, the commander of the garrison in Jerusalem, found himself in the same predicament as Pilate a few years before.

PAUL RETURNS TO THE TEMPLE

He had no reason to proceed against Paul, but it was his duty to maintain order.

He allowed Paul to be brought before the Great Council and once more the town was on the verge of civil war.

The Pharisees and the Sadducees had long since repented of their hasty coalition brought about for the purpose of killing their common enemy Jesus and they had engaged in a series of bitter quarrels which forever kept the people of Jerusalem in a turmoil of religious excitement.

Under those circumstances it was impossible for Paul to expect a fair trial and Lysias wisely removed him to the castle where he was safe from the mob.

And then, as soon as it could be done without attracting too much public attention, he sent Paul to Cæsarea where the procurator resided.

Paul remained more than two years in Cæsarea and during that time enjoyed almost complete liberty.

But he grew tired of the endless accusations made against

PAUL GOES TO ROME

him by the members of the Sanhedrin and finally he asked that he be taken to Rome and allowed to explain his case to the Emperor, as was his good right as a Roman citizen.

In the fall of the year 60, Paul left for Rome.

It was a most disastrous voyage.

The ship which carried the apostle was shipwrecked and thrown upon the rocks of the island of Malta.

After three months' delay another vessel took Paul and his companions to the Italian mainland and in the year 61, Paul reached the city of Rome.

Here too it seems that he enjoyed a great deal of freedom. The Romans really had nothing against him. They simply did not want him to be in Jerusalem where his presence might have caused a riot. They were not interested in Jewish theology and certainly did not mean to try a man for crimes which were not recognised by their own courts.

Now that he was no longer a menace to the safety of the state, he was allowed to come and go at will and he made the best of this unexpected opportunity.

He rented a quiet room in one of the poorer quarters and once more turned missionary.

His courage during these last years was sublime. He was an old man, almost broken by the hardships of the past twenty years. But the jail sentences, the scourgings, the stoning (which he had received once with almost fatal results at the hands of his own compatriots), the endless journeys on ship and on foot and on horseback, the hunger and the thirst, all counted for nothing compared to the opportunity of explaining the ideals of Jesus personally to the capital of the civilised world.

MALTA

How long he continued to preach or what became of him finally we do not know.

In the year 64 there occurred one of those senseless anti-Christian outbreaks which were soon to be very popular. The Emperor Nero encouraged the mob when they started out to plunder and murder all those who belonged to the new faith.

Paul seems to have been one of the victims of this pogrom.

After that day we never hear his name mentioned again.

But the modern church stands as a monument to his genius.

Paul was the bridge which led from Galilee to Rome. He saved Christianity from degenerating into another little Jewish sect.

He made it the religion of an entire world.

THE ESTABLISHED CHURCH

CHAPTER XXIX

SHORTLY AFTERWARDS, ANOTHER DISCIPLE BY THE NAME OF PETER WENT TO ROME TO VISIT THE SMALL COLONY OF CHRISTIANS ON THE BANKS OF THE TIBER. HE HIMSELF PERISHED DURING ONE OF THE MANY POGROMS ORGANISED BY THE EMPERORS WHEN THEY BEGAN TO FEAR THE INFLUENCE OF THIS NEW RELIGIOUS ORGANISATION. BUT THE CHURCH EASILY SURVIVED THOSE ATTACKS. THREE CENTURIES LATER, WHEN ROME CEASED TO BE THE POLITICAL CENTRE OF THE WESTERN WORLD, THE CHRISTIAN BISHOPS OF THE CITY MADE THEIR RESIDENCE THE SPIRITUAL CAPITAL OF THE ENTIRE WORLD

O F Peter, whose name is so closely connected with the change of our spiritual centre from Jerusalem to Rome, we know much less than we do of Paul.

We saw him last when in terrible distress he fled from the house of Caiaphas after he had just denied that he knew Jesus. Then we catch a glimpse of him at the crucifixion. Thereafter for many years we lose sight of him altogether, until he turns up as a very successful missionary, writing very interesting letters from distant cities whither he had travelled to preach the words of his Master.

A man of much less education than Paul, a simple fisherman from the Sea of Galilee, Peter lacked that personal magnetism which made Paul the dominating figure of every society in which he moved, whether Jewish or Greek or Roman or Cilician.

But his momentary cowardice at the trial of Jesus must not make us decide that Peter was lacking in courage.

ST. PETER

Some of the bravest soldiers and some of the most famous regiments have done strange things at unexpected moments. Afterwards, however, when reason has come back, they have invariably made up for their sudden fall from grace by a renewed faithfulness to duty.

And so with Peter.

Besides, he was a man of parts who did a very useful piece of work in a very efficient manner. Being aware of his own limitations he left the more spectacular work to Paul, who spent his days abroad, and to James, the brother of Jesus, who had become the acknowledged head of the church in the old country.

Meanwhile, he contented himself with the less important countries on the outskirts of Judæa, and together with his faithful wife, he trudged the long roads from Babylon to Samaria and from Samaria to Antioch and told the people what Jesus had taught him in the old days when they fished together in the Sea of Galilee.

What finally brought him to Rome, we do not know.

In a strict historical sense, we have no reliable data upon this voyage of Peter. But the name of the apostle is so closely connected with the early development of the church as a world-wide institution, that we must devote a few words to this wonderful old man whom Jesus had loved beyond all others.

A chronicler who wrote in the middle of the second century mentions that Peter and Paul had worked in Rome at the same time and had been killed by the mob within a few months of each other.

Such wholesale killing of the heretics was a new departure in Roman history.

The former indifference of the Roman government toward the followers of Jesus was gradually beginning to turn into hatred.

As long as the Christians had been merely "queer people" who came together occasionally in obscure houses in equally obscure parts of the town to inspire each other with stories about a Messiah who had died the death of a runaway slave, no danger was to be feared from their meetings.

But as gradually the words of Christ began to reach more and more people, there was an end to the patience of the authorities.

It was the old, old story.

First of all, those who depended for their living upon the worship of Jupiter began to complain. They were losing money. The temples were being deserted. The Romans were giving all their gold to a foreign divinity of very obscure origin and the loss on the part of the cattle-dealers and the priests was very serious.

Having assured themselves of the co-operation of the police, the interested parties then began a campaign of slander against the Christians. The half-savage mob of disinherited peasants, living miserably in the suburbs, was delighted to hear such vile accusations against those of their neighbours who offended them by the decency of their conduct. These people winked at one another meaningly when one Roman housewife told another how "those Christians kill little children every Sunday and drink the blood, just to please their god," and suggested that the time had come to "do something."

It mattered little that all the reliable authors of that day agreed upon the saintliness of the lives of their Christian neighbours, and held them up as an example to those Romans who were for ever bewailing the disappearance of the "good old times" while practicing all the vices of the bad new days.

THE SLAVE

But there was still another and a more powerful group which from purely selfish motives feared the success of Christianity. The necromancers and the oriental mystics and the purveyors of a hundred new mysteries which they had only recently imported "exclusively" from the east, found that their business was being ruined. How could they hope to compete with a group of men and women who by preference lived in poverty and who refused to charge a single denarius for explaining the doctrines of their Galilean teacher?

All these different parties, inspired by greed, soon made common cause and went to the authorities and denounced the Christians as wicked and seditious criminals who were plotting against the safety of the Empire.

The Roman authorities were not easily frightened and for a long time they showed great unwillingness to take definite action. But the strange stories about the Christians continued to be repeated, first here and then there, and with such a wealth of detail that they seemed to be based upon solid fact.

Meanwhile the Christians themselves, in their zeal for a new and better world, helped those suspicions along by certain deep and dark references to the Day of Judgment when the entire planet was to be purged by the lightning from Heaven.

When Nero, in a drunken fit, set fire to the greater part of his own capital, people remembered those Christian prophecies which had foretold the destruction of all the big cities.

In an outburst of fear, the Romans lost all sense of reality.

Jews and Christians were hunted down like rats and were thrown into jail. Torture made them confess the most incredible plots against the state. For weeks at a time the executioners and the wild animals were kept busy and it was upon one of these occasions that Paul and Peter both were hacked to death.

But as the Romans were to learn, steadfast martyrs are the best possible advertisement for a new creed. Thus far the Christian doctrines had found most of their adherents in the kitchen. Now the parlour began to take an interest. Before the end of the first century, many high officials and women of noble rank had been executed because they were suspected of Christian leanings and had been unwilling to show their loyalty to the Empire by offerings to the old gods.

Persecution caused resentment and the Christians, who in the beginning had been very meek and humble, began at last to take steps to defend themselves. When it was no longer safe to gather in the open air or in the dining-room of a private house, the church went underground.

Deserted stone quarries in the neighbourhood of Rome were hastily transformed into chapels and there the faithful came together once a week to listen to the sermons of some pious wandering minister, and to find comfort in repeating the stories told a hundred years before by the carpenter from Nazareth.

ROME BURNED

This made all Christians members of a secret society, something which they had never been before.

The Roman officials, for good and plentiful reasons, feared secret societies beyond all other things. In a country where eighty per cent of the people were slaves, it was not safe to allow surreptitious meetings which could not be controlled by the police sergeant.

Reports began to come in from the provinces about the spread of the Christian affliction. A few wise governors kept their heads and quietly waited until the people had regained their senses. Others allowed themselves to be bribed into silence by their Christian subjects. Still others arranged pogroms and tried to find favour in the eyes of the Emperor by the wholesale execution of men and women and children, who in any way could be connected with the suspicious "Galilean mystery."

And everywhere and all the time the authorities met with the same response on the part of their victims. Invariably they denied all guilt and their magnificent behaviour on the scaffold made them so many friends that public executions were always followed by an increased number of candidates for the Christian brotherhood.

Indeed, when the persecutions came to an end, the small congregations had grown to such proportions that it became necessary to appoint certain officers whose business it was to represent the church before the law and to administer those funds which pious people were giving for charity and for the relief of the sick.

First a few of the older men, the so-called "Elders," were asked to undertake the management of the daily affairs of the community. Next, for the sake of a more effectual co-operation, a number of churches in a given town or in a given district combined forces and appointed a Bishop or general overseer to direct their common policy.

These bishops, by the very nature of their office, were supposed to be the direct successors of the apostles. Naturally, as the church grew richer, their power increased. And of course, the bishop of a village in Judæa or Asia Minor had less influence than the bishop of a big city in Italy or France.

It was inevitable that the other bishops should come to regard their colleague in Rome with a certain amount of awe and respect. It was also inevitable that in Rome, the city which had been accustomed to rule the destinies of the world for almost five hundred years, there should be a larger number of men experienced in statecraft and in diplomacy.

And it was only logical during the days of Rome's decline, when there was no longer a chance for energetic young men to make a career in the army or in the civil service, that they should turn to the church to find an outlet for their ambitions and their need of enterprise.

For most unfortunately, the old Empire had fallen upon evil days

Bad economic management had impoverished the small farmers who from the beginning of the republic had been the mainstay of the armies and who now flocked to the cities, clamouring for bread and amusements.

Disturbances in the heart of Asia had driven large hordes of barbarians westward and these were steadily encroaching upon territory which for generations had been in the possession of Rome. But the disorganisation in the provinces was as nothing compared to political conditions in the capital. One Emperor after another was first placed upon the throne and then killed within the walls of his palace by the foreign mercenaries who were the real masters of the Empire.

ROME THE SPIRITUAL
CENTRE

At last it was no longer considered safe for the Roman Emperors to reside in their own city. The successors of Cæsar left the shores of the Tiber and went to live elsewhere. When that happened, the bishops of Rome automatically became the most influential men of their community and assumed full leadership. They represented the only well organised power that was left and the Emperors, removed from their old capital, needed their support to retain a semblance of prestige in the Italian peninsula.

They were willing to make a bid for it.

In the year 313, a formal edict of tolerance made an end to all further persecution. A century later Rome was acknowledged as the spiritual capital of east and west and north and south.

The Church stood triumphant.

And ever since, above the noise of battle and strife, have been heard the words of the prophet of Nazareth, asking those who loved him to cure the ills of this world by that perfect love which understands all things.

5000 - 4000 B.C. THE BEGINNING OF CIVILIZATION IN THE VALLEY OF THE NILE.

4000 - 3000 B.C. BEGINNING OF CIVILIZATION IN MESOPOTAMIA

3000 - 2000 B.C. HAMMURABI THE BABYLONIAN KING GIVES HIS PEOPLE THEIR LAW.

THE PYRAMIDS ARE BUILT

2000 - 1500 B.C. THE JEWS LEAVE THEIR OLD HOME AND MOVE WESTWARD.

EGYPT CONQUERED BY THE HYKSOS

RISE OF ASSYRIA

1500 - 1300 B.C

CRETE THE CENTRE OF CIVILIZATION.

RISE OF PHOENICIA

THE JEWS MOVE INTO EGYPT.

1300 - 1200 B.C

MOSES GIVES HIS PEOPLE THEIR LAW.

GREECE IS SETTLED BY PEOPLE FROM THE NORTH

ITALY IS SETTLED BY PEOPLE FROM THE NORTH

THE JEWS LEAVE EGYPT.

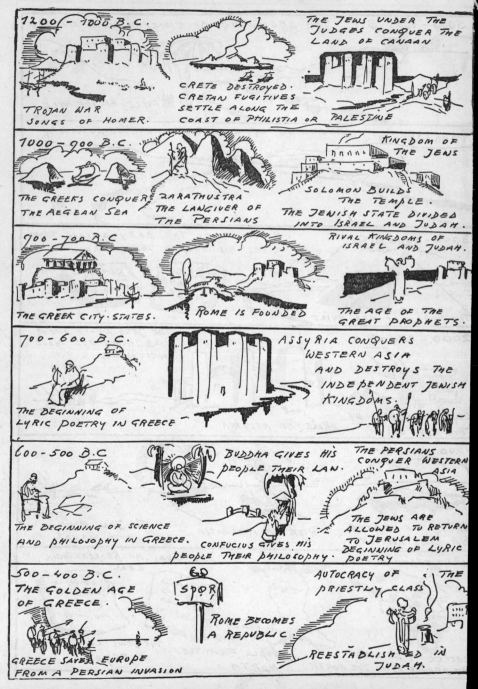

1200 - 1000 B.C.

THE JEWS UNDER THE JUDGES CONQUER THE LAND OF CANAAN

TROJAN WAR SONGS OF HOMER.

CRETE DESTROYED. CRETAN FUGITIVES SETTLE ALONG THE COAST OF PHILISTIA OR PALESTINE

1000 - 900 B.C.

THE GREEKS CONQUER THE AEGEAN SEA

ZARATHUSTRA THE LAWGIVER OF THE PERSIANS

KINGDOM OF THE JEWS

SOLOMON BUILDS THE TEMPLE. THE JEWISH STATE DIVIDED INTO ISRAEL AND JUDAH.

900 - 700 B.C

THE GREEK CITY-STATES.

ROME IS FOUNDED

RIVAL KINGDOMS OF ISRAEL AND JUDAH.

THE AGE OF THE GREAT PROPHETS.

700 - 600 B.C.

THE BEGINNING OF LYRIC POETRY IN GREECE

ASSYRIA CONQUERS WESTERN ASIA AND DESTROYS THE INDEPENDENT JEWISH KINGDOMS.

600 - 500 B.C

THE BEGINNING OF SCIENCE AND PHILOSOPHY IN GREECE.

BUDDHA GIVES HIS PEOPLE THEIR LAW.

CONFUCIUS GIVES HIS PEOPLE THEIR PHILOSOPHY.

THE PERSIANS CONQUER WESTERN ASIA

THE JEWS ARE ALLOWED TO RETURN TO JERUSALEM BEGINNING OF LYRIC POETRY

500 - 400 B.C.

THE GOLDEN AGE OF GREECE.

GREECE SAVES EUROPE FROM A PERSIAN INVASION

SPQR

ROME BECOMES A REPUBLIC.

AUTOCRACY OF THE PRIESTLY CLASS

REESTABLISHED IN JUDAH.

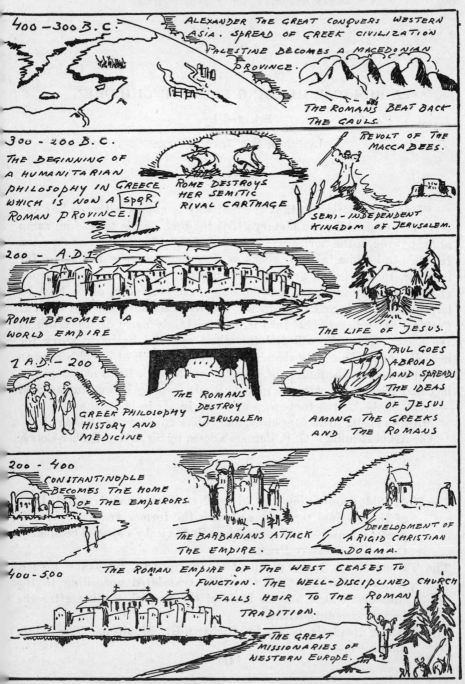

400 – 300 B.C.

ALEXANDER THE GREAT CONQUERS WESTERN ASIA. SPREAD OF GREEK CIVILIZATION PALESTINE BECOMES A MACEDONIAN PROVINCE.

THE ROMANS BEAT BACK THE GAULS.

300 – 200 B.C.

THE BEGINNING OF A HUMANITARIAN PHILOSOPHY IN GREECE WHICH IS NOW A ROMAN PROVINCE.

SPQR

ROME DESTROYS HER SEMITIC RIVAL CARTHAGE

REVOLT OF THE MACCABEES.

SEMI-INDEPENDENT KINGDOM OF JERUSALEM.

200 – A.D.1

ROME BECOMES A WORLD EMPIRE

THE LIFE OF JESUS.

1 A.D. – 200

GREEK PHILOSOPHY HISTORY AND MEDICINE

THE ROMANS DESTROY JERUSALEM

PAUL GOES ABROAD AND SPREADS THE IDEAS OF JESUS AMONG THE GREEKS AND THE ROMANS

200 – 400

CONSTANTINOPLE BECOMES THE HOME OF THE EMPERORS.

THE BARBARIANS ATTACK THE EMPIRE.

DEVELOPMENT OF A RIGID CHRISTIAN DOGMA.

400 – 500

THE ROMAN EMPIRE OF THE WEST CEASES TO FUNCTION. THE WELL-DISCIPLINED CHURCH FALLS HEIR TO THE ROMAN TRADITION.

THE GREAT MISSIONARIES OF WESTERN EUROPE.

A BIBLICAL READING LIST FOR CHILDREN

Selected by

LEONORE ST. JOHN POWER

"I daresay, after all, that the best way is not to bother a boy too early and overmuch with history; that the best way is to let him ramp at first through the Scriptures even as he might through 'The Arabian Nights': to let him take the books as they come, merely indicating, for instance, that Job is a great poem, the Psalms great lyrics, the story of Ruth a lovely idyll, the Song of Songs the perfection of an Eastern love-poem. Well, and what then? He will certainly get less of 'The Cotter's Saturday Night' into it, and certainly more of the truth of the East. There he will feel the whole splendid barbaric story for himself: the flocks of Abraham and Laban: the trek of Jacob's sons to Egypt for corn: the figures of Rebekah at the well, Ruth at the gleaning, and Rispah beneath the gibbet: Sisera bowing in weariness: Saul —great Saul—by the tent-prop with the jewels in his turban:

"All its lordly male-sapphires, and rubies courageous at heart."

"The Art of Reading," G. P. Putnam's Sons; by Sir Arthur Quiller-Couch.

THE BIBLE

The Holy Bible; containing the Old and New Testaments translated out of the original tongues: and with the former translations diligently compared and revised by His Majesty's special command. Oxford University Press.

The Twenty-Four Books of the Holy Scriptures, by Isaac Leeser. Block Publishing Co. Carefully translated according to the Massoretic text, on the basis of the English version after the best Jewish authorities.

The Modern Reader's Bible, by Richard G. Moulton. The Macmillan Co.

A fine rendering of the Old and New Testament into a modern
literary form. Two volumes of stories from the Old and the
New Testament make up the Children's Series in this collection.

The Bible for Young People: arranged from the King James Version
with twenty-four full page illustrations from old masters. The
Century Co.

A very satisfactory edition printed in large type. The Stories
are given in Bible language omitting only genealogies and doctrines and whatever is generally regarded as unprofitable to
young readers.

The Doré Bible Gallery, illustrated by Gustave Doré. William T.
Amies.

One hundred illustrations, and a page of explanatory text facing
each. This wonderfully vivid presentation of Biblical scenes
is now out of print but may sometimes be found in second-hand
book shops.

A Child's Guide to the Bible, by George Hodges. The Baker &
Taylor Co.

An interesting account of how the Bible came to be written, together with an account of the historical settings of the Old and
the New Testaments.

STORIES FROM THE BIBLE

The Garden of Eden, by George Hodges, illustrated by Walter H.
Everett. Houghton Mifflin Co.

Stories from the first nine books of the Old Testament told sympa-
thetically and dramatically in very good style.

The Castle of Zion, by George Hodges. Houghton Mifflin Co.

More stories from the Old Testament.

Bible Stories to Read and Tell, selected and arranged by Frances
Jenkins Olcott. Houghton Mifflin Co.

These stories are selected from the King James Version of the
Old Testament. The powerful language and forceful imagery
of the original is well preserved.

The Children's Bible, translated and arranged by Henry A. Sherman
and Charles Foster Kent. Charles Scribner's Sons.

Telling Bible Stories, by Louise Seymour. Charles Scribner's Sons.

A study of the relation of children to the stories of the Old Testament, and an interpretation of the stories for religious teaching.

THE COUNTRIES OF THE BIBLE

The Book of the Ancient World, by Dorothy Mills, with illustrations and maps. G. P. Putnam's Sons.

An interesting and well arranged account of the Egyptians, the Assyrians and the Babylonians, the Hebrews, the Persians and the Phœnicians.

Ancient Assyria, by Rev. James Baikie. A. & C. Black.

A description of an Assyrian city 2800 years ago.

The Civilization of the Ancient Egyptians, by A. Bothwell Gosse. T. & C. Jack.

A fascinating book, profusely illustrated, telling of the domestic life, the art, the science, the religion and the literature of the ancient Egyptians.

Legends of Ancient Egypt, by F. H. Brooksbank. Thomas Y. Crowell.

"In all about them the Egyptians saw the hand of God—in the rising of the Nile and the fertilizing soil; in bird and beast, in sun and moon, in sky and earth and sea."

Ancient Man, by Hendrik Willem van Loon. Boni and Liveright.

How the human race developed through the ages and finally founded Jerusalem, the City of Law, and Damascus, the City of Trade.

Our Young Folk's Josephus, simplified by William Shepard. J. B. Lippincott.

An abstract of the two great works of Flavius Josephus, "The Jewish War" and "The Antiquities of the Jews," written A.D. 75-A.D. 93 to familiarize the Roman people with the history of the Jews as it is recorded in the Scripture.

Jewish Fairy Tales and Legends by Aunt Naomi. Bloch Publishing Co.

Charming legends dealing with the boyish exploits of the great Biblical characters, Abraham, Moses and David, rewritten from stories in the Talmud and Midrash.

The Arabian Nights, selected and edited by Padraic Colum, illustrated by Eric Pape. The Macmillan Co.

Tales of wonder and magnificence which form, not a book, but a whole literature which goes back to Persia and China and India, as well as to Arabia and Egypt, for its origins.

Ottoman Wonder Tales, translated and edited by Lucy M. J. Garnett, with illustrations in colour by Charles Folkard. A. & C. Black.

"There are religious and semi-religious legends connected with the Prophet Mohammed and his family and with the holy men of Islam; mythical stories concerning the magical exploits of King David and King Solomon; wild romances concerning Djinns, Peris and all allied Supernals; fables with a moral and humorous stories innumerable."

Eastern Stories and Legends, selected and adapted by Marie L. Shedlock. E. P. Dutton & Co.

"Long, long ago the Wisdom Child that should in time become the Buddha was born a King."

The Golden Age of Myth and Legend, by Thomas Bulfinch. George G. Harrap & Co.

The Adventures of Odysseus or The Children's Homer, by Padraic Colum, illustrated in colour and black and white by Willy Pogany.

An attractive, poetically rendered edition of this great story.

Pictures from Greek Life and Story, by The Rev. A. J. Church. G. P. Putnam's Sons.

Pictures from Roman Life and Story, by The Rev. A. J. Church. D. Appleton & Co.

The Story of Mankind, by Hendrik Willem van Loon. Boni and Liveright.

"History is the mighty Tower of Experience, which Time has built amidst the endless fields of bygone ages."

THE DAWN OF CHRISTIANITY

When the King Came, by George Hodges. Houghton Mifflin Co.

Stories from the Four Gospels telling how the King was born, how He lived unknown for thirty years, how He went about the land of Galilee with His Disciples, and how He came to Jerusalem and was betrayed.

The Story of Jesus, by Rosa Mulholland. Benziger Brothers.

Simply and reverently told for little children.

The Story of Jesus, pictures and descriptive text from the New Testament, selected and arranged by Ethel Nathalie Dana. Marshall Jones Co.

Exceptionally beautiful colored prints from the old masters, Giotto, Fra Angelico, Duccio, Ghirlandaio, and Barna da Siena. A distinctive contribution to both art and literature for children.

The Life of Our Saviour Jesus Christ, three hundred and sixty-five compositions from the Four Gospels with notes and explanatory drawings by J. James Tissot. 4 volumes. The McClure-Tissot Co.

J. James Tissot was so attracted by the figure of Jesus and the touching scenes recorded in the Gospels that he went to Palestine in 1886 hoping to trace in the landscape and the character of the inhabitants the scenes of antiquity. The result is four volumes of colorful drawings and many beautiful studies in black and white depicting the life of Christ.

The Christ-Child in Art, by Henry Van Dyke. Harper and Brothers.

An interesting and unusual book, not written for children but much concerned with them, showing the influence of the Christ Story upon the art of the old and new masters of painting. Fully illustrated.

Christ Legends, by Selma Lagerlof. Henry Holt & Co.

Rarely beautiful stories including "The Emperor's Vision," "Saint Veronica's Kerchief" and "Robin Redbreast."

CHAMPIONS OF CHRISTENDOM

Child's Book of Saints, by William Canton, illustrated by T. H. Robinson.

Stories of angels, hermits, abbots and kings whose faith brought about strange miracles.

Stories of the Saints, by Miss Caroline Van Dusen.

"By request of the Rev. Phillips Brooks this book is dedicated to the children of Trinity Sunday School, Boston, for whom it was written."

Pilgrim's Progress, by John Bunyan, with four coloured and several other illustrations by H. J. Ford. The Macmillan Co.

An attractive edition for children arranged by Jean Marian Matthew.

The Seven Champions of Christendom, edited by F. H. Darton.

How St. George, St. Denis, St. James, St. Anthony, St. Andrew, St. Patrick and St. David fought with enchanters and evil spirits to preserve the Kingdom of God.

The Age of Chivalry, by Thomas Bulfinch. Lothrop, Lee and Shepard.

Part 1, King Arthur and His Knights; Part 2, The Mabinogion;

Part 3, Knights of English History—King Richard and the Third Crusade.

The Boy's King Arthur, edited by Sidney Lanier, illustrated by N. C. Wyeth.   Charles Scribner's Sons.

"It is in these tales that we get our earliest glimpses of the modern gentleman, the modern soldier, the modern patriot, the modern lover."

The Story of the Grail and the Passing of Arthur, written and illustrated by Howard Pyle.   Charles Scribner's Sons.

"But now hath the time come that he must quit us, for the period is imminent when the search for the Holy Grail shall be begun, and this is he who shall achieve the Grail."

Stories of Charlemagne and the Twelve Peers of France, by The Rev. A. J. Church.   The Macmillan Co.

Stories from the old French and English chronicles telling of the great Charlemagne and his crusades against the Saracens.

The Story of Roland, by James Baldwin.   Charles Scribner's Sons.

"Taillefer, who sang very well, rode before the Duke, singing of Charlemagne and of Roland and of Oliver, and of the vassals who died at Roncevaux."

Una and the Red Cross Knight and Other Tales from Spenser's Faëry Queene, retold by N. G. Royde-Smith, illustrated by T. H. Robinson.   E. P. Dutton & Co.

"His silver shield bore the dints of many a fierce blow given in battle and on his throat he wore a blood-red cross, so that men called him from that time The Red Cross Knight."

Stories from the Chronicle of the Cid, by Mary Wright Plummer.   Henry Holt & Co.

Telling of the great Spanish hero Rodrigo Diaz de Bivar, called El Seid, and his victory over twenty-nine Moorish Kings.

Jerusalem and the Crusades, by Estelle Blyth, with eight plates in colour by L. D. Luard and a series of reproductions of pictures of historic interest.   T. C. & E. C. Jack.

The Book of Saints and Heroes, by Mrs. Lang.   Longmans Green & Co.

"When Christianity came first to be known to the Greeks and Romans, and Germans and Highlanders, they, believing in fairies and in all manner of birds and beasts that could talk, and in everything wonderful, told about their Christian teachers a number of fairy tales."

Saints and Heroes to the End of the Middle Ages, by George Hodges. Henry Holt & Co.

Stories of Cyprian, Ambrose, Chrysostom, Gregory the Great, Wycliffe, Savonarola and others.

Saints and Heroes Since the Middle Ages, by George Hodges. Henry Holt & Co.

Luther, Loyola, Calvin, William the Silent, Cromwell, Bunyan, Fox, Wesley and others.

FESTIVAL AND SONG

Divine and Moral Songs for Children, by The Rev. Isaac Watts, D.D. L. C. Page & Co.

Spiritual teaching in a very attractive form.

The Children's Hymnal, by Eleanor Smith, C. H. Farnsworth and C. A. Fullerton. American Book Co.

Carols, by William J. Phillips. E. P. Dutton & Co.

Their origin, music, and connection with mystery plays.

Christmas Carols, selected and edited by L. Edna Walter, harmonised by Lucy E. Broadwood, illustrated by J. H. Hartley. The Macmillan Co.

Old English Carols for Christmas and other Festivals.

Festivals, Holy Days and Saints' Days, by Ethel L. Urbin. Simpkin, Marshall, Hamilton, Kent & Co.

A study in origins and survivals in Church ceremonies and secular customs.

Apples and Honey, edited by Nina Salaman. Doubleday, Page & Co.

A collection of stories, poems, historical and biographical material collected from various Jewish writers.

Festival Stories of Child Life in the Jewish Colony in Palestine, by Hannah Trager, with a preface by The Very Rev. Dr. Hertz, Chief Rabbi. E. P. Dutton & Co.

"The human appeal of these tales is sure to give the Jewish child who reads them a deeper affection for the Sacred Occasions of the Jewish Year."

New York City.   September, 1923.

INDEX

447